A Portrait of Claude Debussy

A Portrait of Claude Debussy

———◆———

MARCEL DIETSCHY

*Edited and translated
from the French by
William Ashbrook
and
Margaret G. Cobb*

CLARENDON PRESS · OXFORD

Oxford University Press, Walton Street, Oxford OX2 6DP

Oxford New York Toronto
Delhi Bombay Calcutta Madras Karachi
Kuala Lumpur Singapore Hong Kong Tokyo
Nairobi Dar es Salaam Cape Town
Melbourne Auckland Madrid
and associated companies in
Berlin Ibadan

Oxford is a trade mark of Oxford University Press

Published in the United States
by Oxford University Press Inc., New York

French edition © Editions de la Baconnière, Neuchâtel (Suisse) 1962
English translation edition © Oxford University Press 1990

First published in hardback 1990
First published in paperback 1994

British Library Cataloguing in Publication Data
Dietschy, Marcel
A portrait of Claude Debussy.
1. French Music. Debussy, Claude, 1862–1918
I. Title   II. Ashbrook, William   III. Cobb, Margaret G.
780'.92' 4
ISBN 0–19–816419–X

Library of Congress Cataloging in Publication Data
Dietschy, Marcel
[Passion de Claude Debussy. English]
A portrait of Claude Debussy / Marcel Dietschy; edited and
translated from the French by William Ashbrook and Margaret G. Cobb.
Translation of: La passion de Claude Debussy.
Includes bibliographical references.
1. Debussy, Claude, 1862–1918.   2. Composers—France—Biography.
I. Ashbrook, William, 1922–   . II. Cobb, Margaret G.   III. Title.
ML410.D28D5513 1994   780'.92—dc20   [B]   93–38762
ISBN 0–19–816419–X (pbk.)

Printed in Great Britain
on acid-free paper by
J. W. Arrowsmith Ltd.
Bristol, Avon.

Translators' Foreword

THE original title of Dietschy's book was *La Passion de Claude Debussy*, but this translation is called *A Portrait of Claude Debussy*. The shift to 'portrait' from 'passion' indicates the translators' approach. Since much of the literature devoted to Debussy has not been free of prejudice or has been concerned with specialized aspects of his work, it has been our thought that there is a place for an objective picture of the man himself, and that by making Dietschy's biography available to a wider readership in a revised and up-dated form we may contribute to a more accurate appreciation of the composer of *Pelléas* and *La Mer*.

The chief value of Dietschy's volume is the presentation of considerable biographical detail, based upon extensive research, material not readily available elsewhere, and this has been faithfully rendered, and corrected where new information has come to light since Dietschy's book appeared in 1962. However, we have condensed and, on occasion, omitted some of his effusive personal comments about the composer's life and works. Enough of these comments have been retained, we feel, to preserve the flavour of the original. Nothing actual about the circumstances of Debussy's life or the performances of his works that appeared in the original text has been removed. Moreover, in some cases we have included, in the interest of general clarity, more extensive quotations from Debussy's letters than Dietschy offered. In the notes, Dietschy's frequently incomplete references to his sources have been amplified, as far as possible, to increase their helpfulness. Where multiple sources exist for letters or other references, we have as consistently as possible cited the original edition. We have made corrections when Dietschy is in error or when new facts have emerged since his book was published. Such editorial work has been performed silently to avoid the visual discomfort of a plethora of passages set off in square brackets; however, where Dietschy's account is obscure or partial, we have felt free to contribute clarifying details in the form of translators' notes, and these are identified by square brackets.

Our primary concern has been to make this translation as useful as possible and as up to date as circumstances permit. Most of this updating occurs in the endmatter, where the catalogue of works (with the addition of the numbering of the Lesure Catalogue), the bibliography, and the index have all been expanded and brought into conformity with current practice.

An effort like this is impossible without the help and support of many *debussystes*. For his invaluable, immensely thorough scrutiny of the Catalogue of Works, David Grayson deserves a very special vote of thanks. Further, we owe particular debts of gratitude to Carolyn Abbate, Myriam Chimènes, Christian Goubault, James Hepokoski, Roy Howat, Richard Langham Smith, François Lesure, Jean-Michel Nectoux, Roger Nichols, Robert Orledge, Marie Rolf, and Charles Timbrell for their sharing of recent information and for their encouragement with this work.

W. A.
M. G. C.
New York
1989

Author's Foreword

---◆---

WITHIN the space of some fifty years (1907–1960) nearly ninety original studies devoted to Claude Debussy have been published in the Western world. In the face of such an accumulation of printed material, we expect to be informed, down to the most intimate details, about the true personality of one of the most extraordinary musicians of all time. Yet it is surprising, in spite of all this material, that we are unable to discern his presence accurately, either as a musician or as a man. We find contradictory or apologetic judgements, ambiguous or disparaging opinions. It seems that this artist who was such a figure of contention in his lifetime, even though he no longer stirs up a type of silent polemic, still remains a psychological puzzle to most music lovers and even to some serious students.

His earliest biographers were unacquainted with his letters which have come to light a few at a time. Preoccupied as they were to fit together and make connections between the isolated facts that formed their valuable and basic documentation, they have scarcely had the time to stand back sufficiently in order to 'reflect' upon the life of Debussy or to contribute any very penetrating portrait of the man. Some very debatable interpretations have been put forward to explain a number of the composer's acts and opinions, and these have been sanctioned because they have been promulgated by his contemporaries—friends, musicians, musicologists, men of letters—whereas it would have been wiser in certain cases to treat these interpretations, if not with suspicion, at least with reserve. Some aspects of the private and professional life of Debussy have ignited passionate reactions, inspired animosity, intensified rivalries, and engendered anecdotes and 'legends', which have been handed down to us more or less faithfully and which have formed a basis for subsequent judgements. People are rarely willing to verify certain assertions, to check certain facts; on the one hand, it is easier to copy what others have written; on the other, people do not investigate intensively for the truth, especially when it proves to be less provocative, less romantic than the legend. Yet it is unacceptable if, in trying to test and to question everything, a writer has not done so with all requisite vigour. It is worse if one has, unawares or insinuatingly or stupidly, added to the uncertainty.[1]

Finally, no one has ever carried out research very far into Debussy's ancestors, his parents, his family, his circle, his childhood, and his adolescence. The summary genealogy established in 1932 by Léon Vallas did not shed much light. Implications, veiled remarks, and specious interpretations have given rise little by little to an air of mystery that at times suggests something scandalous. The reserve of the heirs and that of the musician himself, perfectly understandable today, have served to perpetuate it.

For several years, in the absence of an organization of friends of Claude Debussy, some patient and discreet *debussystes* have applied themselves to clarifying specific aspects of the great artist's life and work, gathering evidence in a frequently laudable manner: Henri Borgeaud, Oswald d'Estrade-Guerra, François Lesure, Edward Lockspeiser, and André Schaeffner have pursued and published helpful work. In the face of the contradictions, the secrets, and the approximations that had characterized the existing biographies of Debussy, in the face of the 'mystery' of his poignant life, some research was truly indispensable, especially if the likely discoveries could bring us closer to the man. By examining the basic documents, hitherto disregarded or difficult to locate, and by exploring systematically all aspects of the musician's life, and, as far as possible, of all the actions, gestures, and words credited to him, I have been able to answer certain questions and to propose some new interpretations. No doubt, more than one point will remain obscure; hypothesis will have to take the place of certainty in some instances. Witnesses have died, some series of letters have been destroyed, some documents have vanished, some letters are still guarded in private collections. Yet in the light of indisputable facts, approximations can become likelihood, and likelihood certainty; then perhaps one will have given a more precise outline to the definitive portrait that will later emerge of that unique poet who was Claude Debussy.[2]

---

[1] The allusion here is to Victor Seroff, *Debussy: Musician of France* (New York, 1956). This work is so full of mistakes, untruths, and nonsense that the unwary are hereby warned to avoid it.

[2] What is later affirmed in this book is only done so when supported by irrefutable evidence.

Author's Preface

———— ◆ ————

FOR many people Debussy's music is still only a playful breeze, a passing cloud, a distant flute, a bell concealed by foliage, a tree that drips with rain—fleeting, exquisite impressions that shift and merge into infinity, giving and even seeming to become the illusions of a poet's perception. His music is remote from those people in its spirit and emotion, in its space and depth.

Debussy's music, however, is complete—and love is central to it, an inexpressible love that finds ecstasy in the moving beauty of the world and grows fearful at the transitory nature of things. In its thirst to seize all that feeds it, in its restlessness, it seeks an ultimate sensual pleasure. His very conciseness exposes this obsession with the rapid passage of time— the feeling of a task unfulfilled adding to his suffering—and with this tragic and painful sense of the final moment when life and death come to grips.

But Debussy understood very early that it is renewal that assures the perpetuity of all things: foliation and defoliation, day and night, ebb and flow. Clearly, these are all manifestations of a basic law. Are there not other palpably eternal things that remind us that this world is a movement back and forth towards some unimaginable close?

I have made mysterious nature my religion. . . . Looking for long hours at the magnificent and endlessly renewed beauty of the darkening sky, I felt an incomparable emotion embrace me. The vastness of nature is reflected in the veracity of my feeble soul. Here are trees whose branches reach out towards heaven, here are fragrant flowers that smile in the plains, here is the sweet earth carpeted with heady grasses. . . . And without being aware of it, my hands assume poses of adoration . . .[1]

Debussy records the vibrations of the world. His genius consists in his admirable sensitivity and receptivity. Susceptibility to love is for him a tumultuous joy, and is essential. 'It is something that is stronger than I,' he could say with Mélisande.

The bewilderment of love is present in all his works, fugitive, cruelly— and happily—too brief for the listener's pleasure. Consider the confusion

[1] Conversation of Debussy with Henry Malherbe (*Excelsior*, 11 Feb. 1911).

produced by the fortissimo in 'Les parfums de la nuit' of 'Ibéria'. Its unexpectedness, the fullness of the harmony, the richness of the orchestration, all have something implacable about them, since here tenderness and violence intermingle. For there are two Debussys who manifest themselves: the harsh and the tender. As Alfred Corot rightly says: 'These two aspects of his life, carefully kept separate, produce a continuous antagonism that creates beauty.'[2]

The material appetite operates no less vigorously than the intellectual; there, too, Debussy would have had to admit it as fundamental, as 'something stronger than I'. Throughout his life, just as he sought precision of expression and tangible perfection in his art, he loved to contemplate fine dishes, silks in vivid colours, yellowed prints, Satzouma vases, and walking sticks fashioned of pale wood. Those who knew him have commented on this inclination: Gabriel Pierné speaks of *timbales* of macaroni; Vital Hocquet of rose-flavoured pralines; Robert Godet of 'curried oysters'(!); Paul Leclercq of tiny salmon trout; Lucien Fontaine of tarts impulsively gobbled; Jacques-Émile Blanche of port savoured in solitude; Lucien Monod of an ivory elephant; René Peter of a sailor's necktie of emerald silk wanted at any cost; and Nicolas Coronio of batiste soft to the touch. Sometimes a raging appetite bestows balance in the guise of a physical response upon a spirit too thirsty for ideas: 'The desire is everything. ... What joy at the moment of possession! That truly is love,' as he wrote to André Poniatowski in 1893.[3]

Debussy is the Seducer, according to Vladimir Jankélévitch.[4] But he is so only in order to be the one seduced. He seeks the woman less openly so that she should not be aware of it to begin with; she comes towards him hesitantly, for she feels that he will make her his possession. All sensuous desire presupposes cruelty perhaps, as does innovation, and Debussy sometimes had a need to be cruel. When opportunity failed him, he returned to his solitude: that is what Pierre Louÿs told one of his secretaries. Yet if the woman attaches herself, the Seducer detaches himself, and here again the law of nature is intensified by that of creative genius. Consider why Debussy sometimes felt the need to knock out of the way those who interfered with his progress. Lamenting his inability to complete the two short operas based upon Poe (*Le Diable dans le beffroi* and *La Chute de la Maison Usher*), he wrote to André Caplet on 22 December 1911:

[2] R. Peter, *Claude Debussy* (rev. edn., Paris, 1944), 14.
[3] A. Poniatowski, *D'un siècle à l'autre* (Paris, 1948), 307.
[4] V. Jankélévitch, *Debussy et le mystère* (Neuchâtel, 1949), 148.

To sum up, one would have to suppress what consumes the best of our thoughts and arrive at loving only oneself with a ferocious concentration. Now it is the opposite that occurs: first, the family, which clutters and obstructs me either with too much tender concern or with a blind serenity. Then there come the Mistresses, or the Mistress, upon whom one does not even rely, so happy is one to give oneself to her, even to the point of oblivion. (1957a, p. 57)[5]

There it is, then, that 'irresistible attraction towards something higher', an aspiration which some people persist in believing to be lacking in Debussy; his compositions illustrate his motto: 'toujours plus haut'. Debussy was not yet fifty when he wrote his confession to Caplet, still another affirmation of the duality that tore him apart. It was a bitter and grievous struggle that illness would exacerbate and which declared clearly enough that death was near. Death haunted him and would take him at an age when the subsiding of passion would have given him a tranquillity that those suffering from cancer never quite seem to experience.

Very different from one another are the women who counted the most in Debussy's life for significant periods.[6] Mme Vasnier, as a singer, is in the early songs, in *L'Enfant prodigue*; Madame Vasnier, as mistress, occasioned the birth of *Le Printemps*, *La Damoiselle élue*, the two *Arabesques*, the *Petite Suite*, the six *Ariettes*, and the most important of the *Cinq Poèmes de Charles Baudelaire*. Gaby, the devoted Gabrielle Dupont, was 'la Maîtresse héroïque', and during her reign there bloomed, not without leaving some trace of her presence, the most beautiful flowers of Debussy's springtime: the String Quartet, the *Proses lyriques*, *Pelléas et Mélisande*, the *Prélude à 'L'Après-midi d'un faune'*, the *Nocturnes*. In contrast, Lilly, the first Mme Claude Debussy, locked her husband up within a working girl's cocoon of happiness which was so little conducive to music that the five years of this marriage reduced his creativity to nothing.* Then, and even before she appeared to him, Emma Bardac, as we shall see, mysteriously inspired *La Mer*. After he had come to know her, he composed the *Trois Chansons de France*, the *Deux Danses* for harp and strings, the second collection of *Fêtes galantes*, *Masques*, *L'Isle joyeuse*, the ineffable 'Reflets dans l'eau', and the tender 'Serenade for the Doll'. Then all the rest of his works were born in

[5] Lockspeiser thinks that Debussy will always appear rather a *maudit*, which is true, but, more specifically, a *maudit* who wound up wearing a bowler hat; a *condottiere retraité* ('a retired mercenary soldier') in the phrase of Georges Pioch. For his part, André Schaeffner fears that Debussy belongs 'to the frightening tribe of Gauguin and Verlaine' ('Debussy et ses rapports avec la musique russe', in P. Souvtchinsky (ed.), *Musique russe* (Paris, 1953), i. 98). This is a questioning fear which, happily, is only a misgiving arising from the imagination and from scruple.

[6] Attempts at suicide by two women he abandoned damage Debussy's reputation.

* [In truth these five years were not quite as unproductive as Dietschy implies.]

the atmosphere that she, as the second Mme Claude Debussy, knew how to create and maintain.

These works, as we shall see, evoke through their very titles the logical and touching sequence of intimate events that reveal the full bloom of Debussy's life, of Debussy dedicated to his art, of Debussy intoxicated by the fullness of desire. The *Fêtes galantes* are the tactful homage of the poet to his fair lady; *Masques* is the necessary pretence before the elopement; *L'Isle joyeuse*, unrestrained passion; 'Reflets dans l'eau', the tremulous repose of the overwhelmed lovers, and 'Serenade for the Doll', the fruit of their unrestrained love: the birth of Chouchou Debussy.

'Art is all of life . . .', he has written. Music was Debussy's passion; it nourished his life and brought beauty into it; it was even his moral sense. Doubtless he will survive as one of the four or five purest musicians of all time. If his works are beautiful, it is because they partake of dreams, of a long dream of love, that constantly monitored passion which fed itself from those springs where visible beauty is transcended. To dispute the primacy of the dream over reality is to fail to understand Debussy.

Contents

List of Illustrations

Abbreviations

RdM   *Revue de musicologie*

ReM   *Revue musicale*

RIMF   *Revue internationale de musique française*

The various volumes of Debussy's letters, listed in the Select Bibliography, are identified there and in note references by their date of publication, e.g. (1942, p. 63).

I

'A Set of Completely Unknown People...'

On 22 December 1911, some six years before his death but already suffering from the disease that would later prove fatal, Debussy wrote to André Caplet: 'Truly, we can do nothing about it; our soul is bequeathed to us by a set of completely unknown people, who, through their descendants, act upon us all too often without our being able to do much about it' (1957*a*, p. 57).

In the middle of the sixteenth century there had truly been an N. de Bussy, 'musicien français'.[1] Furthermore, if he was Burgundian, which he scarcely seemed, he could have had for a descendant the Nicolas de Bussy named below, who was of the composer's family, but without formal proofs one cannot claim him as an ancestor of Claude Debussy, another 'musicien français'. Nor can one claim the Chevalier Claude de Bussy, the lord of Eyria, of Bussy, and of Crangeac, referred to in a list of the nobility, even though the village and château of Bussy-le-Grand is situated fifteen kilometres from Benoisey, the cradle of Claude Debussy.

The 'set of completely unknown people' who could have had an effect upon Claude Debussy were originally gathered in the modest little village of Benoisey, in the Côte-d'Or, half-way between Montbard and Laumes, situated on the side of a hill, at the foot of which runs the Brenne. Mont-Auxois dominates the landscape physically, historically, and religiously, for on its south-west slope had stood the Alésia where Vercingétorix was captured, near the Alise of Sainte Reine, which is named after the Christian martyr (there are several women named Reine de Bussy in the family line).

The civil registries show to what extent the de Bussy family flourished at Benoisey in the seventeenth century. Branches of the family were sired by a dozen children: Bridot, Cathelin, Nicolas, and Blaise among others. These people were all labourers or wine-growers who shared the sur-

---

[1] The composer of twenty-one songs for three and four voices, published in Paris by A. Le Roy and R. Ballard in 1553, and, according to Hugo Riemann, 'worthy of comparison with the best works of his better-known contemporaries'.

rounding fields with six or seven related families. Then they spread into the surrounding communities, notably at Montigny-Monfort on the other side of the hill (where there was a Clément de Bussy, a tavern-keeper), in Lantilly, at Champ-d'Oiseau. Bridot de Bussy, born about 1615, who married Edmée Denaut, is probably an ancestor of the composer Claude Debussy. But the line is ascertained only to the sixth generation back: to Edme de Bussy, a wine-grower, born at Benoisey in 1639, who married Léonarde, child of the labourer Jehan de Bussy and Bastienne Bouguereau. They had eight children, the sixth of whom, Valentin, born 11 January 1682, married at the age of forty-two, at nearby Seigny, one Marie Carré, who bore him six children, of which Pierre I, born 2 February 1727, was the great-great-grandfather of the composer.[2]

The misery of those Burgundian peasants was intense: frozen crops in 1709, floods in 1710, famines in 1725, 1739, 1740, and 1750, various tithes, spying by the tax-collectors, peasant revolts: the writings of Vauban, Boisguillebert, Valentin Duval, and La Bruyère show their distress. Perhaps it was these events that induced several of the de Bussys to leave their land and their ancestral village. Little by little, others went away, and today the family is no longer represented at Benoisey.[3]

Pierre I de Bussy, Valentin's son, set up as a farrier in Semur-en-Auxois, where the horse is king. His son, Pierre II, born in 1768, went farther afield; in the company of a baker, he left Burgundy, thanks to the Revolution (but not before 1792) and settled in Paris, where he married Anne-Claudine Boyeldieu, of whom nothing is known except that she was no connection of the composer of *La Dame blanche*. Widowed early, he consoled himself with the daughter of a shipwright on the quai d'Orsay, one Marie-Suzanne Saussay, and he opened a locksmith's shop near Saint-Germain-des-Prés, in a narrow street that has disappeared today: rue Childebert. Three children arrived one after the other: in 1800, Suzanne-Virginie, who married a carpenter, son of a master cabinet-maker; Pierre-Louis, born in 1803, who became a locksmith in the rue de Charenton; Achille-Claude, born in 1805, also a locksmith, who died at the age of twenty-five, before the birth of his daughter. All three were

[2] Another Valentin de Bussy, also born in 1682, earned sufficient consideration at Benoisey from his occupation as merchant to attain the title of 'Maistre'; his wife was called 'dame Jeanne Carré'.

[3] According to Mlle the Mayor of Courcelles-lès-Montbard, the last Debussy of Benoisey was Victor, nicknamed Victor Noir, an eccentric who died about 1940, having lived in the hamlet of La Bergerie, playing the violin in nearby cafés where the young people danced. Coming from that same stock was Ernest-Alfred Debussy, a deputy from the Côte-d'Or between 1896 and 1906; he was a shopkeeper and a radical socialist of the far left.

baptized without delay; the godparents included a shipping agent, a seller of wood for boatbuilding, and a dressmaker.[4]

A fourth child came somewhat later, on 16 June 1812 (at which time his father, Pierre II, was forty-four): he was Claude-Alexandre, the grandfather of the composer. He set up as a carpenter and did not delay in taking a wife, marrying early, at twenty-two, the daughter of a mushroom-grower of Chelles, one Marie-Anne-Françoise Blondeau. Her sensitive features, her eyes apparently blue, her mouth modestly tight, suggest the Nordic type. She was a fringe-maker and did not know how to write, but she gave her husband nine children, the two eldest of whom played a role in Debussy's life: Manuel-Achille, his father, and Clémentine, godmother, benefactress, and prophesier of his future. But no role was played by this other 'musician', the first in the family, Jules-Alexandre, born at the end of 1849, who was working at seventeen, a volunteer at nineteen, and a prisoner of war in 1870—and one who did not rejoin his company. He moved to England and settled in Chorlton, near Manchester, where he married a butcher's daughter in 1877. One wonders what led him to England. There he claimed to be an 'artist musician' (a performer, a teacher?). According to Yvonne Tiénot, reporting in 1960, his grandson, Alex de Bussy, was still living in Leeds, where he worked for a firm that designed clothes.[5] Jules-Alexandre was therefore thirteen years senior to his nephew, the composer of *Pelléas*. We know nothing definite, but it scarcely seems possible that he could have influenced his nephew's choice of a career.[6]

In 1823 the family moved to Montrouge: 120 route d'Orléans. There the great-grandfather, Pierre II, died in 1829; there also the young carpenter Claude, Debussy's grandfather, changed his profession shortly before his marriage, and became a dealer in wines. Apparently this occupation fared badly, for he took up his carpenter's tools again and went back to Paris, under the cover of the Revolution of 1848. He was

[4] A description of Pierre-Louis at the age of twenty: 'hair and eyebrows black, eyes grey, forehead straight, a big mouth, high cheekbones, thick lips'; that is to say, much room and strength in the jaw, and very little above (Record of the military census, Archives de la Seine, Paris).

[5] Y. Tiénot and O. d'Estrade-Guerra, *Debussy: L'Homme, son œuvre, son milieu* (Paris, 1962), 10 n.

[6] As to the other six children who survived: one daughter became a milliner in Boulogne-sur-Mer, and apparently died 'of a broken heart'; another girl was kidnapped at eighteen months; one son became a carriage-builder; there were twins, one of whom was apparently stillborn; and, finally, two other sons, of which one, Achille-Clément, would become, according to Mme Marie Sirret, a director of a cement factory. Among the godparents, only two were not labourers: an architect, and a professor at the École des Chartes whose godson was the 'musician' Jules-Alexandre.

there, at 11 rue du Colisée, when the insurrection of 24 February broke out. Then he moved to 17 rue de Ponthieu, and, finally, to 13 boulevard des Capucines, where Clémentine opened a 'Maison Debussy, couture'.[7]

Debussy's father, Manuel-Achille, was born on 10 May 1836 at Montrouge. His portrait at twenty shows him as coldly resolute, but lacking the appearance of moral or intellectual firmness. In another portrait, when he was about forty, he appears sensitive, charming, even flirtatious: indeed, he is a handsome man, although short (measuring 1 m. 645): he has a lively eye, and his hair is wiry, as his eldest son's would be; he was attractive to the ladies, all in all, he made a very striking appearance. He enjoyed adventures, gallant ones among others, and he had several according to Mme Sirret. But he lacked firmness of character and perseverance; he passionately sought success, without positive results, relying firmly upon his eldest son to acquire the glory and the agreeable life that he had failed to achieve for himself.

At the age of sixteen he was already living as a bachelor at 18 boulevard Montmartre, doubtless employed by the porcelain manufacturer who had a shop at that address. At eighteen he enrolled for a seven-year enlistment in the 2nd Infantry Regiment of Marines, and this gave him the opportunity to sail at the end of 1856 for a distant island—perhaps Guadeloupe or New Caledonia; the archives of the colonial forces in Paris fail to specify. He was discharged on 11 July 1861, seven years later to the very day, and re-enlisted at Levallois (15 rue des Frères-Herbert). Here he lived with his mistress, whom he had got to know while he was stationed in Paris and who would become his wife. During the next ten years he became successively a seller of china, a broker, a clerk in a printing plant, a civil servant, a member of the Garde Nationale, and an outlawed captain without a commission. After one year's imprisonment he was employed, on 15 January 1873, by the Compagnie de Fives-Lille in the rue de Caumartin; he was fired abruptly on 12 April 1887 and went back to work there on 1 January 1895 until his retirement in 1906.

Paul Arosa, the son of Debussy's godfather, has told me that his father had to intervene once or twice to help M. de Bussy out of difficulty. And Henry Prunières has written (in the *Revue musicale* of May 1934) that Debussy's father 'had a reputation of being not very scrupulous'. From

[7] According to Mme Sirret, who from 1886 until 1952 was an intimate friend of Adèle Debussy, the composer's sister, one member of the family left quite young to go to America as a carpenter and, becoming a gold-prospector with another Frenchman, amassed a sizeable fortune. After various changes of fortune, he returned to France, having lost most of his wealth. This story, apparently true, would perhaps explain the adventurous spirit of Debussy's father, and the family's inclination to search at all costs for success, glory, and material rewards.

this one infers that the inopportune break in the relationship between the de Bussys and the Arosas had been inevitable. This break was a bitter consequence of the events of 1871, as we shall see, and it explains the 'distant manner' of Debussy in regard to his godfather and also the expression 'the old rogue' which he sometimes used when talking about his father, as Edward Lockspeiser has pointed out.[8]

Debussy's mother, Victorine Manoury, was twenty-five, the same age as her fiancé, when she was married on 30 November 1861, at Clichy, a little after her brother, who was an employee of the Customs and married to a lacemaker. A coloured portrait shows us her not very pleasing appearance: wary eyes, straight hair, thick nose, not ugly certainly but not charming either, and possibly hot-headed. She gives the impression of being only slightly maternal, passionate, violent, and very independent. Perhaps she bore a slightly tainted heredity: her father was a former wheelwright in the rue Saint-Lazare, and he died at almost sixty in the psychiatric hospital in Clermont-de-l'Oise.[9] Her mother, a Burgundian girl from Tonnerre, came to Paris as a private cook—Debussy's fondness for good living doubtless came from her.[10]

Immediately after their marriage Debussy's parents moved to Saint-Germain-en-Laye, renting at number 38 rue au Pain an old three-storey house, with a china shop on the ground floor. It was there on 22 August 1862 that Debussy first saw the daylight at 4.30 a.m. The light from the oil lamp revealed his strange forehead, this 'double forehead' which made an impression on his immediate circle of friends, and which must have been immediately striking, for Paul Arosa, the son of Debussy's god-father, has given an account of this physical peculiarity. The new-born was called Achille-Claude, in memory of the young locksmith who had died in Montrouge in the flower of his youth. Eleven months later a second child was born, Adèle-Clémentine.

In this little town of thirteen thousand inhabitants, music was respected: there were concerts on the terrace of the château, and concerts in

---

[8] E. Lockspeiser, *Debussy* (5th rev. edn., London, 1980), 4.

[9] The death certificate of Louis-Amable Manoury, dated 28 May 1859, is at the Maison de Santé No. 1 in Clermont (Oise). The records that would explain why he was committed are not available. But as there are records of Manoury in Paris up to 1855, it is likely that he had not been committed long, and that, therefore, he could have been seized with a general paralysis, which would have been a fairly specific medical symptom, considering the period.

[10] Her maiden name was Delinotte; Edward Lockspeiser notes that she was related to Edme Delinotte, known during the Revolution of 1789 as a 'rebellious soldier'. Furthermore, Debussy's maternal grandfather had a cousin, François Manoury, who had participated in the revolt of 1848 (Archives de la Préfecture de Police, Paris).

its gardens, by the musicians of the band of the Empress's dragoons or of the lancers of the Imperial Guard; concerts by the Orphéon; Sunday concerts in the park at Le Vésinet; concerts twice a month (in 1864) by the first violinist of the King of the Belgians. As for the programmes: Verdi, Rossini, Halévy, Ambroise Thomas, Gluck, Auber, and the composers of polkas and galops.

2

Clémentine de Bussy

THERE is a woman at each crossroad of Debussy's life. Certainly women of all ages seemed fascinated by him, and they attached themselves to him like ivy to a wall. First of all there was his mother; then his aunt and godmother, Clémentine, the eldest daughter of the carpenter Claude de Bussy, and the benefactress of the family; she before anyone else understood Debussy's nature and offered him piano lessons.

In 1860 Clémentine was twenty-five. Hers was a tender, generous, and very devoted nature, and she adored children, not having had any of her own. The belated reminiscences of Debussy's sister, then a woman of eight-six, represented her, intentionally, as 'a deeply pious lady'.[1] However, among her acquaintances she was known—and this is more realistic—as easy-going and as one of those women of a regular *demi-monde*, that world of which Alfred Stevens would make himself the unrivalled portrayer. Paul Arosa even described her as the same type of girl as the 'belle Otero'.* Yet it is correct that she was the sole church-goer in her family. A dressmaker living with her parents at 13 boulevard des Capucines, at the age of twenty-eight she became the mistress of a man of quality, and a very conventional one—Achille-Antoine Arosa, thirty-five years old, a stock jobber with a Spanish father.[2] After five years or more of this relationship in Paris, she attached herself to Alfred Roustan, an innkeeper in Cannes, becoming the manager of an inn down there, renting rooms to foreigners during the season. In 1871, at thirty-six, she married Roustan, who was twenty-five. Then illness struck: there were

[1] J. d'Almendra, *Les Modes grégoriens dans l'œuvre de Claude Debussy* (2nd edn., Paris, 1950), 61.
[2] The stock jobbers carried out the same business for an account as did the brokers of the stock exchange, in consideration of a lower commission. The law did not recognize them, and they offered no guarantee to their clients, since they were not, like the brokers of the exchange, government officials. They owed to their probity the credit which they, for the most part, enjoyed in the business world of Paris.

* [Carolina Otero (1868–c.1962) was not only a singer and dancer in reviews, but one of the most visible demi-mondaines of the 1890s. Protected by Gaston Calmette, director of *Le Figaro*, she made her Paris début at the Eldorado in 1889, later appearing at the Cirque d'Été and the Folies-Bergère.]

repeated cures at Aix-les-Bains, and she died of uremia at the age of forty-seven in Suresnes.

It was probably she who in 1864 suggested to her brother that Achille-Claude should be baptized, offering herself and her protector, Arosa, as godparents.[3] Relations were established from that moment between the shopkeeper and the financier, and also between him and the other members of the Debussy family. Arosa, for instance, acted as a referee when Jules-Alexandre Debussy, the musician's uncle—mentioned above—volunteered for the 1st Regiment of Artillery. Yet it seems likely that it was M. de Bussy, proud of his long service as a marine, who chose the career of sailor for little Achille-Claude. These other relatives—the adventurous seeker after gold and the ship's carpenter—would also have supplied a vivid example.

No one knows why Debussy was not baptized until two years after his birth. The musician's parents, uncles, aunts, brothers, and sister had usually been taken to the baptismal font without delay. His parents certainly did not intend to keep Achille absolutely away from the Church. It is more likely that, as young married people, they had not found a godfather and godmother to their liking straightaway. Whatever the reason, Debussy's tardy baptism seems to prove that in 1864 the liaison between Clémentine and Arosa was still recent. It can hardly have lasted beyond 1868,* for it is unlikely that Arosa would have permitted his godson not to be entered at school at the age of six, as was then customary. Unlike his brothers and his sister, Debussy is nowhere cited in the registries of admission in the public and private schools of either Paris or Cannes.

The mistaken notion of Arosa in his role as alleged father of Debussy has been almost entirely dissipated;[4] yet most biographers want to claim

[3] At his baptism, on 31 July 1864 in Saint-Germain, she signed herself with an assumed name, doubtless at Arosa's instigation, who suggested to her—maliciously?—Octavie de la Ferronnière (an allusion to the mistress of François I or to a fashionable coiffure then in style?). The hesitant fashion with which she wrote this sonorous name on the certificate (she forgot one of the two 'n's in Ferronnière) shows that this was a tactful alias.

[4] Henry Prunières (*ReM*, May 1934) accused Léon Vallas of insinuating that Debussy was the son not of his official father, but of his godfather Arosa. Vallas subsequently denied any such suggestion. See Lockspeiser, *Debussy*, p. 5.
This unfounded accusation has caused and still causes trouble to certain people. If it is not absolutely refuted by the fact that Debussy was born 265 days after the marriage of his parents, a fact which argues against any suggestion of illegitimacy, this accusation is even more outrageous for Debussy's mother, a woman whose character was anything but loose. It can be easily refuted by a comparison of Debussy's youthful portraits with those of his legitimate father and those of Arosa.

* [It might have lasted only until 1866, if the dated photograph of Debussy's three-year-old sister taken in Cannes means that Adèle was visiting her aunt Clémentine there.]

that his godfather exerted a significant function in the formation of the great artist. Their suggestions or their affirmations derive from Arosa's taste for painting and from his material prosperity, and also from the fact that his brother Gustave, a stockbroker, became the sponsor of Paul Gauguin. Certainly, Arosa, who was only a clerk of the Bourse in 1863, was a collector of paintings, but no one has ever established that he already possessed, in 1865 at the age of forty-one, the four Corots, the three Delacroix, the four Jongkinds, and the two Pissarros which his son, Paul Arosa, remembered and some of which formed part of this 'collection of M. A.A.' (Achille Arosa), offered for sale on 6 May 1891 at the Hôtel Drouot. Even if he had owned them at that time, it is difficult to imagine that Achille Debussy at the age of three or six was marked by this 'prodigious' influence.[5]

In 1954 I met Paul Arosa, who died in 1957, and he told me all that he knew of the relationship between his father and the Debussy family. From the manner in which he recalled his memories, it seemed to me that one should be very careful in interpreting them. In fact, Paul Arosa was able to declare only that his father had never gone to Cannes, and he said that the only music his father had liked was bel canto (he was an habitué of the Théâtre-Italien), that he had gone to visit Jongkind in his studio, that he had broken off relations early on with Debussy, whose 'distant manner' he hated, and for whom he later predicted a dishonourable future, and that behind the composer's back he had nicknamed him 'the blackguard' [*l'arsouille*]. Further, on one or two occasions he had 'helped' Debussy's father when he was in difficulties. (This might refer to the episode of the Commune which will be discussed in the next chapter.) Yet Paul Arosa could specify neither the frequency nor the duration of the rapport between Arosa and the Debussy family, nor the conditions under which his father might have served as intermediary, even as financial benefactor, at the time when Debussy's musical destiny was determined. Nevertheless, Achille Arosa died in 1908, six years after the triumph of *Pelléas et Mélisande*, and, even though he might have disapproved of the

---

[5] Soon after this (after 1873) Debussy met another great lover of painting elsewhere: his first professor at the Paris Conservatoire, Marmontel. Gabriel Pierné reports that, about 1875, Debussy

persuaded me that together we would cut out these illustrations [from *Le Monde illustré*] to decorate his bedroom. The crime was quickly executed, and I remember that Debussy carried off some reproductions of famous pictures, those of Meissonnier in particular, surrounded by huge margins. I don't need to tell you how angry my parents were' (*ReM*, 1 May 1926, p. 11).

However Marguerite Vasnier, evoking the Debussy of 1880–5, specifies the opposite: 'paintings and engravings . . . , at that time at least, hardly interested him at all' (*ReM*, 1 May 1926, p. 20).

marital behaviour of Debussy in 1904, he would certainly have tried, at least within his family circle, to acknowledge the role he had played in the formation of the *Maître*, had he played one, even a passive one. We can conclude therefore that Arosa was a generous and attentive godfather: he had brought about his godson's baptism, he had given him some lavish toys.[6] He probably afforded his godson a passing glimpse of a world different from that of the small shopkeeper of Saint-Germain, of a world where money permitted comforts, pleasures, and refinements that are not the lot of most people. This is probably the limit of Arosa's influence.[7]

Mme Marie Sirret has described the composer's mother as 'a very independent woman' who 'found her children were a responsibility that frustrated her, and she separated herself from them as much as she could'.[8] She entrusted Adèle to her sister-in-law Clémentine, and later she turned Alfred over to her. Oddly enough, she kept Achille-Claude and Emmanuel near her, both of whom were strong-willed. She did not hide the fact that her eldest child seemed more gifted than the others. All the family's ambitions were settled upon him.

Born in 1863, Adèle possessed a difficult nature. She became a seamstress in fashion houses in Stuttgart and Paris, and later was employed by a decorator. Disillusioned in love, she never married. Emmanuel, born four years after Adèle, was intractable; often his mother had to go looking for him at the police station. According to a school report of 1874, he was 'not at all bright, very slow to progress, behaviour satisfactory'. He left home early and wandered about the countryside, trying a number of jobs, and ended up as a farm-hand. He was married in 1894 and sired four children, of whom the youngest, a boy, settled in Bordeaux. This last had three daughters and a son (born in 1934), who is the end of the male line of the family. Born three years after Emmanuel, Alfred was raised by Clémentine along with Adèle. One of his school reports describes him as 'very intelligent, good attitude, excellent character'. He had an easy existence, becoming a buyer for a railway company

---

[6] Perhaps the painter's palette of which Debussy was fond, Léon Vallas suggests. But it must be specified that Clémentine de Bussy and Alfred Roustan also gave a number of handsome presents to their godsons, Achille-Claude and Alfred.

[7] On 8 Nov. 1871 Arosa made an important marriage, with the Spanish Ambassador as a witness, and from then on he resided in Croissy, where his son Paul was born in 1874. In 1889, when Debussy was looking for subscribers for his *Cinq Poèmes de Charles Baudelaire*, he sent an announcement to his godfather, but this document was not to be found among Arosa's papers after his death.

[8] And sooner than one would think. The census list of Saint-Germain, at the end of 1864, named 'Debussy (Manuel-Achille), his son Claude (two years old)'. There is no mention of Adèle. (Archives de la Mairie de Saint-Germain.)

in Cardiff. From his first marriage, to a dressmaker with mental problems, was born one daughter, who died unmarried in 1949. Alfred's second marriage, which took place in 1931 when he was sixty-one, was childless. The fifth of Manuel-Achille's and Victorine's children, Eugène-Octave, born in 1873, was to die of meningitis before his fourth birthday.

At the end of 1864 Manuel-Achille was on the road to bankruptcy, and the de Bussys turned over their business to their predecessor Mallet, leaving Saint-Germain, apparently for Clichy, to live with Mme Manoury in the rue des Frères-Herbert. According to Mme Sirret, it would seem that Debussy's father had 'run away' from his family; in any event, trace of him is lost. Through a photograph that bears a date, Adèle is found again in Cannes, where she had been at least since late 1866 with her Aunt Clémentine, but the family does not resurface again until the middle of the following year, by then in Paris, at 11 rue de Vintimille. It was at this address that the third child, Emmanuel, was born, on 19 September 1867. M. de Bussy had become a travelling salesman in household goods, and his wife had to work as a seamstress.[9]

In 1868, his commissions apparently having also proved inadequate, Debussy's father took a post in the shop of Paul-François Dupont, a deputy from the Dordogne, who ran a printing and lithography business near the Magasins du Louvre.[10] He immediately settled his family in the neighbourhood, on the fourth floor of 69 rue Saint-Honoré.[11]

It is not certain when and how many times Debussy went to Cannes. Undoubtedly at least twice: in 1870 and in 1871. It is quite possible that he had already been there, for in his letter of 24 March 1908 to Jacques Durand he wrote: 'My memories of that place go back to the age of six' (therefore to 1868). In any event, in another letter, from 1905, referred to below, he recalled with the same details staying in Cannes when he was eight. Only two visits can be definitely confirmed; these reveal that when Debussy was eight and nine he was on the Côte d'Azur. In 1870 Mme de Bussy had come to Cannes to give birth to her fourth child, Alfred, on 16 February, safe and sound. The Doctor Roustan who delivered her, at Clémentine's inn, was doubtless a relative of Alfred Roustan, Clémentine's fiancé. Victorine had taken her two sons, Achille and Emmanuel, there with her without her husband, as it is known that M. de Bussy was

[9] The register of properties does not mention the de Bussys between 1862 and 1872. They must have stayed less than a year in the rue de Vintimille, or perhaps they shared a lodging with Mme Manoury, who, oddly enough, is referred to as 'Marquise de Manoury'!

[10] Later this printing house had a small music department. Debussy sold several of his early compositions to Dupont's son, notably the *Nocturne* for piano.

[11] Registry (Archives de la Seine, Paris).

then living in Paris with his father at 3 impasse de l'École. Achille had probably already returned to Paris in April 1870; in fact, Alfred's baptismal certificate, dated 24 April, bears a child's signature, 'Adèle de Bussy'. If Achille had been at the ceremony, he would surely have signed it as well, and above his sister, for he was the elder.

In 1871 Debussy again went to Cannes, perhaps as a result of the government's orders at the beginning of the year concerning 'useless mouths' during the siege of Paris. In any case he later said that he had received his first piano lessons in Cannes in 1871 from a teacher whom we hear of only as 'an elderly Italian professor named Cerutti'. In fact, this was Jean Cerutti, a violinist, forty-two years old, who was married to a German, Elisabeth Neuweiller, aged twenty-two. They lived in the boulevard Pihoret in Cannes, sharing the house with a painter and two other 'artists'.[12] Since he was the only Cerutti then living in Cannes, there is no doubt that he was Debussy's first teacher. He was not then the 'old' professor that he was described as being, but a boy of nine might judge as old a man of forty-two, who probably had greying temples. Nothing is known of him: perhaps he formed a part of the orchestra at a large hotel or belonged to the *corps musical* created in 1871 to give concerts at the Cercle Nautique. The *Revue de Cannes* does not mention him performing as a soloist nor did it include advertisements of his lessons, as it did of other teachers, of English, of German, of French, of painting, of singing, and of piano particularly, of whom there were a number. Therefore, Cerutti was a violinist of small repute, probably an attractive man, to judge from the age of his wife. He might have been a friend of Roustan or of Clémentine. However it may be, Debussy has reported that this teacher instructed him in 'the first rudiments' of his musical education, 'but he noticed nothing remarkable'.* He mentioned this only to Laloy, author of the first biography of Debussy in French, dating from 1909.

How long Debussy remained in Cannes on each of these visits is not completely certain. In 1870, probably for at least two months; in 1871, perhaps three or more.[13] Society life was exciting in the famous seaside resort: the newspapers of the region listed the French and foreign visitors who were expected or had arrived and reported on the activities of these distinguished persons of leisure who promenaded, took boat rides, enjoyed regattas, and patronized tea-rooms. The musical life was richly

---

[12] Census registry of Cannes for the year 1872 (Archives des Alpes-Maritimes, Nice) and the birth certificate of Jean-Baptiste, son of Cerutti, dated 10 Aug. 1873.

[13] Debussy's paternal grandparents, also in Cannes in 1871, were witnesses at Clémentine's civil marriage ceremony on 12 June. Since they were not at the religious ceremony (13 June), it is likely that they had returned to Paris with Achille, summoned hurriedly to assist Madame de Bussy in the misfortune that had just befallen her, as we shall learn.

* [L. Laloy, *Claude Debussy* (Paris, 1909), 11.]

varied. For several years an Italian troupe had been performing operas, such as: *Il trovatore, Il matrimonio segreto, Don Pasquale, Don Checco, Don Democrito*, and *Crispino e la comare*; on 22 February 1871 Verdi himself conducted the Finale of *La traviata*. There were concerts at the Cercle Nautique; matinées of classical music; some recitals, particularly that of 25 March 1871, at the Grand Hôtel, where the singer Cinti-Damoreau* accompanied by the 'celebrated' pianist Laussel, interpreted Weber, Brahms, and Gounod, and then played, four-hands, the March from *Tannhäuser*. It is not known what Debussy heard, but the important thing was Clémentine's initiative, which would be rich in results, in spite of the lack of sagacity on the part of Jean Cerutti, if he truly lacked it. This initiative was instigated by Achille's first efforts upon the piano (Clémentine had the use of a piano where she was staying), by his dreamy ways, and by his fondness for solitude.

Debussy's sister Adèle remembered that in Cannes, even though he sometimes entertained himself eagerly with a cardboard theatre that she had been given, he would more often spend 'entire days seated in a chair and dreaming, about no one knew what'.[14] The only youthful memory he would refer to when he was in his forties was that of the sea at Cannes and the roses; perhaps of all our childhood emotions we want to keep one single memory complete that sums up everything that has touched our sensibility, a recollection that binds us to that youthful time, something that nothing can wither. 'I recall the railway that passed in front of the house and the sea at the rim of the horizon. ... Then, too, the road to Antibes, where there were so many roses that in all my life I have never seen so many of them all at one time....'[15]

Later, Clémentine de Bussy took charge of the education of Adèle and of Alfred; she was mother to them both until she died. What did they not owe her, each and everyone![16]

[14] J. Lépine, *La Vie de Claude Debussy* (Paris, 1930), 18.

[15] Letter from Debussy to Jacques Durand, dated 24 Mar. 1908 (1927, p. 59). In an unpublished letter of 20 Apr. 1905, written to Marcel Baschet (a comrade from Villa Medici days), Debussy also invoked the time spent 'in Cannes at the age of eight and the pleasure of smelling the roses and looking at the sea' (communicated by François Lesure).

[16] Mlle d'Almendra claims that Achille was turned over to Clémentine at two, but this is demonstrably untrue. We have already encountered several proofs that contradict such a statement, which would derive from Adèle Debussy (cf. Lépine, *La Vie de Claude Debussy*, p. 18). The other facts that she furnished concerning the childhood of Debussy really relate to the musician's brother Alfred, who lived continuously with his godmother until her death in 1882, that is, for twelve years.

* [This could not have been the famous Laure Cinti-Damoreau, who died 25 Feb. 1863, but her daughter Marie, who made her début at the Opéra in 1862 and later married Jean-Baptiste Weckerlin (1821–1910), Librarian of the Conservatoire from 1876 until 1909.]

3

Captain de Bussy

On 12 July 1870 occurred the incident which unleashed the Franco-Prussian War. In mid-November Debussy's father lost his job at the Dupont printing house due to lack of work. He remained idle for two weeks and then was hired to serve in the supplying of provisions for the headquarters of the 1st Arrondissement, which was already a centre of revolt. On 15 March 1871 he was released; perhaps he resigned to see more active service, for he enrolled in the National Guard as a private. The insurrection broke out three days later. Doubtless he had already accepted some 'subversive ideas', for he was promoted sub-lieutenant. He became a communard, and assumed, on 3 May, the rank of captain of the 2nd Company of the 13th Federate Battalion, which was not considered to be among the politically 'moderate' battalions. If his side prevailed, he would be a liberator, a hero of the Commune; and, if things turned out differently, dishonoured, imprisoned, deported, or shot.

At two o'clock in the morning of 8 May 1871, Captain de Bussy, at the head of his company, reported at Issy with the battalion. At three o'clock, Commandant Corcelle, having been kicked by a horse, was obliged to withdraw; and he turned over the battalion to Captain de Bussy, with orders to occupy the fort at Issy. Verlaine was near by, on the same side of the barricade. Debussy's father, the former shopkeeper, led the attack. But at the first shots from the Loyalist riflemen, his men abandoned him. He gave himself up to the chief of staff at Issy, who had him arrested immediately. Released on 10 May, he returned to Paris. And on the 22nd the Commune defeated, Captain de Bussy was imprisoned at the fort of La Muette and later moved to Satory, where he was tried and sentenced on 11 December 1871 to four years in jail.[1]

From the documents of that time we gain insight into the terrible plight of Mme de Bussy. She did not know whether her husband would be deported or even shot without a trial, as happened to so many others. She

---

[1] See the files at the Bureau Historique de l'État-major de l'Armée (Château de Vincennes). Debussy's father was twelve years old at the time of the uprising of 1848, which can be considered as the second revolt—and defeat—of the workers, the first having been that in Lyons in 1831.

asked for the support of the people of the neighbourhood, of his former employers. Their statements, even the police report, were favourable. She herself wrote, on 8 June 1871, to the military authorities in defence of her husband: 'Having four children, we experienced great financial difficulties in our home. In extenuation, he decided in April of this year to accept the rank of Captain in the National Guard, so that his wife and children might eat. This consideration alone dictated his course of action.'

But the official report denied such a justification: 'By accepting the rank of Captain, Debussy [sic] placed himself in an even more prominent position. ... As to the occupation of the fort at Issy ... he formally intended to accomplish that mission, and he would have done so ... had his men not deserted him.' It cannot be denied. Debussy's father had accepted his rank during the active struggle between the communards and the Loyalists. Nevertheless, his dossier, which is still in the Archives Nationales, shows that he was regarded as having 'a weak character'. After one year's imprisonment, his sentence was commuted to four years' deprivation of his civic, civil, and familial rights.[2]

Helpless, Mme de Bussy left the rue Saint-Honoré and returned to 11 rue de Vintimille, where she rented a tiny flat for 'dame de Bussy', as the property rolls show. At the end of 1871 she moved with Achille to 59 *bis* rue Pigalle (his grandfather lived at number 49), not on the courtyard side, but on the fifth floor overlooking the street. This little two-room attic was rented to 'dame de Bussy' for 400 francs per year. There is no doubt that Clémentine (and perhaps Arosa) again came to the aid of her brother's family.[3]

Here, then, is the secret of Debussy's childhood. Here, without any doubt, is the explanation of his silence about his earliest years, his resolute reticence. These events left their mark on him, they accentuated the introversion of his nature, and for a long time after they left him with a secret grudge against all things official. It protected his ambition, first rather aggressive in his youthful naïvety, where it revealed both his desire to avenge his father's setbacks and a drive to impose himself upon a

[2] At Satory, the communards were jammed together in a large, unroofed courtyard, surrounded by walls three metres high, and they had to submit to inhuman treatment, from which Debussy's father, then thirty-five years old, must in one form or another certainly have experienced some after-effects.

[3] According to the property rolls of the Archives de la Seine, Paris, 59 *bis* rue Pigalle is now the Hotel Piccadilly. It should further be noted that Corcelle, leader of the 13th Federate Battalion, who had been living in the rue du Bouloi not far from the Debussy's flat, had been found guilty and condemned, twelve years previously, for theft, fraud, and forgery. There is no doubt that he must have had an unfortunate influence on Debussy's father.

society where the most scrupulous people received no compensations from life. It was a cruel page, but a decisive one, and it illustrates the slow and turbulent freeing of the labouring classes. It determined, in fact, the career of the future composer, and one can see to what extent the insurgent Captain de Bussy had involuntarily prepared his eldest son's future. To the fanciful, Debussy's prelude '"General Lavine"—eccentric', which, in fact, was suggested by the musical hall appearances of an American,* might be construed as an attempt to settle the score for his father's military humiliations.[4]

[4] 'You know that I have no courage, even less a military character—never having had an opportunity to handle a gun; add to that the memory of '70, which prevents me from yielding to enthusiasm . . .', Debussy wrote to Jacques Durand, 8 Aug. 1914, at the start of the First World War (1927, p. 123).

And to Messager, 12 Sept. 1903: 'You are perhaps unaware that I was promised a fine career in the navy and that only the caprices of fate took me down another path . . .' (1938, p. 74).

* ['"General Lavine"—eccentric', *Préludes*, Book 11, No. 6. The reference is to 'General' Ed La Vine, a clown and acrobat, who appeared at the Folies-Marigny (Paris) in 1910 and 1912. In *Complete Works of Claude Debussy* (1. v, p. xvii), Roy Howat states that Debussy 'may have been asked for music to accompany Lavine's act, though none beyond this prelude is known'.]

4

Megalomaniac
Music-lovers

IN 1871 there appeared a third woman: the mysterious Mme Mauté, surnamed de Fleurville. Her daughter, Mathilde Verlaine, reveals in her unreliable memoirs that her own brother, Charles de Sivry, was arrested for being a communard in June 1871 and led off to Satory. She adds without further explanation, 'from this time stems his acquaintance with Debussy's father'.[1]

We can, therefore, take it as plausible that the former shopkeeper met the son of the late 'Marquis de Sivry' in the dreadful courtyard of Satory. He emptied his heart to him; and Charles de Sivry spoke to him of his mother, Mme Mauté de Fleurville, who he said had been a pupil of Chopin. Full of solicitude, she visited Mme de Bussy to listen to Achille's attempts at playing the piano and to get some idea of his musical potential. She encouraged Mme de Bussy to direct him towards a career as a virtuoso, and she gave the child such a solid preparation at the piano, and free of charge, that he was ready to compete for a place in the classes of the Paris Conservatoire on 22 October of the following year.

Perfect fiction, one would believe; but, however embroidered, probably authentic. Yet not so incredible as the fine legendary names with which Mme Mauté adorned her story and herself. In fact with the names of de Sivry and Chariat (the maiden name of Mme Mauté), one is dealing with a strange kind of bravado and with an unrestrained imagination. None of their titles nor their use of *de* to indicate ownership of land and noble birth stand up against the reality of legal documents; the whole family, even though they were in fact musicians, engaged in pulling unsuspecting legs.

To begin, there was Sophie Leroy (Leroy d'Honnecourt, adds Mathilde in her memoirs), widow of M. Decamp (M. de Camp, disjointing the name for vanity), who was married for a second time in 1815 to Antoine Chariat, a music teacher, and gave birth in Cambrai on 30 November

---

[1] Ex-Mme P. [Mathilde] Verlaine, *Mémoires de ma vie*, ed. F. Porché (Paris, 1935), 176. In fact, Sivry was arrested at Néris-les-Bains on 8 July 1871, transferred to Satory on the 20th, and received pardon on 18 Oct. 1871 (Archives de la Préfecture de Police, Paris).

1823 to Antoinette-Flore, the future Mme Mauté de Fleurville. This trio arrived in Paris about 1830. In the spring of 1847, and at the age of twenty-four, Antoinette-Flore, according to Mathilde, married the Marquis Louis de Sivry, a man of letters. But at Saint-Germain-en-Laye, the official registries reveal that the supposed Marquis de Sivry was the son of a hatter, one Michel Sivry, who required the services of a roofer to be a witness for the baptism of his son Louis. According to the unreliable memoir-writer, Louis spoke at least half the known foreign languages at thirty-six, and at the age of thirty-eight, in spite of his learning, was laid in a pauper's grave.[2]

A widow at twenty-six, Mme Sivry had the consolation of her son Charles, whom the noble polyglot had found time to give her some four months before his death. Next, she married in 1852 one Théodore-Jean Mauté, landowner and son of a grocer (with an income of between ten and fifteen thousand francs, according to a police report), to whom she gave two daughters, Mathilde and Marguerite. Then on 11 August 1870 they acquired their only son-in-law: Paul Verlaine. Deceived by her renewed plebian status, she envied her sister-in-law, Rosalie Mauté, who, by coincidence, had also married a Sivry, but one with a position: Charles Poinsinet de Sivry, a magistrate. Therefore, Antoinette-Flore started to erect the requisite scaffolding to rival her sister-in-law's façade. She remembered, for instance, that Chopin had died in the same year as the 'marquis'. One wonders from where she plucked the fragrant name of Fleurville. Certainly not from the works of the Comtesse de Ségur, whose *Bibliothèque Rose*,* which contained a Mme de Fleurville, did not appear until 1857. She adorned herself therefore with the plumes of Chopin and yoked Fleurville to Mauté.

How can one believe either of them, mother or daughter! Mme Mauté, a pupil of Chopin? 'Music teacher' is her description in legal documents. She gave lessons in several noble families, notably the Rohans and the Beurges (this is confirmed by a police report). At best she could have heard Chopin play, and have been familiar with certain recommendations he had made, but one cannot go beyond that. Whatever her knowledge of Chopin was, it was acquired at second hand. Further, Sivry, in his memoirs published in *Les Quat'z'arts*, declared that he had taught

---

[2] There is a Louis de Sivry, author of a *Dictionnaire des pèlerinages* ... and of a *Précis historique de Saint-Germain*, etc. If the parish record of the Sivry–Chariat marriage reveals a 'hôtel' as the residence of the literary pretender—in reality, a lodging house in the rue Gaillon—his death certificate attests to the impecunious but not dishonourable condition in which he left his wife.

---

* [The *Bibliothèque rose* was in fact a series of popular children's books.]

himself music:* yet it would have seemed natural that a former pupil of Chopin would have wanted to transmit to her only son, and a musician furthermore, such a precious pianistic tradition. And finally, it goes without saying that Mme Mauté does not figure in any listing of Chopin's pupils.[3]

No details are certain concerning when and where Mme Mauté gave her lessons to Debussy. Probably between October 1871 (the time of Sivry's liberation from Satory) and October 1872 (when Debussy was admitted to the Conservatoire); and, not inconceivably, even after that. It is astonishing that Mathilde Verlaine, having such a fine opportunity to vaunt the generosity and endowments of her mother, says nothing about them in her memoirs. She confines herself to relating that her brother and her mother 'were the first to discover the astonishing musical potential of the child and persuaded his family to encourage him in that path'.[4] Sivry, for his part, in his 'Souvenirs sans regrets' (published in Les Quat'z'arts), recounts how his mother (Mme Mauté) 'was a musician who was curious about all musical oddities'. Certainly, at the beginning of 1872, when poor Mathilde had just given a son to her husband ('Pauvre Lélian'), who thanked her with blows, the Verlaines had lived, since September 1871, with the Mautés at 14 rue Nicolet. And Achille had been at the Conservatoire for eight months when Mathilde vainly tried to disengage her husband from his association with Rimbaud. That is, during the whole time that Mme Mauté would have been giving Debussy lessons, Mathilde could not have been better situated to have known about it. It just might be that her mother, without Mathilde's knowledge, went to the Debussy's flat at 59 bis rue Pigalle to give those lessons. It is obvious that Debussy would not have referred to Mme Mauté in his correspondence unless there was some reason to do so.

[3] There is a police report, dated 4 July 1871, addressed to the chief commissioner of police at Versailles, which judges Mme Mauté, her children, and her son-in-law Verlaine very severely, but it is certainly exaggerated. 'Madame Mauté (de Fleurville) ... woman of about forty-five, loose morals at least in the past, she pretends to be an honest woman when she is in noble company ... An ardent apostle of Rochefort and of Hugo ... Mediocre writer, she works for music journals and supplies articles to Le Rappel.' Charles de Sivry: 'distinguished musician, member of all the secret societies ... bad poet ... a very harmful person.' Mathilde Mauté: 'out-and-out communist and free-thinker. She has done everything possible to attract the attention of Rochefort ...' Verleine [sic]: 'agent of the Internationale ... very ambitious, very cowardly ... a useless person ... dangerous due to the falsity of his character and his base sentiments.' (Archives de la Préfecture de Police, Paris.)

[4] Ex-Mme P. Verlaine, Mémoires de ma vie, pp. 176–7.

* [He composed operettas and popular songs. In his fifties he was an occasional pianist at the Chat Noir cabaret, which Debussy frequented in the 1890s.]

Interested as she was in the youthful personality of the future Debussy, quick in her enthusiasms and her distortions, attracted by the prospects, fortified by her unverifiable title as a former pupil of Chopin* and by the reference to noble pupils belonging to the Rohan and Beurges families, Mme Mauté, surnamed de Fleurville and ex-Sivry, would not have had any trouble in persuading Achille's parents to direct their eldest child towards a career as a virtuoso pianist. (It is not surprising, therefore, that among all these authentic and apocryphal nobiliary particles, the child Achille Debussy believed he should choose one for himself to ensure success.) The efficacy of Mme Mauté's lessons are attested to by her pupil's admission to the Conservatoire on 22 October 1872. Perhaps Jean Cerutti in Cannes had done more than make a crude beginning for Achille. Here, in any event, a serious question arises: Debussy speaks of Chopin's recommendations concerning the use of the pedal, which undoubtedly suggests an advanced knowledge of pianistic technique. Would it be unreasonable to imagine that Mme Mauté could also have given some lessons to Debussy *after* he was admitted to the Conservatoire?[5] However it might have been, nothing can detract from Mme Mauté's perspicacity and generosity. This usurper of the title of former pupil of Chopin, pseudo-marquise, pseudo-aristocrat, excellent pianist, Antoinette-Flore Mauté shares with Clémentine de Bussy the honour of having directed Debussy towards music as a career.

This, then, was the atmosphere in which Claude Debussy passed his first ten years. This was the 'set of completely unknown people' (or almost so) who had some influence upon him. It is important to stress this crucial period in his life, because no light has ever been shed upon the true nature of that climate: instability, insecurity, lack of money, rebellion, hunger, fear, delusion, shame, defeat. Debussy suppressed the impressions he received then and jealously protected the secret of his childhood. It was from this background that he slowly extricated himself; and this makes it that much easier to appreciate just how precious to him was the support

[5] In 1872 there were 157 aspirants entered for the competition to be admitted to the Conservatoire as piano students: 119 girls and 38 boys. Only 39 were accepted: 31 girls and 8 boys, among them Debussy (Pierre Constant, *Le Conservatoire National de Musique*, Paris).

* [In January 1915, when Debussy was preparing an edition of Chopin for his publishers and friend Durand, he wrote to him on the 27th: 'It is a pity that Mme Mauté de Fleurville, to whom I owe the little I know about the piano, is dead. She knew many things about Chopin' (1927, p. 131). And again, on 1 Sept. 1915: 'With all respect to his great age, what Saint-Saëns says about the pedal in Chopin is not quite right, for I well remember what Mme Mauté de Fleurville told me. Chopin wanted his pupils to practise without using the pedal and to use it only sparingly when performing!' (1927, p. 150).]

he encountered throughout his career. First, whatever is said, there were his parents, who, at least until he was twenty, knew how to impose upon him a sense of discipline and to inculcate sound principles. But it is evident just what an effort he made to acquire all that had been denied him as a child, and to reach the summit which he attained.

Debussy's musical life began at this point. Traditionally, he should have entered school in 1868, but he never did; his mother took its place. From the first she distinguished the eldest from the younger children, but what caused her to do so is no longer clear. In 1868, when she would not yet have had any idea of her son's musical disposition, she was still determined he should have an exceptional career—in the navy, in particular—that is to say, a career understood from the outset to be well paid—and decided that it was useless or a hindrance to send him to school. (Education would become obligatory in France only in 1882.) Later, Debussy himself spoke of those tenacious hopes that his parents had for him, mentioning them to Prince André Poniatowski, in February 1893, as 'the castles in Spain that have been built upon my glorious future...'.[6]

Doubtless from his tenderest youth Debussy must have emitted those mysterious vibrations that foretold genius germinating.[7]

---

[6] Poniatowski, *D'un siècle à l'autre*, p. 307.

[7] I published some of these details for the first time in 'The Family and Childhood of Debussy', trans. E. Lockspeiser, *Musical Quarterly*, 46 (July 1960), 301–14.

5

Defeat of the Child Prodigy

THIS much is clear: early on Debussy's parents had relied on him to obtain glory and material prosperity for the family. We can imagine what particular significance they found in their son's admission to the Paris Conservatoire on Tuesday, 22 October 1872. Three days later he attended a piano class, and then on 7 November he began a class in *solfège*. The former was taught by Antoine Marmontel, then fifty-six, a teacher of high repute, a dedicated lover of painting; the latter, by Albert Lavignac, twenty-seven, not yet permanently appointed, a keen amateur astronomer. Achille-Claude was then ten years old. The attractive photograph of 1874 shows him at twelve: his left eye smiling, the other watchful; the fold at the corner of his mouth contradicts the full lips; he appears very self-contained; and there is a little suggestion of something faun-like which even then predicted his aggressiveness.

The essentials of Debussy's first years at the Conservatoire—his teachers' evaluations of his capabilities—are known, thanks to Vallas. Here are some further details: on 15 January 1873 his father began employment as an auxiliary accountant for the Compagnie de Fives-Lille; his brother Emmanuel started school; his mother was expecting her fifth child, Eugène-Octave, born 10 November; he went to a few opera performances, notably *Falstaff** and *Le Trouvère*, which bowled him over, as Raymond Bonheur remembered. On 1 September 1874 his family moved to 13 rue Clapeyron, to a flat consisting of two rooms and a hall overlooking the street, on the fifth floor.[1] It is further known that he showed an interest in his father's collection of butterflies and a penchant for pictures with wide margins, for he decorated his little room with them:

[1] The Debussys lived in the rue Clapeyron for fourteen years. Achille's maternal grandmother shared this flat and died there in 1875. In 1877 Debussy's youngest brother also died there. We can imagine what an impression these two lifeless bodies in the cramped family flat made upon an adolescent of thirteen, and then fifteen.

* [This, of course, could not have been Verdi's last opera, which dates from 1893, but probably Adolphe Adam's, first performed at the Théâtre-Lyrique, 18 Jan. 1856.]

Napoleonic cavalrymen by Meissonier and riflemen by Neuville, recalling 1870—little realistic studies, not at all impressionistic.

He did not make a trip to London in 1875, as has been reported; that is a fiction that must be exposed, along with all those other tales told by that ingenious creator of stories, André (or Andrew) de Ternant, of London. Other fables involve Debussy meeting Verdi and Boito in Rome, and Brahms in Vienna in 1888, a crossing to England with Saint-Saëns in 1895, and Debussy's project to write his memoirs when he reached sixty.[2]

Debussy began his musical studies in a relatively calm atmosphere. He must have been aware of the difference of environment between his impoverished home and his impecunious family in the rue Clapeyron, and the studious atmosphere, the institutional gravity of the old Conservatoire, and the middle-class dignity of his teachers. Both of them were noisy milieus, however, inspiring in Debussy a dreamy solitude and accentuating his taste for almost imperceptible sounds, his appetite for colour, and his sense of the life hidden within things.

After a year of study Debussy was accounted as very weak in theory but 'very gifted', in the opinion of his *solfège* teacher. It is rather extraordinary that at this same time, Marmontel, who had to evaluate Debussy as a pianist, described him only as a musician and shrewdly observed that Achille was more a creative artist than a virtuoso: 'A charming boy; true artistic temperament; he will become a distinguished musician; very promising future.'[3] Not long after, Lavignac specified: 'A very excellent pupil, intelligent, a worker, and particularly well organized musically.'[4]

Thus it was in 1874 that the twelve-year-old Debussy first distinguished himself. When he was fourteen, in 1876, he showed his first signs of dissatisfaction. He began to argue about the teaching of *solfège* at the Conservatoire, mocking Lavignac for the rhythmic monotony of the examples in the texts, asking him searching questions; later his teacher would claim that he himself had benefited from them.[5] At that time the professor was intrigued and did not want to show himself worsted. 'Remarkable intelligence, admirably organized, but he does not work hard enough and trusts too much in his facility' (January 1876). In June of the same year Lavignac wrote this highly indicative estimate: 'Perfect in sight-reading and dictation; still feckless in theory, although he knows

[2] Edward Lockspeiser undertook a thorough investigation of de Ternant's claims and came to the conclusion that they should be rejected as mere inventions.

[3] Antoine Marmontel was a great-nephew of the more famous Jean-François Marmontel (1723–99), author of the *Contes moraux* and *Bélisaire*.

[4] Léon Vallas was the first to publish these evaluations of Debussy by his teachers (*RdM*, July 1952). See also *Claude Debussy et son temps* (rev. edn., Paris, 1958), 15, 17.

[5] See M. Emmanuel, *Pelléas et Mélisande* (2nd edn., Paris, 1950), 13.

it well enough.' This last phrase suggests that Achille was not in agreement, or no longer in agreement, with the way the course was taught and that his instincts caused him to glimpse an unexplored path and leave behind the routine exercises of that creaking fortress, the Conservatoire.

Although he won in succession all the prizes in *solfège*, including the first medal, as well as a first honourable mention in piano, playing the second *Ballade* of Chopin, nevertheless he failed in the competition of 1876 with the Opus 111 of Beethoven, a composer whom he did not particularly enjoy and played heavily. Marmontel was disappointed. 'Reckless, inaccurate ... blundering a bit ... he does not accomplish what I had expected of him.' Yet it was not just that Achille was at a difficult age and moody. Mme de Bussy stiffened her discipline. The emphatic boxes on the ear that Achille remembered date principally from this time.[6]

The year 1877 brought new confidence to the de Bussy family. Competing as one of fifty-eight, Achille won second prize in piano by playing the first movement of Schumann's Sonata in G minor. But neither the winner nor his parents were aware that the reward was 'granted more to the musician than to the virtuoso'.[7]

From then on, Chilo, as his family nicknamed him,[8] would win no more prizes in piano, nor did he ever win the first prize. Is it just that the highest award was refused to one who would become a performer of great persuasiveness and unequalled originality—all who heard him were in agreement on that—to one who was still regarded as a child prodigy?[9] Marmontel would observe in June of 1878 that he 'possessed very great qualities of execution, but very great inequalities as well'. Two schoolmates of Debussy (Pierné and Vidal) reported that he was not a faultless pianist. It is possible that, at an age when a hypersensitive temperament provokes unexpected reactions, Debussy's personality had already declared itself, negatively. Surely these successive setbacks must be attributed to his dislike of performing in public, and perhaps to the natural

---

[6] 'I come entirely from Chopin's Ballade No. 4,' Debussy is reported to have said to André Gide, according to André Gauthier. This sounds similar to Debussy's famous statement about *Boris Godunov*: 'There is all of *Pelléas* in it.' See G. Jean-Aubry, *La Musique et les nations* (Paris, 1922), 49.
[Debussy's fondness for hyperbolic *bons mots* is well known.]

[7] See Emmanuel, *Pelléas et Mélisande*, p. 15.

[8] According to the same elliptical style, Alfred becomes Frédo and Adèle, Délo.

[9] In the pages of *La Liberté* for 2 Aug. 1875, Debussy was for the first time described as a 'child prodigy'. Further, when Debussy made his first public appearance as a pianist, in January 1876, at thirteen and a half, accompanying the singer Léontine Mendès in a concert organized by the brass band of the factory workers of Chauny, the reviews stressed the fire of young Achille. This testifies to the strong reactions he inspired at this time when he was having his discussions with Lavignac.

strain aroused by competitions, or to the inhibiting obsession with a victory too eagerly desired. To all these explanations might be added the domestic pressure of the vision of his father's angry face and his mother's hand always ready to administer reproof.

Chilo suffered a setback in 1878 with Weber's Sonata in A flat and another one in 1879 with Chopin's *Allegro de concert*. Disenchanted since the previous year, Debussy's parents were overwhelmed, and even more so when, on 24 November 1877, Achille competed in the harmony class of Émile Durand and did no better—a disappointment after eight months of study; there would be another disillusionment the following year. Nevertheless, Durand thought him 'very gifted in the study of harmony' (June 1879). What he described as 'a discouraging thoughtlessness' was only the student's disdain for the subject-matter as it was taught—that is to say, for conventional harmony—and his refusal to apply himself to those traditional set-pieces which Maurice Emmanuel mentioned, which had to be 'reproduced at different pitches within a single key or modulating from one tonality to another'. Worse: he was thought to be physiologically incapable of detecting 'the individual style of a composer'. Emmanuel has judged Émile Durand very harshly, not hesitating to describe him as a 'tactless fellow'. Certainly the repeated failures that Debussy experienced in his class, and the resignation of this professor four years later, made it look that way. However, Durand 'talked things out' with his pupil, who, for his part, must have had some esteem for him: a year later* Debussy dedicated his Trio in G to Durand 'with many friendly thoughts'.[10]

If the setback in piano was irrevocable, and particularly in the case of Debussy, who was temperamentally ill-suited and intellectually opposed to virtuosity, the setback in harmony perhaps concealed a true gift. It was a defeat in a positive sense, considering the true essence of the two disciplines: virtuosity implies technique and method; harmony evokes inspiration and content. Evidently no one took this into account at that time. But let us not deceive ourselves. If Debussy's teachers in their end-of-term reports judged him as inattentive half a dozen times, they were only partially right, and the problems of puberty were also relevant: inattention is basically a denial. Clearly, the first stage in his development dates from 1879: at the age of seventeen, after seven years at the Conservatoire, Chilo already clearly revealed his independence. His ear, his instinct, proclaimed his independence, as did the priority he gave

[10] Émile Durand, then in his fifties, was married to the granddaughter of Boieldieu.

* [That is, in 1880.]

inspiration over formula. His conversations of 1879 with Émile Durand were a preparation for those of 1889 with Ernest Guiraud.[11]

Some time between 1877 and 1880, Debussy briefly attended the organ class of César Franck. For a while he liked Franck's compositions, but later he drew away from them. We know that Franck himself had little appreciation of Debussy. Of the younger composer's works he had heard or read *L'Enfant prodigue* and the six *Ariettes*, certainly, and perhaps the *Cinq Poèmes de Charles Baudelaire*. He characterized it as 'trifling music'.[12]

It only remains to say that at the age of seventeen Chilo Debussy was at an impasse: not doing well enough in either piano or harmony. What would become of him? One can imagine how his parents, filled with hope by his first successes, now tormented him with reproaches. Perhaps even more because he had begun to compose and to separate himself from them by reading a great deal—Musset, Bourget, Leconte de Lisle, Banville. He was aware of his cultural limitations, of the need for some support that would moderate and direct his instinct and exalt his feelings and elicit inspiration. With poetry he could escape from his exercises and from his academic discipline. It was probably out of kindness that Marmontel recommended Debussy, in August 1879, to go and spend several weeks at Chenonceaux, whose owner had wanted a pianist 'to fill elegantly those nights she spent trying to sleep', as Robert Burnand puts it.[13]

And so another woman entered the picture. She was Mme Marguerite Pelouze-Wilson, then forty-three years old, the daughter of the Scotsman who had made his fortune by illuminating Paris with gaslight. She had private access to the President of the Republic, Jules Grévy, who was the father-in-law of her brother, the deputy Daniel Wilson. She had bought the château of Chenonceaux and restored it at great expense; she had received Flaubert there in 1876, 1877, and 1878; she maintained a trio of black musicians, who wore white shirt-fronts beneath their scarlet waistcoats and plumed turbans on their heads. She was worthy of succeeding the 'Grandes Dames de Chenonceaux' of former times.[14]

Debussy had been designated as a substitute for her pianist Jimenez,

---

[11] 'Another [student] arrived late after the class was already under way ... all out of breath from having run. I noticed his bulging forehead under his black hair, and his forthright eyes revealed a tenacious personality. That fellow was called Debussy and his first name was Achille.' ('Souvenirs' of Julien Tiersot in *Le Ménestrel*, 9 Nov. 1912.)

[12] C. Oulmont, *Musique de l'amour*, i (Paris, 1935), 40 n.

[13] R. Burnand, *La Vie quotidienne en France de 1870 à 1900* (Paris, 1947), 161.

[14] A. Arault, 'Les Grandes Dames de Chenonceaux' (unpublished). The newspaper *Le Curieux* in December 1887 offered this description of Madame Pelouze: 'very prepossessing ... blonde and English to her fingertips.'

who had returned to Spain. Unfortunately, we know nothing about Chilo's stay at Chenonceaux. Doubtless he had the chance to become acquainted—or to better his acquaintance—with the works of Flaubert, who would remain one of his favourite authors. It is to be expected that he revealed to Mme Pelouze his ambition to become a composer, and, granting her character and personality, she would have encouraged him. Perhaps she intervened with Debussy's parents. This much is sure: on 7 October 1879 Chilo joined the class in accompaniment taught by Auguste Bazille, and from that time on his family insisted he teach a piano student, in order to turn the six years of disillusioning studies to some account.

On 11 June 1879 *Le Figaro* published a strange article about the candidates for the Grand Prix de Rome:

One can see the barred windows of the studios facing the church of Saint-Eugène. . . . Certainly, the life of a young composer is difficult. Never was there a greater contrast between dream and reality. Courage therefore, young prisoner in the studio. . . . Who knows! Perhaps you are the new musical genius that our time and our country awaits. Perhaps it will be you who will rid our ears for ever of Richard Wagner, that German nightmare.

This prophetic wish was going to be realized practically to the letter. Even if they had been aware of this prediction, M. and Mme de Bussy were very far from believing that it would be their son who would bring it about.

6

Victory of
L'Enfant prodigue

———◄•◆•►———

AT this new turning-point in Debussy's life two other women appeared, almost simultaneously: Mme von Meck and Mme Vasnier. They would help him achieve a decisive victory in his development and his character. It might be said that they came into his life due to his setbacks: the first, thanks to Marmontel, the second, thanks to Paul Vidal, both of whom were witnesses to his parents' angry disappointment.[1]

In the class in accompaniment, the first results were encouraging. On 17 July 1880 Chilo shone in the competition. Bazille judged him as 'good at harmony, a little too imaginative, much initiative and animation'. A month earlier, a rich foreigner had inquired at the Conservatoire for a pianist willing to accompany her on a touring holiday. Just as in the preceding year in the case of Mme Pelouze-Wilson, it was Debussy who was recommended for this position and probably for the same reason. It served as a compensation for the great bitterness that his family had expressed at his failures, and surely, as well, because he was recognized as a particularly able sight-reader.

Mme von Meck's name is familiar; on her mother's side she was a descendant of Potemkin, the favourite of Catherine the Great; at seventeen, she had married Karl Georg von Meck, an engineer, from a well-established noble Lithuanian family. After fifteen years of married bliss and motherhood, her untimely widowhood, in 1876, induced such an excessive love of music in her grief that she sought out an irrationally eclectic remedy in Tchaikovsky, whom she regarded as the god of music. She made a very ostentatious, even provocative, use of the large fortune bequeathed to her by her husband; she was, quite simply, a parvenue. Debussy met up with her on 8 July 1880 at Interlaken, and then went

---

[1] His parents, however, remained attached to their son, even more than he realized, secretly hoping that they would be rewarded by his obtaining the Grand Prix de Rome. They were to be disillusioned again between 1890 and his first success in 1893 with *La Damoiselle élue*, followed by a dashing of their hopes with his marriage, then a resurgence thanks to *Pelléas et Mélisande*, and euphoria in 1905, at the time when Debussy moved into a private house in the Bois de Boulogne.

with her to Arcachon, after having stopped in Paris on 17 July to take part in the competition of his accompaniment class. Then they travelled on to Venice, Florence, and Vienna, where he heard *Tristan*.* He began a symphony, which he worked out in Italy, undoubtedly at the sumptuous Villa Bonciani, finishing it in Paris and dedicating it and sending it to Mme von Meck.[2] She thanked him in these terms:

Brahilow, 8/20 February 1881.

Dear Monsieur Debussy,

Although the pleasure of corresponding with friends is *forbidden fruit* for me (because of my painful nerves), in the present case I cannot deny myself the pleasure of writing you these few words to tell you how touched I am by the lovely surprise you have given me by sending your charming symphony. I strongly regret that I do not have you here to play it for us. For me it would be a double pleasure, but alas, men are always slaves to someone or something, and there is no alternative but for me to rest my hopes on the future. And now I thank you very much, very sincerely, dear Monsieur Debussy, and I wish you all good things, and above all the most brilliant future in your fine career. Accept my most affectionate compliments.

Nadine de Meck

PS I beg you to say many kind things from me to your dear parents. M. Anfray[3] will send you a little souvenir from me, which I pray, Monsieur, will serve *always* to remind you of me. It is an object wrought in Moscow and represents a completely Russian subject: the picture shows Vanya, the contralto role in Glinka's opera *A Life for the Tsar*. Can you believe that I have almost completely given up music, first because I am very occupied here, and then because my partner (Petrouchka) possesses so few attractions in his function as pianist, that he takes away my appetite for music? My daughters send you their compliments.[4]

This letter gives us some insight into Mme von Meck's taste and the Russian composers that she then enjoyed. It makes clear to us that Petrouchka was not a nickname given to Debussy. It further shows us Debussy, the future liberator of French music, placed by Mme von Meck under the aegis of this *Life for the Tsar*, which forty-five years earlier had liberated Russian music from Italian influences.

[2] It was not orchestrated. One movement of it, scored for two pianos, was discovered in Moscow and published there in 1933. It had its first performance in Paris on 12 Jan. 1937, when it was played by Simone Crozet and Pierre d'Arquennes.

[3] M. Anfray might have been an engineer or a tutor, or even a seller of books and engravings of which there was one with this name, in 1880, in the rue de Steinkerque, below the Sacré-Coeur—not built at that time.

[4] This letter is in a private collection.

* [What Debussy heard were probably orchestral excerpts, for *Tristan* was not staged in Vienna until 4 Oct. 1883.]

We know little about Debussy during the four months he spent with Mme von Meck. He gave lessons to her children, he accompanied Julia's singing, he played four-hand works and was a member of a trio. Towards the end of 1879, he began a Trio in G,* which he gladly dedicated to his teacher Émile Durand, perhaps to win his forgiveness; it followed his *Danse bohémienne* for piano, a work in which Tchaikovsky found little pleasure. In October, Debussy transcribed for piano four-hands several dances from Tchaikovsky's *Swan Lake*, which were published shortly afterwards. Debussy gave himself airs, coming under the bad influence of a young student, a tutor in the household. Yet his character was adjudged good. He was carefree, teasing, and bantering; he got carried away; he was still very youthful.† He accompanied Mme von Meck again in 1881 and 1882, in the latter year going as far as Russia.

On his return to Paris, he was admitted on 28 December 1880 to the composition class taught by Ernest Guiraud, then forty-three, an agreeable fellow, less perceptive than he is sometimes credited with being, but flexible. At his first examination, the teacher described Achille as 'intelligent, promises to make a good composer'. A year and a half later he judged Debussy to be 'of unstable nature, but intelligent'. Twelve months later still, Guiraud was worried; he had a presentiment about Debussy's personality, misjudging him: 'a strange character, but intelligent. He writes music badly' (9 January 1883). Guiraud was certainly correct. In the judgement of a middle-aged man in 1883, Achille did write music badly. He refused to accommodate himself to formula; he was looking for something else, and he was not always successful. His music would have appeared eccentric to a composer of music typical of that period.‡

In that same winter of 1880, through the offices of his schoolmate Paul Vidal, Chilo obtained a salaried position as the piano accompanist for the singing class of Mme Moreau-Sainti.§ Held twice a week in the rue

* [This trio was published in 1986 by G. Henle Verlag, Munich. Ellwood Derr, who edited it, says in his Preface: 'According to letters from Mme von Meck to Tchaikovsky, Debussy's *Premier Trio en sol* was completed at Fiesole in the summer of 1880.']

† [Mme von Meck's letter of 28 Aug. 1882 to Tchaikovsky describes Debussy at twenty in these terms: 'he is going to bring life to the entire household. He is Parisian to his fingertips. He is a true *gamin*, witty, and he excels at imitations . . .' (quoted in Tiénot and d'Estrade-Guerra, *Debussy*, p. 24).]

‡ [Guiraud is best remembered today for the recitatives he supplied to substitute for the spoken dialogues in *Carmen* and *Les Contes d'Hoffmann*.]

§ [Mme Marie Moreau-Sainti made her début at the Opéra in June 1856 in the reprise of Verdi's *Les Vêpres siciliennes*. Her father (1799–1860) sang at the Comique and from 1847 until his death taught at the Conservatoire; her mother, who died in 1856, was an actress of note. Retiring from the stage on her marriage to Baron Roux, Mme Moreau-Sainti, a widow by 1880, had opened an exclusive singing school. In 1882 Debussy dedicated *Nuit d'étoiles* to her, his first published work.]

Royale, the class attracted a number of young wives of the bourgeoisie and legal profession, who gave expression to their nagging regret for their lost youth in nostalgic songs. Chilo was first noticed by Mme Émile Deguingand, then twenty-eight, the wife of a forty-year-old notary from Chatou. To her he dedicated *Fleur des blés*. Soon afterwards another pupil became interested in him. This was Marie-Blanche Vasnier, then thirty-two. The daughter of a printer and man of letters, Jules-Constant Frey, and of a music teacher of delicate beauty,[5] she had been married at seventeen to Eugène-Henri Vasnier, eleven years her senior. He was not an architect, as has often been stated, but a registrar of buildings, which is to say that he had nothing whatever to do professionally with the arts.[6]

He was a member of La Marmite, a liberal club with anticlerical leanings, born in the aftermath of the Commune and to which progressives of all leanings belonged: men such as Paul Bert, Denfert-Rochereau, Scheurer-Kestner, the two Coquelins, some senators, deputies, senior functionaries, and second-rate literary and artistic types: men like Jules Claretie, Émile Goudeau, Bartholdi. M. Vasnier was a cold man, secret, an obsessive worker, a teetotaller; as a young man his resemblance to Debussy was striking. Mme Vasnier was the exact opposite of her husband. She was one of those women of character whose husbands end up being only husbands. She was lively, he was ponderous. She loved society, he fled from it. She was up to date, he belonged to a society of French antiquarians. She travelled with her daughter, he pored over established masterpieces. Both of them were anticlerical. Courted and praised, she assumed poses; her rounded arms hinted at her dream of being a singer of elaborate arias. She had red hair, 'shading towards brown' in the phrase of Jacques-Émile Blanche, and her green eyes were adept at being provocative. Her final attraction was contained in her throat. She had the delightful voice of a songbird and possessed an exceptional upper range. She sang, according to *Le Ménestrel*, 'with a perfection that one does not often encounter among professional artists'. Gold she found 'tiresome'; she did not wear jewellery.[7]

Her drawing-room was good of its type, with Louis XV-style black lacquered furniture, curtains of embossed red velvet, dazzling white cushions, Moorish tables, pedestals adorned with dried flowers, paintings

---

[5] At least so she appears in her portrait, painted in 1848 by J.-D. Court, a pupil of Gros.

[6] A registrar of buildings has the same function as a registrar assigned to a judge. He inserts the legal technicalities into the reports of the experts, and transcribes them for delivery with seals. He also writes letters announcing meetings and undertakes to recover the fees owed to the experts.

[7] After a first daughter called Marguerite, who died at the age of two, the Vasniers had a second Marguerite, born in 1869, then a son Maurice, two years younger.

adroitly hung, heroic bronzes, and a selection of delicate bibelots.[8] Unaffectedly, Chilo Debussy invited himself to 28 rue de Constantinople, and the Vasniers received him regularly in their home, where he felt more at ease than in his own. They set aside a room for him to work in. Over a four-year period he visited them during the afternoons and evenings, and every day in the summer at the villa they rented at Ville-d'Avray. It was an abandonment of the familial hearth. Forty-five years later Marguerite Vasnier wrote that Debussy was not happy 'between his father, who was pretentious and not very intelligent, and his mother with her narrow, shabby ideas' (*ReM*, 1 May 1926, p. 17). But this spinster was judging the young man in retrospect, in the light of his later accomplishments. Really, one should pay tribute to Debussy's mother, to her strictness, to the discipline that she knew how to impose upon her son, discipline which allowed him to advance himself decisively.[9]

Mme Vasnier adopted Debussy; beyond his role as an accompanist, she saw him as an escort and, even more, as a handsome dark-haired fellow. Music united them. He composed for her, he accompanied her at the piano in private and in public, and even at costume balls. She gave him only her voice, her presence; she was not in a hurry to offer him anything more. Foreseeing his future accomplishment, she felt that he should owe her something. One wonders if she did not subordinate the granting of her physical favours to make an offering to Apollo's altar, to his obtaining the Grand Prix de Rome. While teaching him the infinite seduction of vocal expression, Mme Vasnier gave him at the same time his first initiation into love. From the charm of her voice, she assumed the character of an ideal woman, whose sensibility, controlled by taste, added a hundredfold to her attraction by the promise of the unalloyed pleasure she seemed to proffer.

For Debussy 1882 was a year of realizations and of affirmations. He turned twenty. It had been ten years since he entered the Conservatoire, and now he wanted to free himself of it, as he had disengaged himself two years earlier from his family home. He had had enough of both. He did not yet feel himself really independent, but ambition had been born in him. His nature was frank and witty, combining high spirits with the

---

[8] This furniture still exists in the home of the Vasnier heirs in Tours.
[9] Paul Vidal gave another picture of Debussy's parents.

His father ... loved music and had instinctive taste. ... Mme Debussy was a mother passionately attached to her son and very excitable. ... She was good-hearted and spoiled me a lot. She was an excellent cook. ... This couple belonged to a very modest social level, but they were not 'of the common run', in the sense that they were interested in everything that was going on around them. (*ReM*, 1 May 1926, pp. 13–14)

sense of humour of an accomplished actor. He was the star of his group of comrades: Pierné, Vidal, Passerieu surrounded him and urged him to play his compositions to them. With one eye on the gallery, he set his imagination free upon what were then considered sprightly poems: 'Pantomime', 'Pierrot', *Mandoline*, 'Fantoches', 'Chevaux de bois'.

At the same time, he was timid, awkward, blundering. His artistic progress was slow, but he pursued it without hesitation, nurturing it with continuous reading. The works that he had written up to this time were charming in their naïvety. They are not those of one in control of his material, but those of a seeker. His first poet was the lively Musset of the *Contes d'Espagne*. He was attracted to these verses because the true poet within him was not yet born. In contact with Banville he blossomed; he matured in the sun of Verlaine. His choice of poets and their poems indicates to us the date of composition of Debussy's early works: approximately 1879: *Madrid* and *Ballade à la lune* (both still unknown), setting verses of Musset, must have been written first. They are followed in 1880 by *Fleur des blés*, and by several settings of Banville poems, of which *Nuit d'étoiles*, his first work to be published, achieved some measure of fame when Octave Séré noticed, in 1921, that the first five chords are the theme of the future Mélisande, containing the essence of Debussy's melody, shaped by his sensibility.[10]

In 1882 Debussy matured and asserted himself. He composed at least twenty songs and began to write for orchestra. He defended Lalo's *Namouna* with enthusiasm.[11] He performed in public with Mme Vasnier. For the first time he was published and earned fifty francs for *Nuit d'étoiles*. He determined from now on to recoup his earlier setbacks to the extent that he boldly presented himself, and failed, in the trial competition for the Prix de Rome. Another jury had already sent him home earlier with the advice that he revise his work. He had been in a separate studio for three days for the counterpoint and fugue tests, which earned him a second honourable mention, when on 14 July his Aunt Clémentine died at Suresnes—she who had been the first to foresee his capabilities. In

[10] Of the four then unpublished songs, on texts by Leconte de Lisle and Banville, sung by Mme Claire Croiza on 29 June 1938 in an all-Debussy concert in Paris—*Jane*, 'Le Lilas', 'Souhait', 'Sérénade'—the first anticipated 'Green' and the last was the most accomplished.

[11] On 27 Aug. 1900 Debussy wrote to Pierre Lalo: 'A very long time ago I was thrown out of the Opéra for having expressed too loudly my enthusiasm for this delicate masterpiece entitled *Namouna*. Your father found marvellous harmonies, which people still considered to be like dangerous explosives' (1980, p. 108).

[*Namouna* is a two-act ballet by Édouard Lalo, the orchestration completed by Gounod; it had its première at the Opéra, 6 Mar. 1882.]

midsummer he rejoined Mme von Meck for the last time, this time in Russia. He had so enjoyed his earlier sojourns with her that he had asked if he could return. He felt that he still needed her. He wanted to please her, to interest her in himself. If he copied by hand, with several variants, and signed two songs which he had not composed,[12] it was to play a trick on Pachulsky, a fellow-member of the trio, who was also a composer; perhaps, equally, it was in order to gain merit himself. But he was less lucky in another endeavour, it would seem: Pachulsky courted Julia von Meck and ended up marrying her. Naïvely ambitious, Debussy is supposed to have settled his choice on Sophie, who was sixteen, and Mme von Meck coldly fired him. Edward Lockspeiser, however, who undertook patient research upon Debussy's visits to Russia, was of the opinion that this story is fiction.

Debussy did become slightly acquainted with Russian music: Rimsky-Korsakov, Balakirev, Borodin. As far as is known, he heard an early opera of Rimsky-Korsakov, some songs by Borodin, assuredly a good deal of Tchaikovsky, and without doubt much gypsy music, since he mentioned it to his first biographer, Louise Liebich, in 1908. Certainly, several characteristics and particular patterns bear witness to Debussy's visits to Russia, but little else. He was influenced to some degree by the atmosphere of these elegant holidays. For four successive years, from 1879 at the château of Chenonceaux, Debussy had detached himself from his family home, becoming accustomed to a world that was new to him, one above all that was free from material concerns, living with people of refined and broad tastes who were open to less prosaic ideas and who enjoyed opportunities for a range of diversions. It should not be assumed, however, that Debussy's critical judgement was blunted by this contact with people of leisure. Mme von Meck's correspondence with Tchaikovsky shows us at more than one point that Chilo had retained his freedom of speech and opinion.

Encouraged by M. Vasnier, Debussy had now decided to seek the Prix de Rome,* and he would win twice and with two cantatas: *Le Gladiateur* and *L'Enfant prodigue*. His seclusion in the studio for the composition of the first (during the competition of 1883) once again coincided with the death of one of his benefactresses: Mme Mauté died on 21 May, and she, like Clémentine de Bussy, was not to learn the destiny of her former pupil.

---

[12] These are the *Chanson d'un fou* of Émile Pessard and *Ici-bas* by R.-L. Hillemacher, which were published in good faith in 1932 under Debussy's name and later deleted from the publisher's catalogue.

---

* [The Prix de Rome were awarded by the Académie des Beaux Arts, one of the sections of the Institut de France.]

It is not known if Chilo had many illusions about his cantata at the moment that *Le Gladiateur* entered the arena.* Léon Vallas is right to mention the weaknesses of Debussy's score, but one wonders whether the cantatas of his competitors were any stronger. The established procedure was that the members of the music section of the Académie voted first to propose to their colleagues of the other sections a cantata for the First Grand Prix de Rome, another for the first Second Grand Prix, and a third for the other Second Grand Prix. At this first voting in 1883, Vidal's cantata was singled out by six members. For the first Second Grand Prix, the struggle was confined between Debussy and Charles René, who had the stalwart support of at least two jurors.† At this first vote, René obtained four votes against three for Debussy; at the second ballot, Debussy gained one vote but did not therefore win the necessary majority of five. Since the third balloting left the two competitors tied, a new discussion, according to established procedure, was held about the relative merit of the candidates. Thus it was on the fourth ballot that Debussy obtained the five votes necessary, with the following opinions: 'A generous musical nature but ardent sometimes to the point of excess; some convincing dramatic accents.' At the second session, when the full Académie voted, Vidal succeeded without problem, winning twenty-five of a possible thirty-two votes. To award the first Second Grand Prix, once again four rounds of balloting were required: at the third of these Debussy and René were tied with sixteen votes apiece; at the fourth, Debussy overcame him, his total reaching twenty. The musical press gave such praise to Debussy's cantata that he was among the first to think that he might win the following year. He was convinced about it, and he felt so sure of his capability that he was impatient for the occasion to come round again.[13]

It was during April 1884 that an extraordinary exhibition occurred when Debussy substituted for Delibes in a class at the Conservatoire and delivered himself of 'a debauchery of chords . . . a stream of arpeggios . . . a gurgling of trills . . .' which were composed of a succession of parallel fifths and octaves, of ninth and eleventh and thirteenth chords. Maurice Emmanuel, who tells of this mischievousness, thought then that two

[13] Succeeding Vidal as accompanist to the Concordia chorus, Debussy met Gounod, who showed great sympathy towards him. In a letter dated 4 Jan. 1934, Henry Prunières wrote to André Suarès that Debussy said of Gounod: 'He had been the first to bring a little perspiration to the expression of things relating to love.'

* [At its public performance, 23 June 1883, *Le Gladiateur* was sung by Gabrielle Krauss, Muratet (a student at the Conservatoire), and Alexandre Taskin, with two-piano accompaniment. See *Le Ménestrel*, 24 June 1883.]

† [One of whom was probably Léo Delibes, René's composition teacher.]

personalities co-existed amicably in Debussy: 'one, a musician freed of the slightest restraint, who had loosed the bridle of harmony; the other, a practitioner so timid that he did not believe it possible to write down the bold things prompted by his brilliant instinct' (*ReM*, 1 May 1926, p. 44).

Emmanuel added that Debussy's cantatas for the Prix de Rome 'are not concessions made with an eye to a successful outcome'. I am not convinced of this, because in fact Chilo was so firmly resolved above all to try to obtain the First Grand Prix de Rome that he made a pastiche of Gounod and Massenet in *L'Enfant prodigue*, perhaps acting upon Guiraud's advice. It is obvious: the Académie awarded the first prize to *L'Enfant prodigue* but severely condemned the work that immediately followed it, the unknown *Zuleima*, his first *envoi** from Rome. 'Today M. Debussy seems tormented by trying to be bizarre, incomprehensible, unperformable...'[14]

If the Debussy of his first years at the Conservatoire had been the 'charming child' as Marmontel said and as confirmed by his photograph of 1874, that of the final years could not have seemed so to all of his fellow-students, to some of his teachers, and to some of the musicians who heard talk of him, nor even to the administrative personnel of that 'venerable' institution. As he gradually acquired the fundamental instruction which he had lacked, absorbed the assigned subject-matter, and found himself at the level of his fellows, he became aware of his inner resources of originality, and he balked. Instead of the 'big fellow ... extraordinarily clumsy and awkward' described by Pierné, the 'self-contained and rather distant' student that Raymond Bonheur knew, and the friend 'with an intense and shy expression', described by Vidal, there appeared around 1880 a Debussy who was impatient, exasperated with the futility of official instruction, and determined upon disruption. He rebelled openly, with spirit, with a youthful and ironically contemptuous violence, which could only bring upon him hostility, above all from those conventional persons who lacked feeling and held fast to their prerogatives. It was really those who played a brief part in his life and were of small importance to him who showed unthinking and enduring antagonism: Camille Bellaigue, Arthur Pougin, Henry Roujon, Théodore Dubois, Léo Delibes, Camille Saint-Saëns, and later Eugène d'Harcourt,

---

[14] André Suarès confirmed this in his letter dated 14 Jan. 1890 to Romain Rolland: 'Monsieur Achille Debussy ... has for his Prix de Rome, like a plunderer, written a cantata (a caricature) on a pattern as Gounod–Massenet-esque as it could be' (*Cette âme ardente* (Paris, 1954), 206).

* [*Envoi* is the term describing a required work, upon which the members of the Académie evaluated the progress made by the various winners of the Prix de Rome.]

and, up to a certain point, Vincent d'Indy and Romain Rolland. The Debussy of the years 1880 to 1884 really must have been most annoying and exasperating. Maurice Emmanuel suggests that he was showing off. The supervisor of the Conservatoire treated him as though he was 'possessed'. But was it just an act? In the eyes of the majority he seemed unscrupulous, as Eugène d'Harcourt put it twenty years later. But more probably, his rebellious pretensions were the spiteful and rancorous reactions of a rather awkward young man who had endured sharp rebuffs in piano, in harmony, and in the preliminary examination for the Prix de Rome competition in 1882. There is no other way to explain the peevishness that certain people felt for him, or the frequently hostile criticisms that he inspired.[15]

The second phase of Debussy's progress towards academic success followed. On 23 May 1884 nine candidates entered their hermetically sealed studios. They had twenty-five full days to write a score to the text of *L'Enfant prodigue*. The Vasniers came to encourage their protegé. Likewise some of the young rebel's friends came too: Grandjany threw him packets of tobacco. The first audition occurred on 27 June,* lasting from noon until four in the afternoon. The sky was cloudy, the atmosphere heavy. The deliberation stretched out interminably. Debussy did not obtain the majority of five votes until the second ballot. The next day, Saturday, the second hearing took place, at the Institute. The publisher Durand remembered the occasion: 'Debussy at one piano, with Chansarel at the other, was nervous . . . but completely in control of himself . . . ; a great sensation with Lia's aria . . . and with Azaël's . . . ; the deliberation of the judges . . . a moment filled with trepidation.'[16]

Then Debussy won at the first vote, by twenty-two out of a possible twenty-eight, thanks to the good will of the painters, it has been said. Some opinions: 'Very marked poetic sense, brilliant warm colours, the music has life and drama.' The 'appearance of disagreement', reported by *Le Figaro* in its account of this victory, was due to a matter of personalities. The protest had been chiefly inspired by 'this poor M. Ernest Reyer', as Debussy would later refer to him, and protracted by

---

[15] Note that Camille Bellaigue, considered from 1890 on as an 'eminent critic', would make a speciality of discrediting all men of outstanding talent.
[For a more favourable view of Bellaigue, see L. Laloy, *La Musique retrouvée, 1902–1907* (2nd edn. rev. & enl., Paris, 1974), 107.]

[16] J. Durand, *Quelques souvenirs d'un éditeur de musique*, i (Paris, 1924), 30.

* [*L'Enfant prodigue* was sung on this occasion by Rose Caron, Ernest van Dyck, and Alexandre Taskin, accompanied by Debussy and René Chansarel at two pianos.]

several like-minded people, among them Arthur Pougin.* It was because Reyer—or to give him his real name, Ernest Rey—had his own candidate, Charles René—or, to give him his real name, Charles Bibard.

Debussy reacted to his success with 'an intense emotion'. He was proud of it, although he tried to seem unimpressed. His teacher Guiraud exulted. His advice had been good. The greatest happiness was experienced by Debussy's parents, and in that their son shared in large part, for he had wanted to win the prize for them. At his father's death in 1910 Debussy confessed to Caplet on 21 November that he had almost never shared any opinions with his father, except for the 'partial admiration' he held for *L'Enfant prodigue* (1957a, p. 48). If it was only a step forward for the composer, for his father, the victorious cantata represented, not so much a hope realized as a compensation for the older and dearer dream of the son who would become a virtuoso. *L'Enfant prodigue* gave him back the image of his own prodigal son, who had disappointed his hopes as a young father, and M. de Bussy, now in his fifties, saw with emotion how his own pitiful illusions, his own setbacks, and his bitterness had at last found a consolation.

From this first victory came Debussy's first verifiable notoriety. On the advice of Vasnier, de Bussy had only to become Debussy. His laurel wreath is his baron's coronet; the Villa Medici, his symbolic barony.[17]

[17] When the prize was awarded, on 5 Aug. 1884, M. Kaempfen, director of the Beaux-Arts (and another member of La Marmite) urged the winners to be patient. 'Do not affront the public too soon, either in the theatre or elsewhere. Don't desert this institution before the time is right. Do not give yourselves the wrong reason for leaving it: that if one stayed longer one would lose one's originality.'

* [Pougin's biased account of the competition appeared in *Le Ménestrel*, 29 June 1884.]

7

'My sojourn no longer
pleases me'

PERHAPS the years of 1885 and 1886 that Debussy spent in Rome were the lost years that he mentioned in his letters to Vasnier and Émile Baron. It is tempting to believe so. There was nothing he could bring back from Rome that he could not have found in Paris: except perhaps a single conviction that he was irremediably different from his companions. If he hated leaving Paris, it was because he loved Mme Vasnier, and if his stay in Rome did not give him any true happiness, if he was in despair there, it was chiefly because he was separated from her. Yet it was also being far from Vasnier himself and his encouragement, and from Émile Baron, that generous bookseller, who supplied him with books, periodicals, and writing paper, who took him to dinner and exchanged ideas with him. These were the regular things that he missed, a friendly, intellectual ambience, perhaps even the cooking, judging from the memory that he preserved of the 'sweet stuff' with its flavour of rancid oil and soured cream that was served to the *pensionnaires* by the cook at the Villa Medici.[1]

It is quite true that Rome bored and oppressed him, that he could find pleasure in scarcely anything there. Nearly twenty years later, he retained the memory only of the trees at the Villa and of 'the violet softness of the Umbrian hills'. In this city, with all its grandeur and majesty, Debussy became an eager collector of little ivory curios.[2] He classified butterflies for his father, treating the specimens with camphor.[3] He liked only the little Anima chapel* among the churches, whose exuberant magnificence shocked him. The muscled realism of Signorelli's *The Resurrection of the Dead* astonished him more than it pleased him. He probably preferred the melancholy sweetness of Sassoferrato's *The Madonna of the Rosary*—a blessed damozel. If at length Rome brought him to despair, it was because he was searching, groping his way, and he did not complete any composition except *Printemps* and the fifth of the Verlaine *Ariettes*,

[1] *Musica*, May 1903.   [2] *ReM*, 1 May 1926, p. 11.
[3] Letter of Debussy to Claudius Popelin, dated 24 June [1886] (1980, p. 16).

* [S. Maria dell'Anima, the church of the German Catholics in Rome.]

'Green', which dates from January 1886, and which he mentioned to Vasnier without naming it in his letter of 19 October.

It may be that he failed to adapt himself to Rome because he was 'still a young, unpolished Parisian' as Henry Prunières has written.[4] Rather, according to Widor, he belonged

to the first of the two categories of 'Romans', by that I mean our *pensionnaires* there ... the first lack curiosity, they live in Rome as they would in Paris, and, becoming bored with Rome, they dream only of seeing the boulevards or Montmartre once more. The second group comprise those curious to see and to learn, who are avid students of the works of Latin antiquity, of the Italian Renaissance, and these enrich themselves with important memories.[5]

That is to say that Debussy, like Berlioz, fifty-four years earlier, already contained within himself the essentials of his nature. He had become aware of the depth of his originality. In acknowledging Debussy's talent, Gounod had affirmed his originality when he told him that he should not be afraid to feel different from other people. Debussy's aesthetic sense was as yet uncrystallized. He made slow progress; however, he never looked back, knowing more or less what he had to avoid, but still hesitant about how to express himself.

According to Article 6 of the Regulations of the Académie de France in Rome, a student was required to be present at the Villa Medici only 'during January of the year in which he takes up his scholarship'. But it was lack of enthusiasm (and perhaps the opportunity to hear the first performance, on 25 January 1885, of *La Sauge fleurie*, Vincent d'Indy's legend for orchestra) which made Debussy defer his departure from Paris until the final days of that month. He travelled by sleeping car (a train journey lasting forty-eight hours), but that was not from vanity, as has been asserted, but the custom, thanks to the 600 francs travel allowance granted by the Académie for the prize-winners' trip to Rome.[6]

Leaving Paris on 27 January under a cloudy sky—all the same, proud enough to be a person of even some small distinction—and arriving in miserable weather, he took a prompt dislike to everything: his fellows, the conversation, the Villa, his room. He was unable to work. Almost immediately he wrote to Vasnier: 'I am afraid I may return to Paris

[4] *ReM*, 1 May 1926, p. 42.

[5] C.-M. Widor, *Fondations: Portraits de Massenet à Paladilhe* (Paris, 1927), 186.

[6] At that time the yearly allowance to the Prix de Rome winners was 3,510 fr. Held back from this amount was 1,200 fr. for board and an additional 300 fr. as a reserve fund, which was returnable at the end of the scholarship. The balance, 2,010 fr., was given them in monthly instalments of 167.50 fr. The musicians also received 50 fr. to cover the cost of copying each *envoi*. Servants took care of their rooms and waited at table.

sooner than you imagine' (*ReM*, 1 May 1926, p. 27). In May he caught a fever and said again to Vasnier, on 4 June: 'The idea has often occurred to me to leave this dreadful barracks. . . . Unfortunately, your letter . . . has opposed my attempts at flight' (*ReM*, 1 May 1926, p. 28). His fellow scholars were to say that he was not very well liked at the Villa Medici. With one or two exceptions, the opinion was mutual. There was a lack of aesthetic compatibility, there was a difference of background, of aims. He formed a short-lived friendship with Gustave Popelin, who had won the prize for painting in 1882, and was the son of the painter and enameller Claudius Popelin-Ducarre, less well known for his *Caesar* at the museum in Chantilly than for his love affair with the niece of another Caesar, the Princess Mathilde. To tell the truth, Debussy courted the Popelins,[7] both father and son, and he benefited from their advice and help and also from the concern of at least one of their friends, Count Joseph Primoli, known as Gégé, a distant cousin of Napoleon III's daughter-in-law.

Right away he confided to M. Popelin that he was madly in love with Mme Vasnier. 'I have become accustomed to only wanting and only imagining *through her* . . . this love which is mad . . .' (1980, p. 16). Agitated and deeply moved, barely over his fever, it is hardly surprising that he could not stand the Villa, which reeked of school, and that he should scorn his studious companions, fellows without problems, mindlessly carefree. Always complaining, perhaps for effect, he gained the sympathy of Count Primoli, who allowed him to use his 'cottage' at Fiumicino. There at last Debussy was satisfied, because he could isolate himself. In July 1885 he spent several rustic weeks of forgetfulness by the sea. The pleasure that he felt then, all alone, is characteristic. One must imagine this lad of twenty-three, free at last from that life in the 'barracks', living in Primoli's delightful villa. In a letter to Vasnier of August 1885, Debussy wrote:

Ah! I could satisfy my unsociable instincts as much as I wanted, not knowing anyone, talking only to order food (which certainly gave me a lot of trouble).

I worked almost well; I took walks, as if I had done so since I was born. Perhaps my seaside was as good as yours, come on! There was a lack of people and casinos, obviously, but that is why I loved it . . . (*ReM*, 1 May 1926, p. 30)

There he found himself again, all alone in an unconstrained atmosphere after five months of communal life at the Villa Medici. He enjoyed

---

[7] It seems likely that Debussy's father was in difficulties at this time. In his letter to Claudius Popelin of 24 June [1886], Debussy wrote that his father was still worried, and regretted that he could do nothing further for him. Debussy's father was fired on 12 Apr. 1887 from the Compagnie de Fives-Lille. (See 1980, p. 16.)

once more—perhaps a little egotistically—the independence and the luxury he had been familiar with previously, at the château of Chenonceaux, at the Villa Bonciani in Florence, and in the Russian houses of Mme von Meck—Count Primoli's villa was in the same class. But the satisfaction of his 'unsociable instincts' meant something more than that to Debussy. He revealed what he did during the day in Fiumicino. He took walks, he even worked; doubtless he read. One can easily imagine him holding mysterious conversations with the sea that scraped ceaselessly towards the shore, giving him sharp impressions of the infinite. Consider the sequence: in Cannes when he was eight he dreamed wordlessly beside the sea, and he absorbed it. In Fiumicino at twenty-three, the sea moved him deeply, he talked to it. In Cancale when he was twenty-seven he revelled in it, he summoned it; later, it inspired him, and always it calmed him. 'Surely it is the thing in nature that heals one most.' And in Saint-Jean-de-Luz in 1917, just six months before his death, he would look at it enigmatically.[8]

When he returned to Rome, he resumed his lamentations. 'It is my intention to hand in my resignation at the end of this year.' Then he grew calmer, seeming to have accepted the inevitable; he heard some concerts and played Bach's organ works on the piano with Vidal. He declaimed Shakespeare and read a lot. When he came back to Paris he was already acquainted with works of Tolstoy, Shelley, Flaubert, the Goncourt brothers, Moréas, Huysmans, Bourget, and Richepin. He was at the Villa as little as possible; one day he made a trip as far as Orvieto. He did not stop complaining about himself and his companions or scoffing at Rome and the Romans. He hated the theatrical churches loaded with sculptures, paintings, and mosaics, where 'the Christ has the appearance of a lost skeleton who inquires in a melancholy way why he has been placed there' (*ReM*, 1 May 1926, p. 33).

In January 1886 a worldly woman visited the Villa and offered him an evening of pleasure to ease his frustration. Doubtless this was Mme Hochon, whom he mentioned in his letters of that time. It is odd that the following month he obtained leave of absence, perhaps thanks to her charming support. He remained away for two months. It is not known what he did in Paris during this time; surely he looked up the Vasniers, especially Madame (and perhaps Mme Hochon), his teacher Ernest Guiraud, some of his fellow-students at the Conservatoire, the bookseller

---

[8] Robert Jardillier, in his *Pelléas* (Paris, 1927), 54, notes correctly 'that the only truly satisfied letters that Debussy wrote from Rome relate to his stay at the seaside in Fiumicino'. This confirms clearly that it was the city of Rome and the Villa Medici that bored Claude-Achille.

Baron, and Gounod, whose daughter was getting married. He put up with the lectures of M. Vasnier and, on his return to Rome on 26 April, he admitted that he had left with the intention of handing in his resignation.[9] He remained at the Villa for another two painful months, then, unappeasable and upset, he managed to obtain a further leave of absence. He announced it on 24 June 1886 to Claudius Popelin, and told Gustave Popelin he would be on his way on 3 July.

I expect to leave for Paris on Saturday. I really want to see you and talk to you. I received a letter from my father, in which it seems that he suspects that I am in Paris. He says that he would have only one thing to reproach me with and that is if I came to Paris and did not see him. We will have to talk about all that, because it is altogether very odd (but that is how it is).[10]

Since his return he had been afflicted with a fever, reinforced, doubtless, by an amatory one. His complaints irritated the registrar so much that Vasnier in his impatience would no longer reply to him. Perhaps he had become suspicious. Then Debussy indulged himself by taking Émile Baron as his confidant, but his letters to him are no less gloomy. Debussy had certainly had enough of Rome.[11]

He sought out his path, drawing nearer to it imperceptibly. His aesthetic ideas were maturing, and he shows this more by the projects he abandoned—*Diane au bois*, *Zuleima*, *Salammbô**—than by those he finished—'Green' and *Printemps*—and sketched out—two more *Ariettes*, *La Damoiselle élue*. And it is certain that he became familiar with Mallarmé's *L'Après-midi d'un faune*, at least by 1886, for the Symbolist review *La Vogue*, which he is known to have read and appreciated, published in its twelfth number (of 12–19 July 1886) a study by Theodor de Wyzewa, which

[9] Léon Vallas claimed there was a receipt from the Italian customs (a document now untraceable at the Bibliothèque de l'Opéra), dated 26 Apr. 1885, giving proof of Debussy's earlier 'flight' from Rome, two months after his arrival. He surely misread it, since the '5' can be easily confused with a '6', and therefore this piece of evidence refers to 1886. [In Lesure's opinion, Dietschy erred. He believes 1885 correct.]

[10] Undated letter of Debussy to Gustave Popelin (in a private collection).

[11] Paul Vidal is of the opinion that in his letters to his Parisian friends Debussy 'has much exaggerated his unhappiness (*ReM*, 1 May 1926, p. 16). Going even further, E. Vuillermoz thinks that one must receive 'with some scepticism the laments of the child-martyr' (*Claude Debussy* (Geneva, 1957), 28). In complaining, and he complained sincerely, although certainly with a romantic exaggeration that is explained by his having read Berlioz's *Mémoires*, Debussy was principally searching, in vain, for an ally who would bolster him in his conviction to leave Rome.

* [That Debussy considered *Salammbô* as an *envoi* from Rome is explained by Massenet's proposal to the Académie, and accepted by it, that 'the *pensionnaires* would have the right to produce, for an *envoi*, the music of an opera in one act' (reported in *Le Ménestrel*, 22 Jan. 1882). Ernest Reyer's *Salammbô* had its première at the Monnaie, Brussels, 10 Feb. 1890.]

seems to anticipate the effect of Debussy's music: 'There is, in *L'Après-midi d'un faune*, a light flow of syllables, some warm languor, an attractively primitive modulation, an alternation of melodies first fleeting then augmenting, according to whether the dream flickers or fades in the sensitive soul of the faun.'

As early as 4 June 1885 Debussy had expressed himself to Vasnier in this way: 'I would always prefer a subject where, in some way, the action would be sacrificed to the expression of the feelings of the soul examined at length. It seems to me that there music can become more human, more alive, that one can explore more deeply and refine the means of expression'. He did not want at all 'to keep falling back into the same old paths'. (*ReM*, 1 May 1926, p. 29)

The following year he described his difficult problem to Vasnier, on 19 October 1886: 'I find myself obliged to invent new forms ... since I would like to arrive at a point where the tone remains lyrical without being absorbed by the orchestra.' In the same letter he spoke of seeking music that was 'supple enough ... so that it could adapt itself to the lyric motions of the soul, to the whims of reverie' (*ReM*, 1 May 1926, p. 39). He was busying himself then with *Diane au bois*, to a text by Banville, which he had begun in Paris. Although the review *L'Art en Italie* would announce its completion, it would never be finished.[12]

According to Léon Vallas, these ideas would have been inspired, if not dictated, to Debussy, by Catulle Mendès in the course of a conversation that took place in 1884, and which Mendès published in the *Revue wagnérienne* of 8 June 1885. One may seriously doubt this, even if one cannot absolutely refute it. Moreover, Vallas did not establish that Debussy was the one conversing with Mendès, whose ideas, except for those which would be normal to two men with a French education, were very far from Debussy's youthful aesthetic, which he had already started to formulate. From Mendès's point of view, everything should be sacrificed to the drama, that is to say, to the action. This is the opposite of what Debussy maintained: 'that the action must be sacrificed to the expression'. Already the musician had shown the signs of his quietism, his contained feelings, his internalization of experience; the critic, on the other hand, wanted brilliance, violence, flair, 'proud, heroic action,

---

[12] It consists of 29 pages from Act II, sc. 3 and 4, as a duet for Eros and Diane (in a private collection). Some fragments of this unfinished work have been examined by Y. Tiénot and O. d'Estrade-Guerra, who describe it as 'not very innovative but filled with a delicate freshness'.

[*Diane au bois* has been discussed at greater length in R. Orledge, *Debussy and the Theatre* (Cambridge, 1982), 37–40. It was first heard on BBC Radio 3, 9 Nov. 1968.]

complication . . . unexpected events'. Mendès recommended the imitation of Wagner, 'not as the poet–composer, but as the writer on aesthetics'. He limited the proper source of a musician's inspiration to popular French songs. Debussy had lost his taste for chivalric adventure; it was man that interested him, not superman. To substitute a Roland for a Parsifal did nothing to change the spirit and atmosphere of a dramatic action. By his first important choice of a subject, *Diane au bois*, Debussy proved that he was not seeking for swords or cuirasses, or for pieces with intricate plots. He had proved it with *Zuleima*, and he would prove it permanently with *La Damoiselle élue*.

Certainly the two speakers in that article in the *Revue wagnérienne* (one of whom could be imaginary) are in agreement about the ludicrousness of traditional opera, in which they find certain Germanic extremes irritating to the French spirit. By implication, they both further criticize empty-headed virtuosity; both of them in fact seem to agree almost too readily. But in the end Mendès does not propose anything, other than Wagner, who might serve as a point of departure for a young French composer. Yet Debussy had written to Vasnier on 19 October 1886: 'I could make use of Wagner, but I do not need to tell you how ridiculous it would be for me even to try' (*ReM*, 1 May 1926, p. 39).

It is not only ridiculous but strange that in 1890, as will be seen, Debussy was unfaithful to himself, weary enough of his search to discard his own aesthetic principles and follow those of this same Mendès into a sort of Latinized Wagnerism in *Rodrigue et Chimène*, which would inevitably remain unfinished.

The Académie had severely judged *Zuleima*, his first regular *envoi*, a work still unknown (or lost), which was judged strange, incomprehensible, and unperformable, even though, according to its composer, it was a work reminiscent of Verdi and Meyerbeer.[13] Saint-Saëns was not prone to appreciate orchestral works written in a key with six sharps. The jury was scarcely less tolerant in the case of *Printemps*, the second *envoi*, finished in Rome in February 1887, in its reduction for two pianos. It was inspired in turn by Botticelli's *Primavera*, and also by the delicate grace of Marcel Baschet's *Printemps*, which the painter had just completed and which was also derived from Botticelli.[14] *Printemps* was Debussy's farewell to Rome,

[13] *Zuleima* should in truth be classified among the lost works, for Louis Laloy had already described it so in 1909, in his *Claude Debussy* (p. 17), written with information supplied by the composer himself. Laloy mentions *Almanzor*; *Zuleima* is its heroine.

[14] It was Debussy's fourth *envoi* from Rome. The original painting, which was at the Université des Annales, has been destroyed, but the sketch survives in the collection of Paul Baschet.

'a dazzling joy at being reborn to a new life', as he wrote to Émile Baron on 9 February 1887 (1980, p. 18).

On 5 March 1887, his required residence strictly at an end,[15] and contrary to what has often been affirmed, Debussy left Rome for good, carrying with him a memento from the Director Hébert inscribed: 'to our very dear musician Debussy, who will be sorely missed'. On his return to Paris, he confronted Vasnier with the step already taken. He had been able to sketch two other *Ariettes* 'C'est l'extase' and 'Il pleure dans mon cœur', as well as *La Damoiselle élue*, based on Rossetti's poem, 'The Blessed Damozel'. He had made notes for a *Salammbô*. He had got to know Maurice Vaucaire, who had proposed that they collaborate upon his adaptation of *As You Like It*, but nothing arose from these last two projects.

Achille Debussy's life in Rome had come to an end. Certainly, he was not yet seeing Mélisande, not even her shadowy silhouette. Now his women were Diane, Salammbô, Zuleima, and the celestial *Damoiselle élue*. Then would come Baudelaire's poetry, which would push aside these pallid, though moving, phantoms of his adolescence. And Mélisande would appear in his dream, in which he would be Pelléas. They could not materialize in that Italian glare, he could not even conceive them, and in Rome less than elsewhere. His feelings were too deep, too passionate not to summon a curtain of mist and a gloomy castle. For love is a sublime wound that sun and orange trees can rapidly heal to the sounds of the guitar, but which opens wide to the mysterious melancholy of forests where light does not penetrate, of ghastly hollows, of forgotten fountains, of grottos that sleep peacefully, of that silence filled by the imperceptible tremor of the invisible. It is within a total fusion of all earthly life that love comes to understand how to earn eternity, in a spasm towards peace-endowing death.[16]

---

[15] '[The *pensionnaires*] are obliged to remain in Rome for at least two years', according to Article 5 of the decree of 4 May 1864.

[16] In Rome Debussy had enjoyed reading the *Mémoires* of Berlioz. Re-reading them, one cannot help but see a relationship of temperament between these two composers, whose most obvious characteristics are the violence of their responses and the impatience of their desires. It is perfectly possible that Debussy might have imitated his elder to some extent. In any case, certain of Berlioz's literary images will recur in pages written by Debussy. For example, in his sixth letter to Heinrich Heine, Berlioz wrote, 'the prickly field of irony, where absinthe and euphorbia grow'. In the same vein Debussy wrote to Chausson in 1893 of 'those paths beside which only rhubarb and poppies grow' (in Oulmont, *Musique de l'amour*, i. 65).

8

'Friendships ... Aesthetics ... the whole Gamut'

FRIENDSHIPS and the clarification of aesthetic aims dominate the six years following Debussy's return from Rome. In 1887 he slipped out of harness and began to make a serious and intelligent use of his regained liberty. He concentrated intensely upon artistic and intellectual questions. If this activity were to be measured merely by the number of men of the first rank whom he met, one can get a very accurate impression of it, and its importance will soon become clear.

In a very real sense, Debussy had never left Paris. His instinct had infallibly shown him that in Rome, 'this city of marble and fleas', he could more easily have withered than flourished, not only because of the character of the place itself, but also because of the mental capacities of his companions at the Villa Medici, none of whom achieved real fame.

Immediately upon his return he sought out his teacher Ernest Guiraud. He felt that he still needed him as a specialist able to give him important advice about technique. They held conversations about music over a period of two or three years, which Maurice Emmanuel has recorded faithfully.[1] Debussy continued to read widely: Shakespeare, Verlaine, Poe, Villiers, Shelley, Swinburne, and Huysmans. He became a close friend of Paul Dukas, who was filled with imposing projects. He met him twice a week, confiding to him his ideas, his plans, and his ambitions, and dedicating to him *La Damoiselle élue*, completed in 1888.

Little light has been shed on Debussy's activity during the first two years following his return from Rome. Beyond two or three letters from Italy, at the beginning of 1887, and nine passionate ones, recently published, addressed either to Gustave Popelin or his father,* which refer

---

[1] In his 'Carnet', published *in extenso* in *Inédits sur Claude Debussy*, Collection Comœdia-Charpentier (Paris, 1942), 27–33. [A translation of these conversations forms Appendix B in E. Lockspeiser, *Debussy: His Life and Mind*, i (2nd. edn., London, 1966), 204–8.]

* [M. Cobb, 'Claude Debussy to Claudius and Gustave Popelin: Nine Unpublished Letters', *19th Century Music*, 18 (summer 1989), 39–48.]

['Friendships ... aesthetics ... the whole gamut' is taken from Debussy's inscription to Paul Dukas, dated 25 May 1897, on a copy of the second edition (1897) of *Prélude à 'L'Après-midi d'un faune'*.]

to Mme Vasnier and undoubtedly date from 1887, no other correspondence from the years between 1887 and 1889 is known. In the latter year Debussy formed a close friendship with Robert Godet. This much, however, is certain. In March 1887 he completed the two *Ariettes* sketched in Rome. He read Mallarmé's *L'Après-midi d'un faune* and worked at orchestrating *Printemps*. He started *La Damoiselle élue*** and began what was to become the fifth of the *Cinq Poèmes de Charles Baudelaire*, 'La Mort des amants' (December 1887). He was accepted for membership of the Societé Nationale in 1888. Probably he attended the first performance of *Lohengrin* in France (3 May 1887);† on 18 May he could have heard Chabrier's *Le Roi malgré lui*; on 9 June, Alfred Bruneau's *Kérim*; on 29 January 1888, Chausson's *Viviane*; on 7 May of that year, Lalo's *Le Roi d'Ys*. It is not true that he went to Vienna and there met Brahms; that is a fabrication, as has been noted, like his trip to London, undertaken to 'negotiate' a performance of *La Damoiselle élue*.[2]

La Damoiselle élue took shape little by little.‡ She is none other than the younger sister of Mélisande, a boarding-school Mélisande. Debussy's choice of subject is highly significant. In the realm of chastity, the adolescent Damoiselle found a place between the virginal Diane and the intense Mélisande. It shows, further, that Debussy was already seeking how to move away from Wagner. It demonstrates above all Debussy's keen attraction towards those mystical idealists who seek in their deepest emotions the wellsprings of their spiritual rapture. Maeterlinck was such

---

[2] Léon Vallas, who had reported these two facts in the first edition of his *Claude Debussy et son temps* (Paris, 1932), acknowledged in the second revised edition (of 1958) that he had been taken in by the fabrications of André de Ternant of London.

* [In this same year of 1887 Debussy's younger brother Alfred, then seventeen, was also engaged in a project relating to D. G. Rossetti. On 8 October he wrote to Édouard Dujardin offering for publication a complete verse translation of Rossetti's *The Staff and Scrip* as *Le Bourdon et la besace*. His translation appeared in the Nov. 1887 issue of *La Revue indépendante*, pp. 185–92.

This work of Alfred's places a different light upon the intellectual atmosphere of Debussy's family than has traditionally been shown. Clémentine had raised Alfred until her death, when he was twelve, and this literary effort testifies to her beneficent influence. Further, Alfred's activity appears to substantiate Paul Vidal's estimate of the de Bussy household, see above, Ch. 6, n. 9.]

† [The first Paris performance of *Lohengrin* was given at the Eden-Théâtre, 3 May 1887, postponed from 30 Apr. 1887, due to public protest and demonstrations (for further information, see *RIMF*, 1 (Feb. 1980), 25–51).]

‡ [Gabriel Sarrazin's translation of Rossetti's poem had first appeared in 1885 in the *Revue contemporaine*, with the title *La Damoiselle bénie*. The text as set by Debussy involved changes in each of Sarrazin's stanzas, frequently approaching Rossetti's English more closely than did Sarrazin (see M. Cobb, *The Poetic Debussy: A Collection of his Song Texts and Selected Letters* (Boston, 1982), Appendix B, pp. 283–90).]

another, to whom Edgar Allan Poe had given incentive. Of Italo-English descent, Dante Gabriel Rossetti combined the calm workmanship of the southern part of his heritage with a cool passion that came from the north. *La Damoiselle élue* came from the tender side of Debussy; *La Chute de la Maison Usher*, which he thought of immediately after, would have been from the other side of his nature.

La Damoiselle élue is a figure from a dream, an ecstatic Mélisande. And this angelic figure from a missal inspired Debussy at the time (1887) when he visited Mme Vasnier at Dieppe, where she was on holiday with her husband in the cottage of the painter Mélicourt. But she was not, like the Damoiselle, leaning 'on the golden bar of heaven'. According to the painter Blanche, 'One night coming back late to Bas-Fort-Blanc with Ochoa, we could distinguish in the shadows a rope ladder, Mme V. [*sic*] at the window, and Debussy clambering up.'[3]

The confidant and accomplice of these rendezvous was Gustave Popelin, who received from Debussy passionate letters that are today in a private collection. Later, only silence. It is true that about 1890, when Mme Vasnier was forty-two, she became buxom, as can be seen in a photograph of that time that shows her in a gown of quilted satin, plump of face, her eyes dry, her arms crossed, the provocative thrust of her breasts balanced by her hips drawn back. Mme Vasnier had taken on the amplitude of one of Rubens's models. Perhaps, too, the registrar had grown impatient, and perhaps he was aware of gossip. Then the Vasniers moved to another quarter of Paris, and changed their summer residence. They departed abruptly from Debussy's life. He never saw them again, which is to say he was no longer admitted to their home. He would make a further offering—'to Mme Vasnier, in grateful homage'—inscribed on a copy of each of the six *Ariettes* which had just been published (1888), a farewell after the more ardent dedications that had preceded it.* There was no such gesture with the *Cinq Poèmes de Charles Baudelaire* of the following year.[4] The Vasniers opened and closed a chapter of Debussy's life. He had encouraged him to persevere. She had initiated him in love. Having arrived at the stage when reality caused disenchantment, he took

---

[3] J.-É. Blanche, *La Pêche aux souvenirs* (Paris, 1949), 224.
[4] M. Vasnier died in 1919, his wife in 1923; both are buried at Pont-Audemer. Marguerite, eclipsed in her mother's dazzling wake, died unmarried in 1935. And Maurice, in a hurry to separate himself from a socially prominent mother and to avoid the knowing smiles of Paris, retired to the provinces, where he died at Nantes in 1932, having led an uneventful life as a tax collector and leaving no issue.

---

* [*Mandoline*, however, bore the simple dedication 'A Madame Vasnier' when it was first published in *La Revue illustrée*, 1 Sept. 1890.]

leave of the Vasniers without too much regret in order to devote himself to friends who were younger, more enthusiastic, more closely involved with the literary and artistic movements of the period.[5]

From this time on Debussy maintained a wide relationship with many varied groups. His closest friendships were, as we have seen, with Dukas and even with Ernest Guiraud, his former teacher. Then he attached himself to the Peters. There was a spontaneous but brief relationship with Michel Peter, and a very close one a little later with his brother René Peter. Others in this group were Étienne Dupin, with his hidden sensitivity, who had inherited from his Scottish mother his blue eyes and his peaches-and-cream complexion; and Eugène Belin, future stockbroker who would serve Debussy as financial adviser; these last four were all related to each other.

In a second group, of bourgeois artists, amateurs of all the arts, we find Raymond Bonheur (the nephew of Rosa, the animal painter), who had been his friend at the Conservatoire, Ernest Chausson and his brother-in-law the painter Henri Lerolle, the violinist Eugène Ysaÿe, the lawyer and music-enthusiast Paul Poujaud, as well as Camille Mauclair and Maurice Denis.

In a third group, of Protestants, there was Robert Godet, from the family of theologians in Neuchâtel, a correspondent for *Le Temps*, a solitary figure whose knowledge was encyclopaedic, with a proud but melancholy mind; Édouard Rist, the famous tuberculosis specialist, who died in 1956; the painter Lucien Monod, and the musician Charles Koechlin.

The Stevens family comprised a group by themselves. At the head was Alfred, the rich and famous 'painter of love-letters', then nearing the end of his career, and his sons and daughter: Léopold, Pierre, Jean, and Catherine.

Beyond these there was a group of musicians he had known at the Conservatoire: among them, Paul Dukas, Gabriel Pierné, Paul Vidal, Xavier Leroux, and René Chansarel. A further circle of professional musicians: André Messager, Vincent d'Indy, Gabriel Fauré, Gustave Doret, Pierre de Bréville, Gustave Charpentier, Raoul Pugno, and Jules de Brayer. In later years he would get to know Isaac Albeniz, Maurice

[5] Debussy's parents moved as well. In 1888 they left the rue Clapeyron for a fourth-floor flat overlooking the courtyard at 27 rue de Berlin (the present rue de Liège). This new flat was roomier. Achille had his own entrance. Birds let out of their cage flew about the rooms. This last may be taken as evidence of the independent spirit that obtained in the household of Mme de Bussy.

Ravel, Charles Bordes, Guy Ropartz, Gustave Samazeuilh, Maurice Delage, and Louis Aubert. His circle of literary acquaintances included: Stéphane Mallarmé, Pierre Louÿs (for a time the closest), Henri de Régnier, Francis Viélé-Griffin, Maurice Bouchor, Georges Courteline, Octave Mirbeau, Jean de Tinan, Léon Blum, Jules Bois, Paul Valéry, André Gide, and Gabriel Mourey. Among critics: Pierre Lalo and Catulle Mendès. Among publishers: Jacques Durand, the earliest and, in all senses, the most astute; and particularly Georges Hartmann, wise and generous, if disorganized. Among painters: Jacques-Émile Blanche, Toulouse-Lautrec, and the sculptress Camille Claudel, the sister of Paul. He got to know the aristocrat, financier, and industrialist, and generous patron, Prince André Poniatowski. Then there were the two related families, connections of Ernest Chausson and Henri Lerolle: the Fontaines and the Desjardins. A further group that had its focus at the Chat Noir cabaret included Alphonse Allais, Raoul Ponchon, Vital Hocquet, Maurice Donnay, and Erik Satie. Others he ran into before 1900 were Maurice Curnonsky, Nicolas Coronio, Paul-Jean Toulet, Raoul Bardac, Marcel Proust, and Reynaldo Hahn, but with these last two he had nothing in common.[6]

Debussy scrutinized interestedly and speculatively all these different people, notables of their day or of days to come, none of them, moreover, intimately acquainted with him. From them he sought those congenial to his own nature. He was seeking himself, and he opened his heart only to those who were sensitive and sincere.

It is known that Debussy's first contact with Wagner's music dates from 1876, at the Conservatoire (if not from 1871 at Cannes), but it is not known what he said about it then. On 20 April 1879 the programme of the Concerts Pasdeloup included the first act of *Lohengrin*. It is also known that Debussy heard *Tristan* in Vienna in the autumn of 1880,* when he accompanied Mme von Meck for the first year. From that time stems his fondness for *Tristan*, which Raymond Bonheur confirmed when he reported that Debussy 'possessed' the score before he went to Russia in

---

[6] Neither of these two liked either Debussy or his music. Hahn was resolutely hostile, spreading his purely personal opinion: Debussy is a false innocent, a fraud. And Proust, even more barbed, went so far as to speak of 'farts' when referring to the music of *Le Martyre de Saint Sébastien*, as Vuillermoz recalled it (*Claude Debussy*, p. 92).

[As far as Hahn's opinion of Debussy's music goes, Dietschy may be overstating his case. René Peter, mentioned that, after one of the early performances of Debussy's opera, Hahn sent the composer a bouquet ('Ce qui fut la "Générale" de *Pelléas et Mélisande*', *Inédits sur Claude Debussy*, p. 10).]

* [Almost certainly this was a concert performance of excerpts.]

1881.[7] For her part, Marguerite Vasnier recollected that he 'used to play and sing some Wagner' when he still came to her parents' house. Finally, on 23 October 1881, the Concerts Lamoureux inaugurated a series of two hundred concerts, given over the next ten years in Paris, and in Charles Lamoureux's programmes the name of Wagner figured 320 times.

Yet it does not seem that the years 1880–4 were particularly Wagnerian ones for Debussy, but rather the five succeeding years. In his known correspondence, the first time Debussy mentioned Wagner occurs in a letter of 19 October 1886 from Rome addressed to Vasnier: 'I could make use of Wagner, but I do not need to tell you how ridiculous it would be for me even to try' (ReM, 1 May 1926, p. 39). Then in a letter from early 1887 to Émile Baron, he wrote: 'The day that you discover that Wagner is not an uncouth boor, you will become for me the most accomplished of my friends' (ReM, Jan. 1934, p. 25). Yet it must be said that Debussy's letters before 1885 are unknown, and this is astonishing. At that time, he was already twenty-three years old. One cannot help wondering what happened to his letters from Russia.

The Revue wagnérienne was started in February 1885. On 3 May 1887 the Parisian première of Lohengrin, the musical event of the year, took place, and among those who went to hear it were Pugno, Dupin, Godet, Fauré, Poujaud, and Chausson. The high point of Debussy's enthusiasm was reached in 1888, when he was invited by Étienne Dupin to make the trip to Bayreuth in August.[8] Undoubtedly, Wagner then exercised an irresistible attraction upon him, as upon the whole artistic and literary world. Pierre Louÿs has left some comments on Debussy and Wagner. One, written by hand and headed 'Tristan played from memory by Debussy', shows that the composer claimed to know Tristan by heart, in spite of himself:

He was challenged to play all three acts; 100 francs, an enormous sum for the young musician, was the bet. He accepted and lost. The basis of this story is true. I suppose it must have been between 1886 and 1891, but who could be certain of it? Who won the bet?[9]

---

[7] ReM, 1 May 1926, p. 7.
[Bonheur's account gives no date for Debussy's first acquaintance with Tristan, but does state that, once Debussy got to know it, it 'never left him after that'.]
[8] In a macaronic letter written together with Bréville, Fauré, and Bagès to Vincent d'Indy from Bayreuth, Debussy commited himself to 'give to the Société Nationale an orchestral composition for the 1888–9 season' (S.I.M., 15 May 1913). This is La Damoiselle élue, which he thought would be a sure thing. One cannot help thinking that this engagement was in the way of being a challenge, and one wonders whether Debussy's enthusiasm for Wagner had not begun to cool by 1888. His reasoned rejection of Wagner, dating from 1886, has already been cited.
[9] The Matarasso Collection, Nice [according to Dietschy in 1962].

Debussy went back to Bayreuth in 1889, and then began the disillusionment: 'What bores these leitmotivs are!... The *Niebelungen*, which
contains some pages that bowl me over, is a contraption. It even causes
my dear *Tristan* to fade, and I regret feeling that I am detaching myself
from it.'[10] Yet, during the same year, but probably earlier, Debussy had
said in a conversation with Guiraud: 'What I love about *Tristan* are the
themes, the reflection of the action. Harmony does not do violence to the
action. Balance.'[11] In fact, Debussy remained attached to *Tristan*, and
passionately so, until his death, even if, after 1893, he attached more
importance to *Parsifal*.

In other notes, transcribed by one of his secretaries, Pierre Louÿs
revealed that, about 1890, leaving Edmond Bailly, of the Librairie de
l'Art Indépendant, he encountered Debussy, whom he had met at
Mallarmé's, and asked him about Wagner. And Debussy answered
unhesitatingly, '*Tristan*'. 'And the rest?' 'The rest ... yes, yes and no ... It
is *Tristan* that gets in the way of our work. One doesn't see ... I don't see
... what can be done beyond *Tristan*.'[12] And Louÿs continues: 'About the
same time, he had naïvely published as the title for a future article:
Concerning the Futility of Wagnerism.' In these same notes, Louÿs revealed:

Fourth period: during and after *Pelléas*. *Parsifal* above all. He loved to quote
certain lines from *Parsifal*, nearly all of which have the same mood: a very gentle
theme, unprepared, which lasts two bars and then fades out. For example: the
theme of the Lake ... the last page of the Good Friday Spell.

He found the prelude to the second act excellent. Simplicity in violence. He
criticized principally the theme assigned to Parsifal himself, which is almost
unchanging, without one's knowing why, and which becomes entirely inadequate at the opening of the last scene.

If I said to him that the first scene of the third act of *Parsifal* is that which most
resembles *Pelléas*, he seemed annoyed at this comparison.

He boasted of having written *La Damoiselle élue* upon his return from Bayreuth
and having succeeded in not imitating *Parsifal*; this demonstrates again the
profound impression that *Parsifal* made upon him.

From the same time. He did not like *The Ring* in its entirety, except for the
Forest Murmurs.[13] At my request he played from memory the prelude to *Tristan*
at Prince André Poniatowski's. He left soon afterwards, as though much moved,

---

[10] Letter to Guiraud of September 1889 (and not 1890, as erroneously stated in *Inédits
sur Claude Debussy*, p. 33, where it was published). There was no festival at Bayreuth in
1890.

[11] *Inédits sur Claude Debussy*, p. 33.
[Dietschy has put together statements from various parts of this rambling discussion.]

[12] Notes that were sold in October 1959 at the Librairie Coulet and Faure, Paris.

[13] G. Robert, *La Musique à Paris: 1895–1896* (Paris, 1896), 56, is of the opinion that the
treatment of a passage from the *Prélude à 'L'Après-midi d'un faune'* 'recalls certain aspects of
the Forest Murmurs'.

and said to me, on the avenue du Bois, in a voice charged with emotion: 'I played that for you', so much had the insensitivity of his hosts wounded his feelings.

Debussy did not know one word of German and judged a drama of Wagner as though it were a symphony. When Debussy wrote *Pelléas*, Wagner dominated the music of the entire world.

In chatting with Debussy, I spoke of Wagner with such exaggerated expressions that they called for contradictions, and I am perhaps the friend to whom Debussy has spoken the least good about Wagner.

None the less, I remain convinced that *Parsifal* and *Tristan* engendered more from Debussy than did the Russians. Quite particularly pages 202–38 of *Parsifal* and the Forest Murmurs. It is a gross mistake to believe that either Debussy plagiarized a master or that he owed him nothing. A great artist, he had no need to plagiarize in order to understand, and to pass beyond.

The extent to which Paris was then subjugated by Wagner should not be forgotten. Literary types studied German. They made it a point of honour to use German expressions to indicate philosophic ideas or the elements of Wagnerian dramaturgy. The yoke of Victor Hugo in literature corresponded to that of Wagner in music. The profusion of small literary and artistic journals showed the reaction taking place, but not yet in music, as is confirmed by two curious articles which we shall see. The Wagnerian banner still floated victorious ten years later, in 1896, and Debussy really seemed to be the only one who had chosen a sovereign way to turn away from Wagner with dignity. In *La Critique* of 5 April 1896, Jules Combarieu, speaking of 'Wagner and the French composers', wrote: 'The group of avant-garde progressives who constitute the revolutionary force have for their leader a man of great learning and lofty inspiration, M. Vincent d'Indy ... [who is] the most brilliant representative of Wagnerism in France.' And with d'Indy's school, he would boldly align Alfred Bruneau, Paul Dukas, Gabriel Fauré, and Gustave Charpentier, a grouping which would earn the writer a trenchant reply from Charpentier that Debussy could have adopted.[14] To continue with the article:

Besides, one might mention those who, improving upon the audacity of French or German masters, work to stress the freedom of the modern style, to push to the limits what is only complex and to reduce to crumbs what had been little more than slices: for instance, Debussy, A. Savard, and Albéric Magnard, next to whom Bach and Wagner seem to be masters of simplification.

[14] 'I have never had anything in common, nor has my music, with the *panurgiens nationaux*, followers of Suns, and I recognize no one as chief, not even and above all "the most brilliant representative of Wagnerism in France".' A slap entirely deserved, aimed both at Combarieu and at those who, impressed by the 'great knowledge' and 'the fine head' of d'Indy, worked to make of this dogmatic Romano-German a guide and an innovator.

Three months later, on 5 July 1896, the same journal 'with an eye to giving an account of the progress recently made by the Wagnerian idea' launched a referendum about the practicability of putting up 'a monument built by Frenchmen in memory of Richard Wagner'. This unfortunate initiative evoked only thirty-four answers, most of them from unknown people: twenty-one favourable, two doubtful, and eleven chauvinistically hostile. Among the most significant, a woeful one from Déroulède,* which referred to Wagner as a 'bandit'; and a very lively one from Willy,† a witty contributor to *Le Canard enchaîné*, which said: 'Wagner is beginning to bore us, my children . . .' Combarieu's article and the referendum in *La Critique* serve to give the temperature and the exact climate of musical Paris at the end of the nineteenth century.

In 1888 Debussy finished *La Damoiselle élue*, the two *Arabesques* for piano, the *Petite Suite* for piano four-hands, the six *Ariettes*, and two of the *Cinq Poèmes de Charles Baudelaire*. In 1889 he started to emerge slowly from the shadows. The report of the Académie des Beaux-Arts on *La Damoiselle élue* was a ray of hope; the tenor Maurice Bagès sang two of the *Ariettes*; the *Petite Suite* was played in a salon by the composer and Jacques Durand, who published it at once. The *Cinq Poèmes de Charles Baudelaire* were completed definitively in March 1889.[15] Debussy played and sang them to Chausson and Godet, but the publishers refused them, and also *La Damoiselle élue*. At that time Debussy did not cut a prominent figure in the musical world, compared with some of his companions. As early as 1887 Pierné had an exclusive contract with a publisher. Vidal had his *Sacre de Charles VII*, his Ave Maria, his incidental music to *Le Baiser*, and his *Hymne à Carnot* all introduced at various concerts. Instead of publishing the *Cinq Poèmes de Charles Baudelaire*, Durand supported Debussy by entrusting to him various arrangements of Saint-Saëns's compositions,

[15] With 'Le Jet d'eau'. It was Debussy who, in the refrain, had substituted the word 'pâleurs' for 'lueurs'; 'pâleurs' does not exist in any edition of *Les Fleurs du mal*. The substitution was decided perhaps with Godet, for in a phrase in his letter of 10 July 1889 Debussy, as though to recall to his friend's mind their earlier discussion, put between quotation marks this word 'pâleurs' . . . 'in mingling our "pâleurs" . . .'.
[Dietschy's interpretation here seems suspect in the context of Debussy's complete letter to Godet, quoted in Cobb, *The Poetic Debussy*, pp. 182–3, and it seems unlikely that Debussy was here discussing the change of text as though it resulted from some earlier conversation.]

* [Paul Déroulède was head of La Ligue des Patriotes and a dedicated anti-Wagnerian.]
† [Pseudonym of Henri Gauthier-Villars (1859–1931), clever and often caustic critic who sometimes wrote under the name of 'L'Ouvreuse'.]

the first of which, *Introduction et Rondo capriccioso*, for two pianos four-hands was published on 24 June 1889.[16]

Having sight-read the *Ariettes*, André Suarès, who was both curious and independent in spirit, observed this new composer with interest: 'His analytical style is very personal. He seems, at last, to have understood Wagner thoroughly, but he does not copy his technique ... a melodic quality that is very subtle ... musical writing of incontrovertible mastery.'[17] In the same letter, Suarès stated that Debussy 'is working at a symphony ... whose idea would seem to be based upon many tales of Poe, particularly *The Fall of the House of Usher*'.

Confirming his taste for Poe is this printed questionnaire that a young woman submitted to him, on 15 February 1889, which he filled out with his customary sincerity.[18]

Your favourite virtue? Pride
Your favourite qualities in men? Will
Your favourite qualities in women? Charm
Your favourite occupation? Reading while smoking rare tobacco mixtures
Your chief characteristic? My hair
Your idea of happiness? To love
Your idea of misery? To be too hot
Your favourite colour? Violet
If not yourself, who would you be? A sailor
Where would you like to live? Anywhere outside the world [*N'importe où hors du monde*][19]
Your favourite prose authors? Flaubert and Edgard-Poè [*sic*]
Your favourite poets? Baudelaire
Your favourite painters and composers? Botticelli, Gustave Moreau, Palestrina, Bach, Wagner
Your favourite hero in real life? Skobeleff[20]
Your favourite heroine in real life? Mme de Beaumont

[16] 'The *Poèmes de Baudelaire* scared off the publishers, as much by the choice of subjects, scarcely suitable to young girls, as by the manner in which they were treated', in the opinion of Georges Servières (*Le Guide musical*, 15/22 Sept. 1895). On the other hand, the first performances of the *Petite Suite* and of the second of the *Arabesques* were given by the students of Mlle Marguerite Balutet on 23 May 1894.
    [C. Goubault, *Claude Debussy* (Paris, 1986), 170, 172.]
[17] Letter from André Suarès to Romain Rolland, dated 14 Jan. 1890 (Suarès, *Cette âme ardente*, p. 206).
[18] This questionnaire was published for the first time in *Le Crapouillot*, Dec. 1903.
    [In the version Debussy filled in, the questions are put in English.]
[19] Although this *N'importe où hors du monde* could be the title of a work by Barrès, it also sounds like Poe.
[20] The conqueror of Turkestan (1843–82). A pantomime entitled *Skobeleff* was then being performed in Paris, at the Hippodrome. Debussy surely went to see it.

Your favourite heroes in fiction? Hamlet
Your favourite heroines in fiction? Rosalind
Your favourite food and drink? Russian food, coffee
Your favourite names? That depends on the people
Your pet aversion? Dilettantes, women who are too pretty
What character in history do you most dislike? Herod
What is your present state of mind? Sad, a seeker, but not on 15 Feb. '89
For what fault have you the most toleration? Errors in harmony
Your favourite motto? Always upward [*Toujours plus haut*]

These various answers reveal much about Debussy. They are valuable in making one acquainted with the man and artist of that time. To be loved is nothing like loving. It is being present; to love, that is dreaming. In fact, Debussy evades the world, as does Poe; like Hamlet he contemplates it. Reading, coffee, tobacco, keep it distant, while the dilettantes and too pretty women are happy to be in the thick of it. His motto betrays the nobility of his ambition. In Botticelli (shades of Rome and of *Printemps*), it is the slender female form that he loves, electric, arousing—in a word, the flesh; the woman here, plaintive and troubled, anticipates moreover Mélisande. On the other hand, in the painting of Gustave Moreau, Georges Rouault's teacher, it is the philosophy he enjoys, the vivid expression of the 'sentiments of the soul'. In time, Turner captured his imagination: in March 1908 he described him to Durand as 'the greatest creator of mystery in art'; then came the turn of Degas, Henry de Groux, Whistler, Velasquez, and, later, Goya. It is remarkable that the Impressionists never aroused his enthusiasm; his attitude seems to have been one of defiance when faced with their 'achievements'.[21] He did, however, enjoy Toulouse-Lautrec.[22]

He saw the sea again on 3 April 1889, when he was invited by Michel Peter and a couple of friends to go to Saint-Énogat, near Saint-Lunaire, where they stayed for two months in Judith Gautier's summer house. Boat trips, in spite of threatening weather, were Debussy's particular pleasure. A tossing sea, a 'tidy' squall: 'Among strong emotions, there was one that

---

[21] According to Robert Godet (1942, p. 43). Perhaps unduly prejudiced by Stevens, Debussy remained faithful to the style of the Second Empire.

[22] Here is what Mme Paul Chansarel, sister-in-law of René Chansarel, one of Debussy's friends, wrote to me:

It was my husband, a friend of Toulouse-Lautrec, who brought the painter and the composer together for the first time. It was one evening when Debussy had dined at my mother-in-law's house, where he was a frequent guest. He and my husband both went to the Moulin-Rouge where they found Toulouse-Lautrec. I do not remember if their friendship was very protracted, but what I am certain of is the admiration these two artists had for each other.

I had never experienced. Danger! It is not displeasing. One feels alive!...' said Debussy.[23]

Completely thrilled, he slipped away from his hosts at Cancale to be alone with the sea for several days in order to 'live again', as he had four years earlier at Fiumicino at Count Primoli's villa. There lies the distant origin of *La Mer*. The sky and the sea thrilled him; their immensity, their restless majesty held for him something implicitly unique and mysterious.

When he returned to Paris, at the end of May, Debussy visited the oriental exhibits at the Exposition Universelle of 1889, which had already been open for three weeks. He enjoyed the strangeness of it. The music of Cambodia, Annam, and Java piqued his curiosity and aroused great sympathy in him. He regarded Eastern music as a sister to Western. He did not assert that Palestrina's counterpoint 'is only child's play' compared to that found in Javanese music. He still counted Palestrina among his favourite composers. Debussy allowed himself to be carried away by the performances of these oriental artists, by a union in which music, dance, and pantomime form inseparable parts, rather than by their technique. The lyric drama was a subject that intrigued him when he saw how these artists developed and communicated it through the expressive power of their free motion, gestures, and music. As he said: 'Action must be sacrificed to expression.'

In August of the same year Debussy returned disenchanted from Bayreuth. He already more than half understood that art, in order to be expressive, has no need of a 'special theatre' or a 'hidden orchestra'.[24] Then at the end of October of the same year, 1889, he continued his conversations with Guiraud, who did not pontificate, and to whom Debussy could expound his theories in order to test them and have them confirmed. He now upheld a new thesis. He believed that music is created to express the inexpressible, that it should come out from the shadows, and the drama should reflect no country, no period of time. He held that music should not be 'developed', but should reject all formulas to become discreet, human, supremely expressive; 'two associated dreams: there is the ideal'.[25]

These ideas are the extension of those that he had tried out on Vasnier from Rome, four or five years earlier, when he had spoken of sacrificing action to expression, of the lyric accent not being drowned by the orchestra, of the music being more human. It was not only the oriental performances at the Exposition of 1889 that strengthened these ideas. He

---

[23] Peter, *Claude Debussy*, p. 123.
[24] This he wrote later in *S.I.M.*, 15 Feb. 1913.
[25] Emmanuel, *Inédits sur Claude Debussy*, p. 28.

was intrigued by Edgar Allan Poe, whom he had identified as one of his favourite prose writers; assuredly Shakespeare too and Villiers de l'Isle-Adam. Thanks to Suarès, we know that in 1889 Debussy was dreaming of, if not actually working on, *La Chute de la Maison Usher*. Probably he had not yet written a note of it; but Poe filled his mind from this time on. Debussy thought about this project, and what appealed to him was Poe's instinct for the invisible, his obsession with death and with existence, his sense of mystery, his fascination with eager, ingenuous women.[26]

This then was the aesthetic that Debussy pursued in 1889. He had some idea of the source for the atmosphere of the lyric drama that he was seeking. A natural progression led him from Shakespeare, through Poe and Villiers, towards Maeterlinck. Nourished by symbolism, Debussy moved imperceptibly towards *Pelléas et Mélisande*.[27] There is no doubt that, from 1888, he dreamed only of writing for the theatre: the proof is in *La Chute de la Maison Usher*, which might have been composed already had he been able to complete his libretto. Further proof is in the *Axël* of Villiers de l'Isle-Adam, for which, according to Vallas, he wrote one scene without going further, doubtless constrained by the often gaudy grandeur of the poem. It is remarkable that his aesthetic fed upon Nordic, particularly Anglo-Saxon, sources: Shelley, Shakespeare, Swinburne, Poe, and later Dickens, Keats, Turner, Whistler, Maeterlinck.

At this point two controversial questions present themselves. What influence did Maeterlinck's *La Princesse Maleine* exert upon the aesthetic of Debussy? What influence did Mussorgsky's *Boris Godunov* have upon his music? Léon Vallas, always a little suspect of being hostile towards Debussy, claimed, without bringing the slightest proof, that Debussy had read *La Princesse Maleine* in 1889 and had been deeply impressed by it; this drama would therefore have directed his aesthetic and would have suggested the ideas that he discussed with Guiraud at this time, those that Maurice Emmanuel raised again in his report.[28] On the other hand, Robert Godet, Debussy's intimate friend, writes that Debussy reacted 'with indifference' to *La Princesse Maleine* (*ReM*, 1 May 1926, p. 77). One wonders whom to believe. Actually, neither the one nor the other, for, if

---

[26] It is known that Baudelaire first read aloud his *Histoires extraordinaires*, his French translation of Poe's *Tales*, at the home of Alfred Stevens in the rue de Calais. Perhaps it was from Stevens's son Léopold that Debussy first became really acquainted with Poe.

[27] 'M. Maeterlinck is ... the only mystic today ... he expresses himself in very clear, very simple phrases, but ones that have a double or a triple sense. ... That is an excellent way to deal with the fantastic ... Poe, the Poe of *The House of Usher*, is assuredly his close master, and Villiers, too ...' (L. Muhlfeld, *Le Monde où l'on imprime* (Paris, 1897), 119–20).

[28] L. Vallas, *Achille-Claude Debussy* (Paris, 1948), 213–14; id., *Claude Debussy et son temps*, p. 143.

at the beginning Debussy had reacted with indifference to this play, one cannot understand why he wanted to set it to music.

Written in 1889 and published in Brussels that year in an edition of 185 copies, *La Princesse Maleine* had made its appearance in France in February 1890. It did not begin to be widely noticed, along with Maeterlinck himself, until after 24 August 1890, the day when Octave Mirbeau in *Le Figaro* brought attention to both of them as he ironically and ostentatiously compared them with Shakespeare. 'I know nothing about M. Maurice Maeterlinck, I only know that no man is less known than he.' Then, he went on to judge *La Princesse Maleine* as 'the most attractive work of its time, superior in beauty to what is most beautiful in Shakespeare'.[29]

It seems evident that Debussy had not read *La Princesse Maleine* in February 1890, since he began work that April on the diametrically opposed *Rodrigue et Chimène* of Catulle Mendès. He waited more than a year to ask Maeterlinck for the rights to set *La Princesse Maleine* to music. On 23 June 1891 Maeterlinck declined to give them to him. June 1891 was, furthermore, the time when *L'Intruse*, Maeterlinck's first play, was performed.

In any event, it seems certain that Debussy had not read *La Princesse Maleine* in 1889. He could have become aware of it in 1890; it is more likely that he became interested in it in 1891. Whether or not he was enthusiastic about it, *La Princesse Maleine* did not determine the direction of Debussy's aesthetic.[30]

It is also difficult to answer the second question: when did Debussy experience the revelation of Mussorgsky, and of *Boris Godunov* in particular? His close friends give different accounts. Raymond Bonheur says laconically, in 1893.[31] Paul Dukas, as related by Robert Brussel acting as a go-between, declares it was 1890; but, he adds, equivocating about the date, that Debussy 'revealed the score of *Boris*' to him 'by playing him the Coronation Scene'. Robert Godet is more explicit: the score of *Boris* was

---

[29] It was Mallarmé who drew Mirbeau's attention to *La Princesse Maleine*, saying to him: 'Read that, it is like a tapestry' (a recollection reported to Oswald d'Estrade-Guerra by his friend, the Symbolist poet, Saint-Pol-Roux). If Mallarmé had not known the play until the first half of 1890, it is scarcely reasonable to think that Debussy would have known of it any earlier.

[30] It matters little to determine whether Debussy owned a copy of the first edition of 1889 or of the second (in duodecimo, Lacomblez, Brussels, 1890), since one still would not know when he actually read through it.

[For a concise account of the question of *La Princesse Maleine*, see Orledge, *Debussy and the Theatre*, pp. 45–6.]

[31] *ReM*, 1 May 1926, p. 77.

submitted to Debussy in 1889, but he was indifferent to it because he could not read Russian, and he paid attention only to a 'very charming little chorus of the Polish maidens'. Jules de Brayer (according to Godet) says: indifference between 1889 and 1896, a total comprehension of Mussorgsky as early as 1901, causing Debussy to publish an emotional report on the song-cycle *The Nursery* in *La Revue blanche* of 1 April. In 1918 Alfred Mortier remembered that Debussy said to him in 1892 or 1893: 'Chabrier, Mussorgsky, Palestrina, those are the ones I like.'[32]

For his part, Debussy wrote, on 23 June 1908: 'I could declare that when I travelled to Russia twenty years ago no one uttered Mussorgsky's name. It is only in France that I began to get to know him.'[33]

Music critics still confuse the issue. Louis Laloy, who wrote his book from information supplied by Debussy, gives 1889 as the date of the revelation of Mussorgsky (but not of *Boris*).[34] Léon Vallas is convinced and is close to affirming that Debussy must have 'heard some works of Russian music' in 1881 or 1882, when he was in Russia with Mme von Meck, but that these included Mussorgsky can be refuted without hesitation, as we have just seen. He thought, as early as 1890, that 'the real, profound, and useful function of Mussorgsky was above all de-Wagnerization'; and Vallas tried to prove it in noting that in *Rodrigue et Chimène* there are eighteen bars that 'bring to mind with great accuracy *Boris Godunov* and *Pictures at an Exhibition*'.[35] On the other hand, Gustave Samazeuilh, who examined this very *Rodrigue et Chimène* and found in it an atmosphere compounded of Wagner, Franck, Borodin, of bel canto, and even an echo of the second *Arabesque* of Debussy, could see no association with Mussorgsky; at least he does not mention it.[36]

André Schaeffner[37] goes much further. He claims that Debussy had known *Boris Godunov* before anyone and had jealously kept it a secret; that he had surreptitiously studied the score and had drawn some decisive

[32] *Le Courrier musical*, 1 Apr. 1918.

[33] Letter to Pierre Lalo (cited at length in Ch. 18).

[34] Laloy, *Claude Debussy*, p. 15.

[Laloy's book is not to be relied upon, as many of the dates are incorrect, even though they were supplied by Debussy.]

[35] Vallas, *Claude Debussy et son temps*, p. 111. Vallas has made a speciality of finding reminiscences of other composers in Debussy's compositions. It is too bad that his instinctive hostility to Debussy the man undercuts the value of his basic judgement and interpretation of Debussy the composer.

[36] *Le Temps*, 25 Dec. 1933. As for Raymond Bonheur, who had heard Debussy play *Rodrigue*, he remembered the end of the act 'where one could already hear the gruff accent of Golaud' (*ReM*, 1 May 1926, p. 5, n. 2).

[37] 'Debussy et ses rapports avec la musique russe', p. 101.

conclusions from it. His hypothesis is based upon two documents and matched by two presumptions. First, there is César Cui's article on *Boris*, which was published in the *Revue et gazette musicale* of 18 January 1880, which, to bolster his argument, Debussy is supposed to have read. Secondly, he claims that in 1889 Debussy had read a socre of *Boris*, said to have been available at the Conservatoire well before then, and had read it with scorn—or pretended scorn—when Godet, believing it was the only example in France, had submitted it to him for his perusal.[38]

A fragile hypothesis, since it rests on the very dubious assumption that Debussy had read Cui's article and been struck by it. Schaeffner does not affirm that this happened in 1880. Amid all the novel information that Schaeffner gives about the matter, one cannot help wondering at the supposition that Debussy would have gone, without being prompted, to consult a journal that had not been published since 1881. This last fact Schaeffner neglects to mention. Who else would have encouraged Debussy to do this, if not Godet, but their friendship did not begin until 1889? Why would Debussy then have studied at the Conservatoire a score of which Jules de Brayer and Godet had shown him a copy that very year, 1889? Why would he have proclaimed his enthusiasm for Wagner and hidden his simultaneous admiration for Mussorgsky? Why, in that questionnaire of 15 February 1889, would he have mentioned just Palestrina, Bach, and Wagner as his favourite composers, and yet affirmed to Alfred Mortier in either 1892 or 1893: 'Chabrier, Mussorgsky, Palestrina, those are the ones I like!' That is to say, why would he create a mystery between 1890 and 1892 of an opinion that he expressed spontaneously after that to Chausson, Dukas, Bonheur, and even to René Peter?[39] The truth is that within the space of two or three years Debussy extols and then renounces Wagner and, simultaneously, first ignores and then becomes familiar with Mussorgsky. It cannot be understood otherwise, since Godet was correct in saying: 'With his friends Debussy was congenitally incapable of dissimulating about matters relating to art' (*ReM*, 1 May 1926, p. 74). Xavier Leroux says something to the same effect in *Les Arts français*, No. 16, of 1918.[40]

In fact, on this whole question of Mussorgsky we are only sure of two points appearing in two letters of Debussy to Chausson. In one, with no

[38] But Schaeffner does not make it clear that Cui placed Alexander Dargomizhsky's *The Stone Guest* above *Boris Godunov*, at the head of all the operas of the new Russian school.

[39] 'The first time I heard the name of Mussorgsky it was spoken by Debussy' (Peter, *Claude Debussy*, p. 131).

[40] In his preface to the Caplet correspondence (1957a, p. 11), Schaeffner tries to show that Debussy contrived mysteries both in his art and in his private life, but the examples he gives are easily refuted.

specific date other than the year 1893, Debussy showed an avid sympathy towards the Russian composer and not the preoccupied but hidden curiosity that Schaeffner describes: 'As I have been very good, bring me some Mussorgsky!' In the second, dated 4 June 1893, Debussy gave Chausson, according to Charles Oulmont, 'important details about Mussorgsky, his most treasured musical concern from now on'.* Now, in fact, he adds some biographical details that are only roughly accurate:

You will know that Mussorgsky is almost contemporary with us. He was an official, then he retired on a small income to a little village, living on the edge of poverty. Note that he was well-groomed and that he would have preferred luxury, but it was for the sake of music that he condemned himself to something approaching exile and fled from the ready pleasures of elegant capital cities. Finally, he died at thirty-nine, around 1880 or 1881. This information comes to me from Jules de Brayer, from whose forehead shine, one might say, prophetic rays when he speaks of Mussorgsky, whom he ranks much above Wagner. He will be very useful to us for a particular project.[41]

This letter of 4 June 1893 from Debussy to Chausson seems decisive.† It almost substantiates the fact that Debussy did not know much about Mussorgsky before 1893. But it is true that his first contact with the Russian composer did date from 1889. That year Rimsky-Korsakov had conducted, on 22 and 29 June, two concerts of Russian music, which included in their programmes: Borodin, Glinka, Cui, Balakirev, Glazunov, and Mussorgsky's *St John's Night on Bare Mountain*.

There is no doubt that Debussy and Chausson in 1893 began a serious study of Mussorgsky's songs and probably of *Boris Godunov* as well. The question of Mussorgsky's influence upon Debussy naturally arises. As a matter of fact, if Mussorgsky had suggested a dramatic climate to Debussy, if he had encouraged him in his researches, and perhaps above all in his intransigeance, if traces of *Boris* had even been found in *Pelléas et Mélisande*, one still could not say that Mussorgsky had determined Debussy's orientation, his aesthetic, or his style. For, even the very early *Nuit d'étoiles* (1880) and *La Damoiselle élue* (1887-8), and the choice of

---

[41] This last phrase, although ambiguous, evidently refers to Mussorgsky rather than to Brayer. (It reminds us of that remark in his letter of 19 Oct. 1886 to Vasnier: 'I could make use of Wagner . . .') The project Debussy referred to was probably either one of the works on which the two friends were engaged at the time: for Debussy, *Pelléas*; for Chausson, *Le Roi Arthus*. Or perhaps it was some emotion or atmosphere to be treated in musical terms that they had been discussing.

* [Oulmont, *Musique de l'amour*, i. 56.]

† [In *RdM* (1962) there are ten letters from Chausson to Debussy, the earliest of which, dated 24 May 1893, inviting him to Luzancy, cites as an added inducement: 'And perhaps the new Mussorgsky scores will have arrived' (p. 49).]

poems up to those of Baudelaire (1887–9) these foretell *Pelléas* specifically. Further it was Wagner who, a few months later, still 'obsesses' Debussy. As he wrote to Chausson, on 2 October 1893: 'I was much too hasty in crowing over *Pelléas et Mélisande* because ... the ghost of old Klingsor, alias R. Wagner, appeared at the turn of a bar, therefore I ripped everything up ...' (1980, p. 55). Perhaps Mussorgsky had assumed for Debussy the value of being an example on a higher plane—that of artistic vocation. When Debussy reported to Chausson what Brayer had told him about Mussorgsky—'that he would have preferred luxury, but it was for the sake of music that he condemned himself to something approaching exile ...'—Debussy was moved by the passion that had inspired his Russian colleague to renounce the ordinary pleasures of life. He probably recognized something of himself in this description, especially because as we are going to see, he was then about to sacrifice his *Rodrigue et Chimène*.

Truly, Debussy had submitted to only one dominant influence: Wagner. Wagner had indeed enchanted Debussy, he had permeated him, as he had subjugated all of Europe. This is the only influence that Debussy had 'submitted to', but he had naturally looked for indications everywhere, and he had solicited contributions from every direction. To free himself he had to find his way: intuiting it, establishing it in advance, drafting it. He detached himself little by little as his progress affirmed itself, as gradually the various ingredients of his art came together and fused.[42] Undoubtedly curious about all types of music in his intense research for a way to perfect what he sought to express, Debussy never halted long before the attractions that he encountered. His incessant march, this undeviating progress, comparable to a stream tirelessly following it course, overturning or evading all obstacles, this progress is confirmed by a remark of Catherine Stevens in her *Notes*: Deubssy 'loved (as do I) the music of Java; one day [he liked] Russian music, another day not. This formed part of his paradoxical nature.'

The heroic jumble of the Exposition of 1889 brought that decade to a climax. During that period Villiers de l'Isle-Adam died humiliated in an asylum. Debussy's grandfather, the old carpenter Claude de Bussy, died two days later at the old people's home at Issy, where he had gone after the death of his wife. But his grandson, the composer Claude Debussy, was not yet Claude, nor even Claude-Achille; he remained Achille throughout his younger years. There survived in him something of the

[42] On the occasion of his enquiry in 1902 into the influence of German music, Combarieu's *Revue musicale* (1, 1 Jan. 1903) reported Debussy's magisterial reply: 'Only those susceptible to being domesticated run the risk of becoming imitators.'

bubbling Achille of his adolescence. It is true that then he seemed to be on an unproductive path. Another one had been foreshadowed, however, from 1876 on, at the Conservatoire, and in thirteen years of research he had conscientiously applied himself to finding his way more clearly. His life, until then, had been a slow ascent, but a continuous one. In 1889 he finally came to see that he could 'make use of Wagner' only to the extent that he could go beyond him. In 1889 the oriental artists had pleased him with their exoticism and their freedom of expression. Villiers and Poe had given him a taste for mystery and the fantastic. Further, in 1889 he had heard two of his six *Ariettes* sung in public; however, he had not found performers for the *Cinq Poèmes de Charles Baudelaire* (printed by subscription), nor for *La Damoiselle élue* (still unpublished), nor for any of his other compositions. The Académie had found fault with his *envois* from Rome; the publishers had ignored him. He still could not get himself noticed anywhere in any important or decisive way. He was obliged to continue the series of transcriptions of Saint-Saëns's works.* In her *Notes*, Catherine Stevens describes Debussy's frame of mind at that time: 'No one wanted to play his music or publish it. He was poor. Léopold (Stevens) took his music to the houses of his friends who were known to support the best music. He brought it back again; no one was interested in it.' †

Tired of waiting, impatient to make his mark, Debussy next undertook the composition of his *Fantaisie* for piano and orchestra (October 1889), and then began this unique period, extraordinary really, when he tricked himself, denying himself in the hope of achieving success, by becoming associated with Catulle Mendès. This period coincides with the entry into his life of an ambitious and energetic woman, Gaby—Gabrielle Dupont—who perhaps personifies the Chimène of *Rodrigue et Chimène*, which the composer was about to begin.

* [These transcriptions included *Caprice pour piano sur les airs de ballet d'Alceste de Gluck*, Symphony No. 2 in A minor, and *Airs de ballet* from Saint-Saëns's own *Étienne Marcel*, all arranged for piano four-hands.]

† [Dietschy has freely adapted and arranged his quotations from these *Notes*.]

9

The Illusory Chimène

An astonishing period—from the end of 1889 to the end of 1892—led Debussy to complete the *Fantaisie* for piano and orchestra, only to bury it unheard, and then to write 126 pages comprising more than two acts of *Rodrigue et Chimène*, only to put that work aside and then, later, to condemn it, to lock it up, and to forbid its circulation.

André Poniatowski informs us that Debussy had probably known Catulle Mendès since 1889. He writes that one day in the autumn of 1890 he encountered 'at a dance at the Hôtel Continental . . . Catulle Mendès, accompanied by Georges Courteline, Claude Debussy, Pierre Louÿs, and one or two other young writers who used to form the usual company of this singular character'.[1]

It is not known whether Mendès had by then made a promise to Debussy or not, but as early as October 1889 the composer had begun his *Fantaisie* for piano and orchestra, which was later to be engraved, thanks to Mendès's support. It derives neither more nor less from the 'loathsome concerto' [*concerto abhorré*], and it is astonishing that Debussy, the delicate, even quietist, poet of his earliest songs, should suddenly develop a taste for fiery virtuosity. Perhaps he felt compelled to give in to the influence of his environment. René Chansarel, to whom the *Fantaisie* is dedicated, had played the Grieg Concerto at the Concerts Lamoureux on 25 November 1888. At the end of the same year, Pierné had given the première of his Concerto in C minor in Marseilles; and Godet remembered a performance of a Borodin symphony, four-hands, at Debussy's flat, 27 rue de Berlin, by Achille and the same Chansarel in 1889 (1942, p. 37). This was the same Borodin composition that Debussy would brand, five years later, as 'crowd-pleasing' in a letter to Pierre de Bréville.

Therefore Debussy began his *Fantaisie* and completed it by the spring of 1890. It was to have been played on 21 April of that year at a concert sponsored by the Société Nationale, but the over-long programme prompted Vincent d'Indy, the evening before the concert, to propose to Debussy the performance of just the first movement of the *Fantaisie*. Whereupon the composer withdrew his score, writing to d'Indy, as Vallas

---

[1] Poniatowski, *D'un siècle à l'autre*, p. 239.

informs us, that there was more value in 'an adequate performance of three movements than in a satisfactory performance of the first'.[2] Debussy confidently displayed the same intransigence in 1896, when he refused to let Ysaÿe conduct some excerpts from *Pelléas et Mélisande* at a concert. And again in 1917, he refused to allow an encore of the 'Intermède' from his Violin Sonata. Yet in 1890 this withdrawal of his composition seems to have been something more than just the scruple of an artist who wants the integrity of his work respected, since later he suppressed his *Fantaisie*. True, nearly a year after the Société Nationale concert he was still waiting to have it played: 'The *Fantaisie* is going to appear soon,' as he wrote to Godet on 13 February 1891 (1942, p. 95). Yet, although he proposed it to Poniatowski on 9 September 1892 for a tentatively projected concert in the United States, he was very doubtful whether that concert would be given, and at the end of 1895 he turned a deaf ear when the publisher Hartmann and the pianist Raoul Pugno insisted that it should be performed in public at last. Then, still later, after he had quarrelled with Chansarel, to whom he had dedicated it, he put it aside once and for all.[3]

Rodrigue et Chimène was next in line. At a performance, undoubtedly a private one, of the *Cinq Poèmes de Charles Baudelaire* in February 1890, the relationship between Mendès and Debussy became closer. Mendès gave Debussy his just-completed book, *Méphistophela*, 'with his hearty compliments for his Baudelairean music and his fine concert'. Then, according to Godet, Mendès arranged to have the *Fantaisie* engraved. So Debussy could scarcely refuse to set *Rodrigue et Chimène* to music, as Mendès subsequently proposed he do. In fact, Debussy accepted this proposition in April 1890. He accepted it because in fact he could scarcely refuse what the then very influential Mendès was offering him. Chabrier had set Mendès's text of *Gwendoline*.* Messager had presented *Isoline* on 26

[2] Apparently Camille Benoît also withdrew his score. In *Art et Critique*, 26 Apr. 1890, E. Garnier wrote:

> Why were two compositions omitted from the programme? If it is true that M. Chansarel was ill and could not perform the work by Debussy, we'll pass by, but that leaves M. Benoît, who, if I am to believe certain rumours, withdrew his composition at the last moment. Was he sincere? That is not what we hear....

[3] On 24 Apr. 1890, three days after the anticipated but suppressed performance, Debussy ceded his *Fantaisie* to the editor Choudens for 200 fr., but Choudens had no faith in Debussy and would not publish the work, and it was re-sold, with other compositions, to Hartmann in 1895.

[The work was not published until 1920.]

* *Gwendoline*, first performed at the Monnaie, Brussels, 10 Apr. 1886, came to the Paris Opéra on 27 Dec. 1893.]

December 1888. Pierné would prepare three ballets—*Le Collier de saphirs* (1891), *Les Joyeuses commères de Paris* (1892), and *Le Docteur Blanc* (1893)— upon texts by this same Mendès. Furthermore, the writer's mistress, Augusta Holmès, had just had performed on 11 September 1889 her *Ode triomphale*, to commemorate 1789. Yet there is no doubt that Debussy accepted *Rodrigue et Chimène* for a more specific reason: his thirst for success. Since Debussy had already set to music poems by Banville, Bourget, Mallarmé, Verlaine, and Baudelaire and was pleased by what he knew of the works of Shakespeare, of Villiers, and of Poe, it is almost inconceivable that Mendès's libretto did not appear straight off to be a glaring vacuity, 'Parnassian bric-à-brac and motley Spanish barbarism', as Paul Dukas would characterize it. It was, however, a work to which he could surrender himself completely, and one which, at that particular time, promised to be both profitable and brilliantly performable. In an almost analogous situation, nearly twenty years later, Debussy accepted *Le Martyre de Saint Sébastien*, but with this essential difference: then he had full mastery over his art.

It is probable that at first he found pleasure in the intimate relationship of Rodrigue and Chimène, for at heart this is a love story. But little by little he became aware that his imagination rose too high above the text, that his sincerity did not harmonize with the poet's artificialities of diction. Debussy had to admit to a certain indulgence for bel canto effects: something that he disdained. Alfred Cortot, who once owned the unpublished manuscript, asked whether *Chimène* might not have given 'birth to a number of episodes of eloquent warmth whose communicable lyricism would surely not have failed to exercise their power upon the public'.[4]

Likewise, Gustave Samazeuilh, who examined the manuscript, noted in it 'certain compromises with traditional operatic style'.[5] Paul Dukas, who had heard Debussy play and sing the score, also remarked in his letter of 1 October 1893 to Vincent d'Indy: 'He also played his opera to me. . . . You will be very surprised, I believe, at the dramatic breadth of certain scenes . . .' (*ReM*, Mar. 1949, p. 7). Dukas wound up his judgement with an observation that shows us that *Rodrigue et Chimène* contained both aspects of Debussy's personality, the bitter and the tender, the Debussy who felt compelled to obtain a public success and the eager and uncompromising Debussy who would end up triumphing over the other one. 'Add that all the episodic scenes are exquisite and of a harmonic

---

[4] A. Cortot, 'Un drame lyrique de Claude Debussy (*Rodrigue et Chimène*)', *Inédits sur Claude Debussy*, p. 16.

[5] *Le Temps*, 25 Dec. 1933.

subtlety that recalls his early songs. Yet the work has everything that makes its failure certain. Let us wish that he might succeed! The text is moreover perfectly void of interest' (*ReM*, Mar. 1949, p. 7).[6]

If Debussy none the less clung to *Rodrigue et Chimène*, it was because he felt the need to bring off an achievement, as he found it wearing to lead a life without hope. The struggle was grim. On 30 January 1892 he had written to Godet '... this intolerable feeling that I sometimes have of living in a city where I am an exile, where nothing awaits me, and where I am fated to follow a melancholy routine' (1942, p. 98).

When he had finished the first two acts, he came to see that to continue with it would be a gesture of futile self-betrayal: 'I am afraid I have won some victories over myself.' He revealed to Godet the implicit basis of his thought: 'It is impossible to be someone without engaging in a little play-acting.' A highly significant admission. In sketching the third act, he was aware that he was still cheating himself. Then he took control of himself, and gave up this work. A proud and admirable renunciation! Yet it was more than that: this miscarried work, long unknown,* is moving, none the less, for *Rodrigue et Chimène* was Debussy's purgatory, *Rodrigue et Chimène* was the preliminary sketch for *Pelléas et Mélisande*.

One can see it very clearly. Debussy was weary with his futile search and with his permanent shortness of funds, and with the *Fantaisie* and *Rodrigue et Chimène* he wanted to write some music to put food on his table, and he indulged in a little play-acting. Here is additional evidence. He was satisfied with the works he had composed between 1885 and 1889: *Printemps*, the six *Ariettes*, *La Damoiselle élue*, the *Cinq Poèmes de Charles Baudelaire*, and the *Petite Suite*; he did not renounce them. He sought to get them published, and those that he could not get printed right away he would publish later, and he would revise them. Now the two works that immediately followed (1889–90), namely, the *Fantaisie* and *Rodrigue et Chimène*, were those which should have displayed a ripening fulfilment of the composer's progress and a reaffirmation of his emerging identity, yet Debussy condemned these two works, buried them until his death, forbidding even their exhumation. More relevant: the short contemporary works—the piano pieces (*Valse romantique*, *Ballade (slave)*, *Tarentelle styrienne*, *Rêverie*,† *Mazurka*) and the songs (*Les Angélus*, *La Belle au bois*

---

[6] Another witness, Vital Hocquet (Narcisse Lebeau) recalled as well: 'I remember this *Cid* of his; it was not in the same vein as *Pelléas*, but much more romantic, stuffed with many concessions [to popular taste]' (Peter, *Claude Debussy*, p. 148).

* [The nearly complete short score of *Rodrigue et Chimène*, as transcribed by Richard Langham Smith, had its first performance, 22 June 1987, in Paris.]

† [The first performance of *Rêverie* was given, 27 Feb. 1899 by Mlle Germaine Alexandre.]

dormant, Fêtes galantes, first series, and *Trois Mélodies de Verlaine*) were not renounced. The *Marche écossaise* which followed them (in 1891) was inserted in a programme of 1894; in 1896 Debussy suggested it again to Ysaÿe, although unenthusiastically, and he orchestrated it in 1908, having found in it 'some scandalous failings'; in 1913 he authorized a first performance. The next works were never in debate: the String Quartet, the *Prélude à 'L'Après-midi d'un faune'*, both begun in 1892, were first performed in December 1893 and December 1894, respectively. Finally, knowing that Debussy never stopped liking some parts of his *Fantaisie*, one must acknowledge that his renunciation of it is even more eloquent, all the more so since, after Mendès's death in 1909, he could then have published his 'Concerto'* (already engraved, we should remember), as he did *Printemps* in 1904 and the *Marche écossaise* in 1911. Certainly, at that time he was not thinking about the *Fantaisie*, but when Godet reminded him of it in 1917, Debussy answered that he did not like it enough to undertake to lighten its too heavy orchestration.[7]

Two questions arise here: who had led Debussy astray, and who brought him back to the right path? We shall answer the second in due course, but let us first consider who had led him astray. His family? Catulle Mendès? Both, without doubt; both were capable of it; but maybe Gaby along with them. There is a very eloquent sequence of dates. Debussy wrote off *Rodrigue* before 1892: in May of that same year, on the occasion of the funeral of Ernest Guiraud, Godet noted with what insulting petulance he resisted all compromise.[8] Catherine Stevens, in her *Notes*, gives another instance of Debussy's touchy intransigence:

One evening I came home and found Debussy with Maman. He had come for dinner. I was carrying in triumph a book by Maurice de Fleury with his gracious dedication. Debussy took the book and said to Maman: 'Madame Stevens, will you permit me to tear out this dedication and throw it in the fire? I cannot understand how one could dare to offer, with a dedication, such an incestuous book to a young girl.' And he tore out the dedication, grinding his teeth.

---

[7] It should be noted, however, that the engraved proofs of the *Fantaisie* seem to have been lost, for Jobert, in 1919, was obliged to re-engrave the score for its first performance, given by Alfred Cortot in London, 20 Nov. 1919.

[We have found no published letter by Debussy to Godet dated 1917 that refers to the *Fantaisie*. Either Dietschy saw an autograph letter or else he erred in the date.]

[8] *ReM*, 1 May 1926, p. 70.

* [Dietschy perhaps exaggerates this 'renunciation' of the *Fantaisie*, for in August 1909 Debussy wrote to Edgard Varèse: 'For a long time now I have been thinking of modifying it [the *Fantaisie*] almost completely ... I have changed my mind about the way to use the piano with the orchestra. Also the instrumentation must be written differently, lest it seem like a rather ridiculous struggle between the two forces' (quoted in F. Lesure, *Catalogue de l'œuvre de Claude Debussy* (Geneva, 1977), 72).

Finally, as Debussy admitted to Poniatowski in February 1893, his family constantly reproached him, for being 'a son who was too unproductive'.[9] This explains their unshakeable ostracism from that time, at least as far as it pertains to *Rodrigue et Chimène*: by his renunciation of the corrupt work, Debussy flouted both the poet and his parents. The *Fantaisie* suffered the consequences, from which one can conclude along with Godet: 'For the good equilibrium of his remorse, or its harmonious appeasement, the composer did not want to have anything further to do with *Chimène* once he had sent her back to Mendès' (*ReM*, 1 May 1926, p. 69).

This extraordinary time is further marked by two unusual events. Debussy began his relationship with Gaby, Gabrielle Dupont. Perhaps it was for Gaby, and in conjunction with her, that he determined to make a frontal attack upon success. In April 1890 he dedicated to her the *Rodrigue et Chimène* that he was beginning to work upon. He wrote 'A Mademoiselle Gabrielle Dupont' ceremoniously upon the still virginal first page of the manuscript. He had just become acquainted with her. Eight years later, weary of waiting in vain for the hoped-for success, she abandoned the impecunious composer for a rich count. Twelve years later Debussy inscribed to her a score of *Pelléas et Mélisande*: 'To Gaby, princess of the mysterious kingdom of Allemonde. Her old devoted friend Claude Debussy. June 1902.' Assuredly, this was an expression of gratitude. It is difficult to estimate a woman's contribution to an artist's work. She was with him when he composed *Rodrigue et Chimène*, the String Quartet, the *Prélude à 'L'Après-midi d'un faune'*, the *Proses lyriques*, *Pelléas et Mélisande*, and even the *Nocturnes*. She helped him; she was his constant companion; she was, all in all, 'the mistress one takes for granted'. Her devotion and her self-effacing character make her an even more touching figure.

Until 1957 nothing was known of her; just that she came from Normandy, that she had green eyes, a strong chin, a lithe figure, and a rosy complexion. Until recently her age, her birthplace, her appearance, and when she died were unknown, but now she is revealed to us as a headstrong, energetic native of the Auge region, born on 11 June 1866 at Lisieux (to a father who was a trimmer of material and of doubtful morals). She became a well-dressed tart and died at nearly eighty on 12 May 1945 at Orbec (Calvados).[10]

Arriving in Paris about 1887, she began living with a black-sheep aristocrat, the Comte de Villeneuve. At first she did not possess the 'royal

[9] Poniatowski, *D'un siècle à l'autre*, p. 307.

[10] H. Pellerin, 'Claude Debussy', *Le Pays d'Auge* (Lisieux, May and June 1957). Gaby was sometimes nicknamed 'the lady with the green eyes', which echoed the title (*La Dame aux yeux verts*) of a novel of contemporary life by Dubut de Laforest, published in instalments in *L'Écho de Paris* from 28 Jan. 1897 on.

demeanour', the 'distant and almost disdainful' air that Henri Pellerin attributed to her, but René Peter, in describing her as 'the least frivolous blonde', also noticed that she possessed the makings of a cocotte worthy of a place in the Gotha of courtesans. When she cast her lot with Debussy, she had to work; her occupation has been variously described as a laundress, waistcoat-maker, corset-maker, or washerwoman. Rather, she was employed as a milliner, affirms Pellerin, and this may have been the 'hard labour' to which René Peter referred. During the eight years of her relationship with Debussy she adapted herself to all situations, courageously eating a skimpy diet, drinking beer, and smoking 'weeds' with him as they strolled the boulevards, and then adjusting effortlessly to the high-life of the avenue Niel, to which she would be promoted by her liaison with Comte de Balbiani, who became her protector, in the wake of Debussy.[11]

Debussy presented her under the assumed name of Gaby Lhéry.* She was intelligent, she read, she wrote without mistakes but without punctuation; she carried herself well; she had a fine figure, which curved provocatively; she was practical and efficient. She loved Debussy jealously, proud to share his life as an artist and to meet the literary figures of his circle. She must have been attached to him and have had confidence in him to remain with him and put up with eight years of hardship. 'Doubtless she was waiting for her recompense to arrive sooner or later...', wrote René Peter. Debussy moved with her to 42 rue de Londres, to a dank attic (the rent: 120 francs a year), where they found a place for a borrowed Pleyel, a bed, three chairs, and a rickety table. Money was lacking, treats were rare and modest, their meals often consisted of bread and chocolate. She worked, while he toiled over the tiresome transcriptions for the publishing house of Durand, work done to provide food, 'imbecile's toil', as he described it to Godet. He did not,

---

[11] Vital Hocquet has recounted how he met Gaby during the first days of her liaison with Comte de Balbiani. She introduced him in this way: 'Dear friend, this is Vital Hocquet; I have never slept with him.' And the count replied, 'I am sorry for you, Monsieur, for you have missed out on something very special!'

[René Peter writes that many years later Alfred Cortot saw Gaby in the Grand Théâtre in Rouen, dressed in the bonnet and apron of an *ouvreuse*. She still owned precious manuscripts that Debussy had given her; although she had been offered large sums of money for them, she was unwilling to part with them. (Peter, *Claude Debussy*, pp. 35–6.)

We know, however, that Cortot once owned the draft of *Rodrigue et Chimène* and the short score of the *Prélude à 'L'Après-midi d'un faune'*, both inscribed to Gaby. This last bears the added inscription: 'Offert à M. A. Cortot par Mme G. Lhéry'.]

---

* [This name was Gaby's invention, striving for a distinction that the name Dupont, a common surname in France, did not possess.]

however, stop composing. From 1890 to 1891 stem the dozen songs and piano pieces mentioned earlier. He was timidly emerging from obscurity.

People had started to ask for him. 'The Vicomtesse de Trédern has taken it into her head to sing my prize cantata (*L'Enfant prodigue*) at her château. She is asking me for the score and the orchestral parts. . . .'[12]

It was doubtless an anonymous act of kindness which prompted a Scottish officer to come to Debussy's flat one day to ask him to write a march for his clan. (He might have been a relative or a friend of Étienne Dupin's mother, who was a Scotswoman.) That is the origin, according to Godet, of the *Marche écossaise*, then called *Marche des anciens comtes de Ross*, for piano four-hands.[13]

The second remarkable fact about this period of bohemianism was Debussy's habit of frequenting not only the Chat Noir cabaret, but even the Auberge du Clou, of going to circus performances, to puppet shows, to billiard matches, and also to the bawdy spectacles of the popular singer Jeanne Bloch. When he visited the Stevens's household, he would accompany Raoul Ponchon and his friends at the piano, and in chorus they would sing the songs of Béranger and the operettas of Hervé and Offenbach. At the Chat Noir he would on occasion beat time for the carefree group of fellows who would bawl popular ditties like 'Le Café' by Ben Tayoux. 'We would sing it, that song, all evening long . . . , and it was Claude Debussy who, in high glee, would direct our frenetic chorus.'[14]

For him it was like a fountain of youth, an escape from the bitterness of his daily life, from the violence he wrought upon himself by making those transcriptions and by working at *Rodrigue et Chimène*. These were the escapades that he was always in search of and would find along with Chausson. Doubtless it was more than that: a defence against academic intellectualizing, a reaction against convention, an instinctive need for independence and imagination. That was the prevailing spirit of the Chat Noir. As Maurice Donnay explains: 'it is not at all easy to define what was "the spirit of the *Chat Noir*". It is easier to say what it was not: it was not

[12] Letter from Debussy to Ambroise Thomas, undated, but probably from 1890–2 (in the Bibliothèque Nationale). The Vicomtesse de Trédern (*née* Say) was a prominent dilettante soprano, who liked to put on performances of operas in which she successfully took the leading soprano parts at her château at Brissac.

[13] The *Marche écossaise* had been announced for performance at a concert on 29 May 1894 by the Société des Grandes Auditions Musicales at the Jardin d'Acclimation, an advertisement which suggests that the orchestration was at least sketched at that time. But the work was not played.

[14] M. Donnay, *Autour du Chat Noir* (Paris, 1926), 32.

pretentious, not servile, not sectarian. The sponsoring spirits at the *Chat Noir* were Independence and Imagination.'[15]

We have mentioned that about 1890 Debussy made friends with Vital-Narcisse Hocquet, the Narcisse Lebeau of the Chat Noir, a 'young fellow filled with wit', as Donnay described him, who had 'a painter's eyes', according to Debussy, and whom Gaby called 'my little zinc dog' under the pretext that he was a plumber. Hocquet was the first of these relaxing friends who were so dear and so necessary to the composer, among whom later would be Pierre Louÿs and René Peter. Debussy thrived on easy relationships with cronies, with frequent arguments and spirited exchanges, a relaxation where the use of *tu* was immediate and as though instinctive. It was Hocquet, from Arras, who some time around 1891 introduced Debussy to Erik Satie, also from Normandy. This association was perhaps the determining element that got Debussy back on the right track.

There has been much talk of Satie's 'genius' and of the 'influence' that he is supposed to have had upon Debussy, but it would be more accurate to attribute to him the lesser role of an inspirer. If Satie's music is raw and thin as a slice of meat, if it evokes the strange advance of a drunken stilt-walker through some lunar landscape, his wit is that of a comedian, of a farceur whose quips are irresistibly amusing. This uncommon man—a student of the occult, a mystic, a visionary, a penniless non-conformist—could not help but appeal to Debussy, perhaps because of his private life. Cruelly deprived of tenderness, unable to open his heart, Satie gesticulated. He both hid and exalted himself in the buffoonery of his writing, and here his success sparkled. Once he said that he wanted to write an opera for dogs and that the curtain would rise to reveal a bone.[16]

Jean Cocteau was one of Satie's earliest supporters and helped to launch him. In the *Revue musicale* of 1 March 1924, he wrote: 'It was in 1891 that Satie composed the music for a Wagnerian parody by Péladan, and this opened, without anyone being aware of it, the door through which Debussy went marching towards fame.' He added that Satie, running into Debussy, said to him, while he was writing his parody *Le Fils des étoiles*: 'Enough of Wagner! It's pretty but it's not native to us. It's important that the orchestra should not make faces when a character comes on stage.... What is needed is the atmosphere of Puvis de Chavannes.'

Satie is supposed to have announced straight out to Debussy that he was thinking about *La Princesse Maleine* and did not know how to get

---

[15] Ibid. 46.
[16] This information was communicated by Mme Jeanne Thieffry.

Maeterlinck's authorization. All of which led Cocteau, unperturbed, to this conclusion: 'Several days later, Debussy, having obtained the authorization from Maeterlinck, began *Pelléas et Mélisande*.'

From this fancy footwork stems all the misunderstanding of the relationship between Debussy and Satie. Once set in motion, it became so embellished as to imply that, if Satie had not existed, Debussy would have remained undeveloped. Here is an extreme example of this attitude: 'Debussy found nothing. It was Satie who thought of everything. He took the chestnuts out of the fire, but it was Debussy who sold them to the public and reaped the profits.'[17] Happily, Satie remained unaware of these aspersions.[18]

It has been claimed that Satie turned Debussy's attention to *La Princesse Maleine* in 1891. In any event, Debussy was interested in it. Using Jules Huret of *L'Écho de Paris* as an intermediary, he asked Maeterlinck for his authorization to set the play to music, and it was on 23 June 1891 that the dramatist, bound by an earlier promise, declined the proposition, as Vallas reported. The question naturally arises whether Debussy made this move for himself, with Satie's agreement, or whether he made it for his friend. It is doubtful that Satie seriously dreamt of composing *La Princesse Maleine*, for two years later he composed a simple prelude for an entirely different work: *La Porte heroïque du ciel* by Jules Bois. However it may have been, it is very possible that Debussy found in Satie a spirit of sufficient independence and originality to affirm his own disgust with *Rodrigue et Chimène*, and to lead him, in the course of conversations they probably had, to take a decisive step ahead on his own personal path by rejecting definitively those ideas and formulas which still held him captive. On 27 October 1892, inscribing a copy of the *Cinq Poèmes de Charles Baudelaire* in words which hint at the prologue of *Pelléas et Mélisande*, Debussy was perhaps rendering a secret form of thanks to Satie when he wrote: 'For Erik Satie, gentle medieval composer, [who] strayed into this century to the joy of his good friend Claude-A. Debussy.'

In the spring of 1891, this is to say a year after he had begun it, Debussy was thinking of giving up *Rodrigue et Chimène*. The final sentence would not

[17] M. Sachs, *Au temps du Bœuf sur le Toit* (Paris, 1939).

[18] André Suarès has left a note, however, describing an occasion when he was a fellow-guest with Satie at a dinner given by Jacques Doucet about 1920. Suarès was irritated to hear Satie boasting about all Debussy owed to him. Sometime later he wanted to publish in the *Revue musicale* an article, half in jest, half in earnest, on Satie, when Henry Prunières urged him to be indulgent, saying: 'Cocteau and his group made a madman out of this good, charming fellow, once so full of modesty, who died a megalomaniac after two years of delirium.'

[According to the New Grove, Satie died on 1 July 1925 of 'sclerosis of the liver'.]

be passed until after two additional years in which he slowly and 'desolately' pursued his hopeless task. Now it seems likely that, secretly freed from *Chimène* as from an impediment, he moved ahead with greater assurance and decisiveness. He seemed to have acquired a certainty that he was constitutionally incapable of writing to order. It was exactly at the end of 1891 that Jules Bois, a specialist in metaphysical conjecture, who had published that same year a verse-dialogue entitled *Il ne faut pas mourir*, suggested to Debussy that he write incidental music to his first esoteric play, *Les Noces de Sathan*.[19]

We cannot be surprised at the composer's refusal to touch a text so abstruse and recondite, but it is curious to find that Jules Bois in his preface points out: 'The dances of Ramayana have been performed in Cambodia since time immemorial by dancer-priestesses, while a narrator declaimed a poetic text, rather in the same way that M. Mallarmé intended *L'Après-midi d'un faune* to be performed. . . .'[20]

As early as 1892 Debussy had determined to work on this *L'Après-midi d'un faune*, having been familiar with it for several years; now he foresaw setting it to music in three parts. Poniatowski was convinced that Mallarmé's poem provided the occasion for lengthy conversations between the poet and the composer, and that Mallarmé played as decisive and influential a role in Debussy's development as Satie had. Except for *Pelléas et Mélisande* and the *Chansons de Bilitis*, by 1892 Debussy had sketched all that he would produce in the remaining years of the nineteenth century: the Quartet, the *Proses lyriques*, the *Prélude à 'L'Après-midi d'un faune'*, and the *Nocturnes*.

The idea of a work for strings was perhaps inspired by the performance in April 1890 of César Franck's Quartet, which Willy described as making a serious impression upon him and 'all the choir of adolescents'.[21] The *Proses lyriques* are Debussy's first poems, and he must have experienced some pride seeing the first two published by Viélé-Griffin in his *Entretiens politiques et littéraires* (December 1892). Their musical setting was undoubtedly sketched at the same time as the poems, for the texts are naïve, slim improvisations that exalt trees, the sea, flowers, night, and which pay allusive compliments to the poets who had enchanted him.[22]

---

[19] According to a letter Debussy wrote to Jules Bois, Feb. 1892 (1980, p. 34). *Les Noces de Sathan* was performed for the first time on 31 Mar. 1892, but with a score by Henry Quittard.

[20] J. Bois, Preface to *Les Noces de Sathan* (Paris, 1892), 5.

[21] In 1893 Debussy wrote to Chausson referring to his Quartet: 'I have not been able to get it as I want it to be, and I am therefore starting it again for the third time.'

[22] They would be followed by *Nuits blanches*, five poems for solo voice with piano accompaniment (the title borrowed perhaps from Albert Samain), which Debussy

Finally, at the same time as he was working on *L'Après-midi d'un faune* he sketched *Trois Scènes au crépuscule* (a title borrowed from Henri de Régnier); these comprised the first idea of what would ultimately become the *Nocturnes*. He proposed these to Poniatowski, in his letter of 9 September 1892,[23] for a projected concert in the United States that never materialized.

Thus, with the illusory *Chimène* put aside incomplete, encouraged by the poets, and his head full of projects and ideas that were ripening, Debussy was moving ahead towards his goal; he had found himself once again. A great many people in the artistic world foresaw and longed for a musical renewal to match the already flourishing revolution in painting and literature. On 5 January 1892 Chabrier wrote in a partially prophetic vein to Charles Lecocq: 'The man of genius, in the new style, frighteningly individual, like Berlioz . . . has not yet been found. But he will turn up, probably in Germany, as always (damn it!).'

He had already been found; he was about to arrive.

---

announced to Hartmann in his letter of 20 Apr. 1899, but they remain unknown or unfinished. An extract [three bars] from one of these poems, both words and music, dated July 1900, has been published by Octave Séré in *Musiciens français d'aujourd'hui* (Paris, 1921), 130.

[23] Poniatowski, *D'un siècle à l'autre*, p. 306.

10

'Voici que le printemps'

THE year 1893 fulfilled all the promise of 1892. It was Debussy's decisive year, fertile and fertilizing, a dawning, besides being the year in which he entered his thirties. The year is memorable for *La Damoiselle élue*, for the *Prélude à 'L'Après-midi d'un faune'*, for the *Proses lyriques*, for the Quartet, for the *Nocturnes*, for *Pelléas et Mélisande*—above all for Debussy's encounter with *Pelléas et Mélisande*. It sealed his affection for Chausson, Lerolle, Ysaÿe, Pierre Louÿs, Bréville, Messager, and Poniatowski. It was the year he formed these firm friendships, as well as continuing those with Godet, Bonheur, the Peter–Dupin circle, and the Stevens family. It certainly seemed that in 1893 all those close to Debussy, his friends and comrades, became aware, if not of his genius, at least of his superiority and his originality. This favourable response was aroused by the performance of *La Damoiselle élue*. This same year marked the first success, the first true recognition of Claude-Achille Debussy, composer. After five years of waiting, *La Damoiselle élue* was finally presented to the public on 8 April. *Le Figaro* did not distort the facts; it expressed exactly what most of the audience felt: 'It has, all by itself, more life than the compositions that preceded . . . It is so good, a breath of youth . . . Here is new blood . . .'

D'Indy, Bréville, Lekeu did not conceal their admiration. Chausson and Lerolle grew closer to Debussy, and for two years gave him their fraternal and most generous financial support. The Stevens family had him to dinner three times a week. He got to know Pierre Louÿs well. In the same way, Godet, Bonheur, Peter, Dupin, Poniatowski, and Messager gathered round him and encouraged him, each according to his temperament, his conviction, and his means.[1]

To explore the question of how Debussy encountered Maeterlinck's *Pelléas et Mélisande* is to deal in hypotheses. The year of the encounter can

---

[1] In Jan. 1893 Poniatowski, notably, had lavished on Debussy a sum sufficient to ensure his peace of mind for a year or two (see Poniatowski, *D'un siécle à l'autre*, p. 310).

['Voici que le printemps' is a song composed in 1884.]

no longer be in doubt, not after the study of Oswald d'Estrade-Guerra;[2] it was 1893. Yet Louis Laloy in his *Claude Debussy*, written in 1909, based upon the inaccurate recollections of the composer, reported Debussy as saying he had bought a copy of *Pelléas et Mélisande* 'during the summer of 1892'. A simple error of a year, and an approximation of the season, 'summer' being intended in the sense of fine weather.[3]

It is chronologically verifiable that on 13 April 1893 the performance of Maeterlinck's *Pelléas et Mélisande* at the Vaudeville was announced for the 21st. On the 19th, it was postponed until the first days of May. On 4 May *Le Figaro* specified that it would be given on the 10th, but at the Bouffes-Parisiens,* then it was postponed until the 17th. On 9 May Octave Mirbeau published in *L'Écho de Paris* a leading article that paid tribute to Maeterlinck and to Lugné-Poe:

A beautiful and lofty manifestation of dramatic art, of art that is simple and profound, will take place in a few days. . . . I have earlier expressed my thoughts regarding Maurice Maeterlinck. I have expressed my respect for this great poet, for his deep understanding of the heart, for his strange sensitivity about the hereafter. . . . The forthcoming performance will mark an epoch in the renaissance of drama, a sign of the increasing effort which will overthrow the conventional and the commonplace and will advance towards pure beauty.

André Hallays, in *Le Journal des Débats*, urged connoisseurs to see the spectacle: 'in ten or twenty years after the evening of the first performance of *Pelléas et Mélisande* at the Comédie-Française, they will be able . . . to boast of having been "maeterlinckiens" from the very first.' Unfortunately, the publicity surrounding Maeterlinck put off some critics, who took their revenge in their reviews.

Informed of the coming performance, Debussy would therefore have bought *Pelléas* (at the Flammarion bookshop, according to Laloy), at the end of April or the beginning of May, for it is inconceivable that he

---

[2] O. d'Estrade-Guerra, 'Les Manuscrits de *Pelléas et Mélisande*', *ReM* (Carnet Critique), 235 (1957), 5–24.
[See also D. A. Grayson, *The Genesis of Debussy's 'Pelléas et Mélisande'* (Ann Arbor, 1986), 133–63.]

[3] It is strange that Debussy, who does not seem to have had a flair for chronological details, has left a note: 'Bought and read *Pelléas* in 1893' [in the Bibliothèque Nationale]. The calligraphy reveals that the note was written at that time, and the lay-out, which a quick folding of the paper reproduced below, with the writing reversed (the ink being not yet dry), proves that Debussy did not want to add anything to these words. There must have been a sentimental reason that inspired the jotting of this note, a circumstance that makes it even more moving.

---

* [By Lugné-Poe's company called the Théâtre de l'Œuvre.]

would not have read the play before going to see it. In a note written by him, in 1902, 'on three large blue sheets', at the request of the Secretary-General of the Opéra-Comique,[4] he specified: 'in spite of the enthusiasm of a first reading. . . .' If he had seen the play before reading it, it would have been the performance that would have awakened the enthusiasm, above all in a Debussy who was so sensitive to auditory stimulus. Gabriel Fabre[5] had, on the occasion of this single performance, composed the music for the song of the three blind sisters (a passage suppressed by Debussy), published in March 1893, under the title 'Chanson de Méli-sande' (No. 3 of *Trois Musiques*) and, oddly enough, dedicated to Maeter-linck's mistress, Georgette Leblanc, who would later passionately claim the role of Mélisande in Debussy's opera, as though foreseeing the dazzling success that *Pelléas* would have in 1902. She meant to avenge the mixed reception that the play had received in 1893, a failure with which she had been indirectly associated.

When Debussy sent his payment to Lugné-Poe for an orchestra stall for the performance of *Pelléas* at the Bouffes-Parisiens, he told him in a covering letter that he knew neither the play nor the author. It is clear from this that he had never seen the play, which is obvious, nor Maeterlinck, whom he would not meet until November of that year.

On 17 May, the very day of the first performance, a matinée, *Le Figaro* published an interview with Maeterlinck. 'There are not twenty people in Paris who know the poet from Ghent.' Maeterlinck spoke modestly about his own work. 'It is a mediocre play, no better, no worse, I suppose, than any other . . .' The following day the critics condemned it almost unani-mously. *Le Temps*, in particular, obviously sought to demolish the author. *L'Écho de Paris* spoke of 'the attempt at a performance of *Pelléas et Mélisande*', a work that 'is not at all designed for the stage, [but] for the medium of painted canvas. . . .' On 20 May, in the same newspaper, Henry Bauër spoke of 'this performance that was a rumble of defeat . . .'. *Le Figaro* judged that Maeterlinck showed signs of 'pigheadedness and of a bias for absolute simplification', but added: 'that which has more value is the *idealistic* striving . . . the impression of a fatality that dominates the characters . . .'.[6]

---

[4] G. Ricou, 'La Générale de "Pelléas et Mélisande"', in G. Ricou (ed.), *Histoire du théâtre lyrique en France depuis les origines jusqu'à nos jours* (Paris, 1935–8), iii. 69–81.

[5] This is Gabriel Fabre, and not Gabriel Fauré, as some have written, no doubt thinking of the incidental music that the latter would write for *Pelléas* some time later, certainly with Debussy's consent.

[6] For Jules Lemaître, Maeterlinck's play was a 'charming trifle of decadence . . . a sweet little baroque poem of united mumbling . . .' (*Journal des débats*, 21 May 1893).

Vallas has written that there was no enthusiasm among Debussy's friends. This seems an exaggeration. Although Pierre Louÿs was unimpressed by it, it is hard to imagine that Lerolle and Chausson did not encourage Debussy to devote himself entirely to *Pelléas et Mélisande*. Both Lerolle and Chausson were, with a rare concern, about to assist Debussy financially and morally: Lerolle had been present at the performance of the play, undoubtedly in Debussy's company, and Chausson was about to set to music the *Serres chaudes* of this same Maeterlinck.[7] The only astonishing thing is that, in his letters written after the performance of 17 May 1893, Debussy did not refer to the drama to which he was about to dedicate himself until 6 September despite his 'enthusiasm' for it. He thought about it, however, doubtless secretly (he will confess it himself, as we shall see), since in July he requested Henri de Régnier to be his intermediary with Maeterlinck with a view to obtaining the rights. Régnier addressed Maeterlinck in these terms: 'My friend Achille Debussy, who is a composer of the finest and most ingenious talent, has begun to write charming music for *Pelléas et Mélisande* that adorns the text deliciously, all the while respecting it scrupulously. He would like, before moving ahead with this work, which is considerable, to have your authorization to pursue it. . . .'[8]

On 8 August, the poet gave his consent. 'I wholeheartedly give him all necessary authorization for *Pelléas et Mélisande*.'[9]

It is important to know precisely what Debussy thought of *Pelléas*. One would suppose, from his declaration of 1902, that his initial enthusiasm was followed by bitter perplexity: the play dismissed, ridiculed by the Press, the poet demolished by certain writers; with all this he might well have questioned the rationality of embarking upon this project. As he wrote in 1902: 'In spite of the enthusiasm of a first reading, and perhaps secretly weighing a possible musical setting, I did not begin to think seriously about it until the end of this same year, 1893.'[10]

It is therefore absolutely certain that Debussy, in his 'enthusiasm'—and Henri de Régnier's letter confirms this—had started almost immediately to make notes and to write fragments of scenes of *Pelléas et Mélisande*, rather than plunging into full-scale composition. But he did not talk much about it, and certainly had no precise purpose, but wrote only for

[7] The first to be completed, No. 3, bears the date 'June '93'.

[8] G. Leblanc, *Souvenirs* (Paris, 1931), 166.

[9] On 8 July 1893 Romain Rolland wrote to André Suarès: 'I have read *Pelléas et Mélisande*. It contains some exquisite scenes of a delicacy that have impressed me, and something truly Shakespearean this time.'

[10] Ricou, 'La Générale de "Pelléas et Mélisande"', iii. 72.

his own personal pleasure, almost in spite of himself.[11] It is not implausible, as two or three of his friends have reported that the scene of *Pelléas* that first stirred Debussy is the overwhelming one of the lover's exhilaration, of the ecstasy following the declaration of love: *On dirait que ta voix a passé sur la mer au printemps* ('One would think that your voice has passed over the sea in springtime'). In fact, by 6 September 1893, he was able to tell Chausson that the last scene of the fourth act was finished.[12] It is also clear that, far from thinking of a practical realization, Debussy, who could have been expecting a refusal from Maeterlinck for *Pelléas*, like the recent one for *La Princesse Maleine*, experienced only the joy of encountering the text he had dreamed of, the landscape, the atmosphere, the characters of 'no country, no period of time', which he had been seeking, and of which the *Rodrigue* of Mendès had been only a caricature.[13]

At the end of May 1893 Debussy and Bonheur went to spend a few days in Luzancy, by way of Saâcy, in Seine-et-Marne, invited by Chausson to the property that Mme de Bonnières rented to his parents-in-law. It is a real château—today a summer camp—with its large park of twelve acres that stretches down to the Marne. This gracious Luzancy, nestling in the silvery verdure of the 'Vallée des Artistes', where not long before Corot had found the model for his misty foliage, is probably where Debussy first read through *Boris Godunov*.* He spent happy days at Luzancy with music, discussions, boating, playing ball, and taking photographs.

'Those few days spent with you have made me your devoted friend for ever. . . . How good it was to be for a while a part of your life, to be in some degree part of your family . . .', he wrote to Chausson. Those days in

[11] Raymond Bonheur confirms it: 'it was not with the preconceived plan of creating a theatrical work that he allowed himself, at first, to be seduced by Maeterlinck's drama' (*ReM*, 1 May 1926, p. 7).

[12] Debussy's hesitation, his fear of committing an error in judgement about Maeterlinck's work, seems all the more likely in the light of his letter of Feb. 1893 to Poniatowski, in which he severely judged Massenet's *Werther*, Gounod's *Faust*, Ambroise Thomas's *Hamlet*, and above all Gustave Charpentier's *Louise* (then called *Marie*), that 'triumph of the *brasserie*' (Poniatowski, *D'un siècle à l'autre*, p. 309).

[13] It is astonishing that Oulmont (*Musique de l'amour*) could write that Debussy, not being among 'the Franck clique', was 'impatient with instant realizations' (i. 61), the Debussy, that is, who was about to renounce *Rodrigue* and the *Fantaisie* and who would demonstrate all his life a noble intransigence where his art was concerned. Going so far as to endow Debussy with 'the character of a virtuoso acrobat' (i. 57), Oulmont proves to us that he has understood nothing about the composer.

* [Charles Koechlin claims that, in the photograph of Debussy playing the piano at Luzancy in the presence of the assembled Chausson and Lerolle families, he was reading the score of *Boris* (*ReM*, 1 May 1926, p. 30 n.).]

the country, free to talk 'about all sorts of subjects', were a liberation for both of the friends, who became youngsters again. As Debussy wrote to Chausson on 5 June 1893:

And don't accuse us too much of 'youthfulness', for there are so many people who do not want to stay young for fear that no one will take them seriously. Then, you must not believe that this quality, transposed into art, fails to give us the faculty of being able to understand all manifestations of feeling as they occur. . . . Therefore let us be crazily light-hearted in order to forget the prison that life too often is; let us also be melancholy and sad like the old ballads; let us never neglect to put our sensibility through its paces, for only very good things can come out of it.

He expressed his admiration to Chausson, which his friend deserved, since he was like an elder brother:

Let me tell you . . . you are much superior to the people who surround you, and that is because of your qualities of sensitivity and of artistic tact, traits which the others seem to me to lack absolutely. They make their way through the meadows of music, crushing beneath their disrespectful feet bouquets of little flowers, without regard for their qualities to inspire feeling, and they make their way where only rhubarb and poppies grow, or couch grass, the spreading flower.*

And it was a delight for him to see Chausson again in his handsome house at 22 boulevard de Courcelles. Camille Mauclair described it like this: '[Chausson's] house was a marvel of good taste and art. Lerolle had embellished it with his delicate designs. It was a museum where Odilon Redon and Degas hung side by side with Puvis de Chavannes and Carrière.'

If Debussy's first notes for *Pelléas et Mélisande* probably date from May 1893, his eager discourse with the characters of the drama started 'officially' in September, as the first manuscripts are dated: 'September–October '93'.[14] In fact, in October Debussy asked for an interview with Maeterlinck, using Pierre Louÿs as an intermediary, thus enabling us to see that by then he had thought about the work in its entirety and was concerned about the general plan of the play. He made some cuts, and in November Debussy went to Ghent with Louÿs in order to discuss these with the poet, who recommended some himself, which were 'very important, even very useful', but rather few—in fact only twenty or so pages out of a total of about 160.

---

[14] In his letter of 25 July 1907 Debussy confirms this to Laloy: 'As to *Pelléas*, I began it in earnest in September '93 . . .' (*RdM*, 1962, p. 26).

---

* [These parts of Debussy's letters to Chausson from 1893, which are not dated precisely, are extracted from Oulmont's *Musique de l'amour*, i. 55–7, 65.]

On this trip Debussy took advantage of his proximity to Brussels to submit the Quartet to Eugène Ysaÿe, as the advice of the violinist, the leader of a noted string quartet, was important. When he got back to Paris, Debussy wrote to him of his anxiety. But Debussy's only quartet aroused 'unrestrained enthusiasm'[15] when it was first played at the Société Nationale on 29 December 1893. The Quartet is chronologically the first of the sovereign works of Debussy, his first masterpiece, sparkling, universal, eternal. What Willy wrote about it three years later in one of his 'Lettres de l'Ouvreuse'[16] must have pleased the composer:

Claude-Achille Debussy['s] Quartet has just been given again by the Nationale. [This composition is] so vigorous, so original in its passion, with disconcerting oddities of writing. [There is] an exquisite perfume of the Far East in the first movement, then a phrase dear to Jean de Tinan, G, F sharp, E, F, restless and nostalgic; then a lovely Andantino, whispering and tender, then the Finale, broadly sketched, where the Titanesque lament strides upon harmonies that Reber had not foreseen. . . .[17]

Doubtless Debussy had immediately talked to his friends about his plans and his work upon *Pelléas*. Since Maeterlinck's approval at the beginning of August, he had begun to play for them the scenes he had already composed. In an unpublished letter to Bonheur, of 27 October 1893, one sees that he had submitted to his friend the final scene of the fourth act, with 'the great chains':

Ah well, that is just fine! You come to Paris, you dine at Vian's, and you do not come to see me? You are just a faithless, wishy-washy person! It is hardly worth the trouble to have special friendships with people who trample upon the simplest laws of friendship! In the name of the mother of us all (of some of us would be more accurate), have some sensitivity! I urge you to come next week to dine with your little friends, under penalty of having you see the gates close. Do you hear the great chains? He who loves you just the same.

C.D.

We have more evidence from a letter of Lerolle to Chausson, this one from 19 December 1894, which is a report of a musical evening at Lerolle's house, in the course of which Debussy, without being 'the hero of the party', played for about an hour the scenes he had already written for *Pelléas*. Obviously, the impression they produced was 'sufficiently

---

[15] G. Doret, *Gazette de Lausanne*, 26 Mar. 1943.

[16] *L'Écho de Paris*, 12 Jan. 1897.

[17] In the 'Chronique du règne de Félix Faure', *Le Centaure*, 2 (1896), 155, Jean de Tinan wrote: 'Since this morning a restless phrase has pursued me—G, F sharp, E, F...—a phrase from the Quartet of Claude Debussy—and it fills me with I don't know what irresistible nostalgia. . . .'

confused'. Paul Poujaud seems to have been one of the rare individuals who truly loved *Pelléas* from the beginning:

We had a little group here yesterday. . . . There was first of all d'Indy, the hero of the party, Poujaud, Benoît, Debussy, the Denises and the Arthurs (Fontaine). I had asked Debussy to bring *Pelléas*, but when he arrived he told me that he hadn't brought it along . . . Then, after dinner . . . d'Indy . . . recounted to us in his most bizarre manner the subject of his third act (of *Fervaal*), then he played and sang it like a little girl who recites her lessons. . . . Then, at a quarter to midnight . . . Debussy doodled at the piano, like somebody who was thinking of something else . . . I said to him that he had perhaps deceived me, and in fact I found *Pelléas* in his briefcase. And he began. We gathered round the piano, while Benoît, furious, went and lay down on the sofa. Debussy was carried away, d'Indy grimaced with his moustache while turning the pages, and Poujaud seemed amazed, as for Benoît, he turned over in boredom, yawning loudly . . . then at the last note, before Debussy could wipe his forehead or lift his hands from the keys, he went off without saying one word to anyone. . . . Then some kind words for *Pelléas*, which, I believe, had really astonished them. . . .[18]

At first Debussy kept Paul Dukas away from these partial performances:

Dear friend, it is you who are the difficult one. And that it is why I will not play *Pelléas* for you. I will explain. The various times I have played it up to now have been necessarily fragmentary performances. The impression they have produced seems to me confusing enough, or even contradictory. I would much rather wait until I have finished an act or two to be able to give you a more complete idea of it. I hope that you will be touched by such self-denial and that you will find in it only a desire to please you better, for it is almost useless to tell you all the value I place upon your criticisms as well as upon your encouragement. (1980, p. 63)

The opinion of his friends really mattered to Debussy, and he obtained from them all sorts of encouragement so that *Pelléas* might fully develop. Early on Chausson and Lerolle encouraged him to find a more suitable flat than the attic in the rue de Londres. In July 1893 they installed him at 10 rue Gustave-Doré, on the fifth floor overlooking the courtyard, in three rooms with a hall, lending him furniture and other necessities. Lerolle added to these a luminous water-colour; Fontaine, a pair of candlesticks. Still worried about Debussy's means of subsistence, Chausson suggested to him, unsuccessfully, a position as an accompanist at Royan (in late 1893). Chausson also organized evenings devoted to Wagner operas at his mother-in-law's, Mme Escudier's, and later at Mme Godard-Decrais's, at

---

[18] The letter is published *in extenso* in the valuable book by Tiénot and d'Estrade-Guerra, *Debussy*, p. 86.

which Debussy played. And Lucien Fontaine offered him the directorship of an amateur chorus that he had just founded.[19]

Here then is Debussy well befriended and on his way, it would seem, to completing *Pelléas et Mélisande*, but a unique work of this scope could not have a simple period of gestation. Mysterious elements took part in its development, and their turbulent character seemed to be the ransom exacted by its creation. Incidents were going to explode from time to time, dross that dims the fire of genius and which incapacitates the great artist. Women came into his life at this point, and others would materialize later. Women, as before, as always—adorable, cruel servitude.

[19] In directing the chorus, Debussy was both conscientious and exacting, not hesitating to embarrass the choristers by singling them out—Madame, sing your part to me!—in order to make them study. Ravel, who succeeded Debussy in this post in 1904, contented himself with beating time abstractedly, always in a hurry to get away. (Reported by the Fontaine family.)

'Nuages' et 'Fêtes'
sans 'Sirènes'*

CHAUSSON and Lerolle, particularly the former, had tried to give Debussy's life 'a necessary regularity, an evenness worthy of his work and helpful to it', as Charles Oulmont has said. They had settled him in a proper flat; they paid for his necessities and, at first, his rent, his gas and coal; they obtained money for him; they encouraged him intellectually and morally. For his part, Debussy exercised a dynamic influence upon Chausson; he opened several secret doors for him. Indeed, Chausson wrote to Debussy: 'You have made me think about things which I would never have considered had it not been for you. . . .'[1] On the other hand, Gaby had never been in the good graces of either Chausson or Lerolle, and doubtless she never accompanied Debussy when he visited them.[2] It is probable that, at least unconsciously, they hoped that Debussy would marry someone suitable and would thereby at last achieve equanimity, would become, like them, 'peacefully happy'.[3]

In fact, at the end of 1893, Debussy again saw Thérèse Roger, one of the soloists of *La Damoiselle élue*, and courted her. She was the second child of an insurance inspector who died during the Commune, and of a music teacher; she had the manner of those girls who are chaperoned too much. At the Chausson's they did not find her talents as a singer above that of a respectable average.[4] Encouraged by Mme de Saint-Marceaux, the wife of the sculptor [René de Saint-Marceaux], Debussy proposed marriage to

[1] Oulmont, *Musique de l'amour*, i. 75.

[2] In his letter of 4 June 1893 to Chausson, Debussy announced to his friend his coming to Luzancy and continued: 'My p.a. (*petite amie*, undoubtedly) has earned all your gratitude, for truly her part is the only awkward one in all this.'

[3] Chausson was seven and a half years older than Debussy; Lerolle, fourteen years. The latter had the same painting teacher as Degas and had studied the violin with Édouard Colonne.

[4] It was she, however, who sang at the first hearing of Chausson's *Serres chaudes*, 3 Apr. 1897. At the age of thirty-six, she made an unfortunate marriage to a divorced engraver, and died four years later, in 1906.

* These are the three parts of *Nocturnes*. They are referred to on p. 104.

Thérèse. Several sentiments probably inspired him: a secret desire for the middle-class security extolled by Chausson, the moral climate, to have a musician for a wife, the seduction of her voice. Everyone was surprised at Debussy's choice, particularly Chausson and Lerolle, and Pierre Louÿs above all, who wrote to his brother, on 24 February 1894, that Mme de Saint-Marceaux was committing 'a grave imprudence in marrying Debussy to a drawing-room singer, Mlle R.; I am convinced that it would be a bad marriage, and I am distressed about it for my friend's sake.'[5]

Nevertheless, when on 17 February 1894 Thérèse Roger gave the first performance of two of the *Proses lyriques*, Debussy himself announced their engagement, and he informed Bréville officially of it. Meeting an earlier obligation, he returned to Brussels for the concert of 1 March given at La Libre Esthétique. It seems that when he got back to Paris a well-intentioned lady (Mme Griset, so it was said) had advised Debussy's future mother-in-law that the composer had not yet broken off his liaison with Gaby and that his way of life offended the conscience of respectable people. René Peter seemed to confirm this: Gaby 'had accepted stoically, one could even say sublimely, the regimen of poverty for two ... not hesitating to take on any sort of work to maintain as best she could the routine of the household'.[6] And Pierre Louÿs, in a letter of 22 March 1894 to Mme de Saint-Marceaux:

The unfortunate telegram which caused the rupture from which my poor friend suffers so much has been ill understood, but I recognize that appearances condemn Debussy ... a young man cannot dismiss as though she were a chambermaid a mistress who has lived with him for two years, who has shared his poverty without complaint, and against whom he has no reproach to make, except that he is weary of her and that he is getting married. Ordinarily, one would extricate oneself by means of some bank notes ... that is the convenient way. You know that Debussy is incapable of making use of it. He believed himself obliged to act circumspectly. ... If there had been less haste in announcing the engagement, Debussy would have had time to extricate himself completely. ...[7]

It is not known whether the engaged pair persisted for a time in their intention of getting married, or if at some point Mme Roger intervened with Chausson and Lerolle to press Debussy to renounce Thérèse.[8] Neither do we know how Debussy's friends carried out this mission or how Debussy received it. However it may have been, Debussy was helpless,

---

[5] G. Millan, *Pierre Louÿs ou le culte de l'amitié* (Aix-en-Provence, 1979), 216.

[6] Peter, *Claude Debussy*, p. 33.

[7] P. Vallery-Radot, *Tel était Claude Debussy* (Paris, 1958), 41–2.

[8] This is what the late Guillaume Lerolle told me in 1954.

and perhaps also defiant when his friends deserted him. Chausson wrote to Bréville on 23 March 1894: 'Yes, I know about the break-up of Debussy's marriage plans. It is very sad from every point of view. And what is going to ensue is not pleasant either.'[9]

This tale caused repercussions for a long time, for on 11 May 1894 Pierre Louÿs wrote to Jean Stevens:

For two months I have supported D[ebussy] against twenty-five people. I am convinced that I have not been mistaken. But yet I would like to have proof of it, and for that there is no other means than that of clarifying what you have said to me. . . . You know my friendship for D., and I hope that you are not surprised by the trouble I am taking so that it will not be broken.[10]

If one goes by the chronology of the known correspondence, there was a complete rupture, lasting for at least two years, with Chausson, Ysaÿe, Bréville, and Godet.[11] Only Lerolle did not immediately withdraw, in spite of the pressure that Chausson seemed to exert upon him and which he resisted for a year. He wrote to Chausson, in October 1894: 'Since you are no longer there, if I could not see him any more, I would end up being too upset.'[12]

Perhaps one can localize here, but without solving it, the puzzle of Mélisande. There may have been an embodiment of Debussy's Méli-sande. Precisely between 1893 and 1895—those years of the beginning and the carrying out of most of the work on *Pelléas et Mélisande*—a young girl appeared before Debussy in the grace of her seventeen years, and with a reserved and touching beauty. She was the daughter of Henri Lerolle, Yvonne, to whom in February 1894 Debussy offered a Japanese fan decorated with birds and flowers, which bore this dedication: 'To Mademoiselle Yvonne Lerolle, in memory of her little sister Mélisande.'

[9] Presumably Chausson feared that Debussy would return to Gaby, but later, when the final break occurred, Debussy's friends addressed other reproaches to him and would fall out with him for life. It is true that there was a revolver, that Gaby tried, without inflicting harm, to kill herself. Had there been no revolver, one wonders what would have been their attitude towards Debussy, who never expected such a desperate outcome.

[10] [Millan, *Pierre Louÿs ou le culte de l'amitié*, p. 218.] The friendship was not broken. At the beginning of June, Louÿs invited several friends to his house to hear Debussy play and sing some excerpts from *Pelléas*. See the letter of 31 May 1894 from Pierre Louÿs to Debussy (1945, p. 32).

[11] 'Some shadows that then passed over the friendship without causing him any harm . . . a Lady with green eyes . . . would have behaved well to have stayed at home', wrote Godet (*ReM*, 1 May 1926, p. 72).

[12] Oulmont, *Musique de l'amour*, i. 83. In a radio broadcast of 1952 (*Regards sur deux anniversaires musicaux*), Gustave Samazeuilh said that he had met Debussy 'as early as 1896 at Chausson's'. It is probable that Debussy had occasion to see his older friend from time to time, up to 1897, but without renewing their previous intimacy.

This Yvonne Lerolle, who has always been presented to us as a child, would be, therefore, in Debussy's imagination, the elder sister of Mélisande: that is to say, the completed work in relation to a sketch, reality in relation to illusion. One cannot help wondering why he offered this gift on the eve of pledging his life to another. Since in this same month of February 1894 he was on the point of marrying Thérèse Roger, his dedication to Yvonne Lerolle seems to take on the meaning of a farewell. Maybe he was saying farewell to a dream that she personified, farewell to what was perhaps his feminine ideal, from the purest and deepest layer of his being, the layer where his mother had left some sacred trace. Those who knew Yvonne Lerolle have testified to her grace, her transparent air, her 'unattainability'. She was as far removed as possible from the energetic Gaby, as from the dull Thérèse Roger. In the winter of that same year, 1894, he also offered Yvonne those then unpublished *Images** which Alfred Cortot, who had just won an honourable mention in piano at the Conservatoire, made her study. One of these, the 'Sarabande', was published in the illustrated supplement of the *Grand Journal* for 17 February 1896 with this dedication: 'May these *Images* be accepted by Mademoiselle Yvonne Lerolle with a little of the pleasure that I have had in dedicating them to her.' A revised version of this 'Sarabande' was included in the suite *Pour le piano*, published in 1901, with a new dedication, simple and sincere like a witness to fidelity: 'To Madame E. Rouart (*née* Y. Lerolle).' For at the end of 1898, when she was twenty-one, Yvonne Lerolle was married to Eugène Rouart. Surely, when the collection appeared, she was no longer so distinct in Debussy's mirror; she lingered only in his memory. Mélisande was definitely conceived and on the point of being created; Yvonne did not torment him any longer. He was married, too, and nearly forty. Nevertheless he thought of her again, when modifying the name of his dedicatee, his Mélisande of 1893.[13]

His engagement was broken, some friendships shaken. As though in reaction, or as though to escape for a time from bourgeois conventions

[13] The *Images* of 1894, without titles, comprise a prelude in the form of a nocturne, the 'Sarabande' (revised when incorporated in the suite *Pour le piano*), and a piece, 'très vite', which is, properly, a sketch of the future 'Jardins sous la pluie' (according to Cortot, who once owned the manuscript). This opinion is perhaps corroborated by Henri Pellerin (*Le Pays d'Auge*, May and June 1897), according to whom 'Jardins sous la pluie' was inspired by the gardens (in the rain) of the Hôtel de Croisy at Orbec (Calvados), where Debussy went with Gaby over Pentecost, 1894.

[This version of the origins of 'Jardins sous la pluie', derives, of course, from Gaby and is generally accepted. For another version, see below, Ch. 15, n. 1.]

* [The title *Images* (*oubliées*) was given to these *Images* when they were published for the first time in 1977.]

that he had seen at too close hand with the 'Franck clique', Debussy began to form a very close friendship with Pierre Louÿs, who was younger, more open, whom he had met for the first time in 1890 at Mallarmé's or perhaps earlier in the company of Catulle Mendès. Their friendship was based upon a common inclination towards pleasure and on their projects which, at first, seemed very similar. Louÿs was a man of the world, Debussy, a loner; both of them were ambitious: the writer to achieve, the musician to realize his potential. If Louÿs, very much the man of letters, had some glimmer, as he acknowledged, of 'the genius' of Debussy, he did not suspect the true grandeur of the artist. But for Debussy Louÿs was not a genius. Louÿs admired Wagner like a god; he hailed Hugo as the prince of poets, while, for Debussy, Hugo was only a resonant giant. Louÿs loved Spain, while his friend, without any acquaintance with it, hated it. Louÿs made faces at *Pelléas et Mélisande*. As for politics, Louÿs was passionately anti-Dreyfus, and Debussy shrugged his shoulders about the 'Affaire', but he was rather in the other camp, according to Peter. None of the projects that they planned in common came to fruition: *La Danseuse*, *Cendrelune*, *Aphrodite*, *Daphnis et Chloé*, *La Saulaie*, nor *Le Voyage de Pausole*. The only ones to see daylight, on the composer's initiative, are the three *Chansons de Bilitis*, two years after their publication in book form.* Referring to *Cendrelune*, which the musician wanted to refine, Louÿs wrote to Debussy on 12 May 1895: 'This religiosity, this triumph of the lily over the rose, and of modesty over love, this is Greek to me' (1945, p. 54). It was here that they differed.

About everything else they were in harmony: that is, about everything that was not fundamental. They hid nothing from each other; they talked, amused themselves, ate together, planned to share a house. Debussy was taken in by the ease, the elegance, the culture, and he enjoyed Louÿs's friends. Appreciating the latter's simplicity, his politeness, his generosity, Debussy sought his advice on everything, wanted his approval. He borrowed his *bons mots*, his whimsies, his money. Where his timidity balked, where he was uncomfortable with the rituals of the literary groups and the protocols of organizations, he asked for the mediation and the counsel of the poet. When he first married, it was because of his friend's example. Undoubtedly, Debussy had no more intimate friend than Pierre Louÿs.

At first sight, it is not quite clear what attracted Louÿs to Debussy: no high spirits, no connections, no money, no influence, a limited and

---

* [Dietschy is in error. Debussy derived two other works from Louÿs's poems: the incidental music for *Les Chansons de Bilitis* of 1900–1 (using texts other than those of the three songs, *Chansons de Bilitis*); and the *Six Épigraphes antiques* of 1914, published in 1915.]

disputed notoriety, self-educated, incomplete, for he lacked a background in the classics. On the other hand, he possessed a pure heart, absolute sincerity, a refined sensibility, an eager artistic mind, an adventuresome and disrespectful wit, and unusual ideas. He further liked Debussy's 'staunch side'. Putting his ear to his friend's chest, Louÿs would murmur to him sometimes: 'I don't hear the A of your heart.'

Louÿs's goodness, his friendship for Debussy, appeared most notably in the invitation that he sent him from Geneva on 13 July 1894 to meet him in Biskra, where he would provide for him 'for two months gratis'. He could scarcely believe that Debussy would agree to make this long journey all alone. There were other reasons as well to keep Debussy in Paris: Gaby, perhaps; the expense of the journey, and, most likely, a lack of enthusiasm for a stay in Algeria that would separate him from his work, especially from *Pelléas et Mélisande*, which was his 'sole companion'. 'My life here is simple like a blade of grass, and I have no other joys than that of working,' he wrote to Lerolle on 28 August 1894.[14] He was indeed working hard: *Pelléas*, the *Prélude à 'L'Après-midi d'un faune'*, which he completed in September, and some 'pieces for violin and orchestra, which will be called *Nocturnes*', after having earlier been called *Trois Scènes au crépuscule*. Above all he worked at night, until dawn. Night is propitious for secret conversations, the accomplice of the most tender dialogues; it amplifies the intimate voices of our dreams. When day broke, Debussy so arranged his world that it was time for sleep. This was the 'happy time of *Pelléas*'.[15]

He was working at full steam, but more than that at peak inspiration, and so much so that he neglected material tasks. He did not want to waste any more time on his Quartet, which had been composed and performed. Badgered by Durand, who demanded the correction of the proofs 'with the yells of a savage', he asked Ernest Le Grand to take over that task. In this way, in moments of feverish pressure, Debussy would find friends (Godet for *Pelléas*, Caplet for *Le Martyre de Saint Sébastien*) who would lend a hand. It seemed that no one could refuse him. 'When I want a thing, I get it,' he said to René Peter. That was profoundly true, in more than one sense.

It has been claimed that at the beginning of August (1893 or 1894) Debussy paid a visit to the Abbey of Solesmes: 'it was on the feast of our

[14] M. Denis, *Henri Lerolle et ses amis* (Paris, 1932), 30.

[15] Ten years later, while composing his *Rapsodie* for saxophone and orchestra, he recalled these days in a letter to Messager, dated 8 June 1903: 'I have been working as in the happy time of *Pelléas*, and again I have seen early mornings breaking with a hangover' (1938, p. 62).

Lady of the Snows (5 August) that a little group of tourists arrived, one of whom was Debussy. Then he was not so important as he became later, but I was not so blind as not to discover the purpose of his visit: modality.'[16]

If this tale was not contrived to satisfy the needs of a thesis, the narrator surely mistook the person, for one cannot imagine Debussy in this role of intellectual spy, mysteriously departing for Solesmes, sitting at the abbot's table, and getting up before 4.20 to be present at matins and lauds—he who could never see a priest without discomfort, or get up in the morning without being sick. Further we are supposed to imagine this recently arrived Englishman neglecting to raise the least question at table, watching with an odd vigilance a Debussy then totally unknown, and remembering these details fifty years afterward.[17]

This year of 1894, which was full of dreams and work, ended with a triumph, a limited and disputed one, but one which made history. On 22 December, the very day of the conviction of Captain Dreyfus to perpetual exile, Gustave Doret was obliged to encore the *Prélude à 'L'Après-midi d'un faune'* at its first performance:

On arriving at the Salle d'Harcourt on the evening of the concert, Debussy betrayed some anxiety with that slight fixed smile that I recognized so well. He shook my hand without saying a word. ... Not without emotion, I mounted the podium. ... The public's silence was impressive at the moment when our admirable flautist, Georges Barrère, played the first phrase. Little by little, I felt behind my back that the audience was conquered and subjugated. The triumph was complete. There were cheers. The orchestra itself applauded. An encore was demanded, and I was forced to grant it. I broke the rules, thinking that it had been a long time since a masterpiece of this class had been presented.[18]

Among musicians, the *Prélude* definitively established Debussy's talent and originality. Among the critics, few opinions were expressed, or they were insignificant. *Le Figaro* said more, but missed the point: 'such pieces are amusing to write, but not at all to hear'. If the *Guide musical* blamed a Wagnerian influence as too dominant, one year later Alfred Ernst, in the

---

[16] Mlle d'Almendra was given this information by a colleague who has since died, an English specialist in medieval music (Almendra, *Les Modes grégoriens dans l'œuvre de Claude Debussy*, 187).

[In *La Musique retrouvée*, p. 68, Laloy mentions the 'venerable' Canon de Bussy, a curé at the church of Saint-Gervais, much interested in early church music. Surely, he is a more likely candidate as the visitor to Solesmes than our Debussy.]

[17] Laloy, in the *Revue musicale* (of Combarieu) of Nov. 1902, had already tried to establish a poetic parallel between 'the grave, sweet song that is breathed by the orchestra at the beginning of *Pelléas*' and the secular influence of the Gregorian chants of the church in the Middle Ages. But Laloy, like Claudel, was then a dedicated convert.

[18] *Gazette de Lausanne*, 19 Nov. 1939.

Revue encyclopédique (15 December 1895), wrote the opposite. 'What is certain is that Debussy does not at all imitate the talented poet–composer and that will be in his favour. . . .' At the same time, two valuable opinions were brought out: 'justice must be accorded, without distinction, to all the innovators—and M. Debussy is, without doubt, one of those',[19] and, second: 'the freshness and suavity of the *Prélude à 'L'Après-midi d'un faune'*, divinely set to music under the inspiration of the beautiful poem of Stéphane Mallarmé by the young composer Debussy.'[20]

Respectfully invited to the première by Debussy, Mallarmé said: 'This music extends the emotion of my poem. . . .' Today the *Prélude*, trembling with sunshine and perfume, maintains all the strength of the eager youth of Claude-Achille Debussy.[21]

From then on Debussy could devote himself exclusively to *Pelléas et Mélisande*. By January 1895 he already foresaw the completion of the work. 'To finish a work, isn't it a little like the death of someone one loves?' he wrote. In April, he worked upon the death of Mélisande; in May, some sketches for the fourth act; in June, once more the death and the final episode. It was not his German origin that kept the publisher Georges Hartmann from appreciating Mélisande's understated death. Debussy reported his reaction to Lerolle, on 17 August 1895:

Look, here is Hartmann, who is certainly a representative of an average intelligence; well then, the way the death of Mélisande is presented does not move him at all. On him it makes no effect! Besides, in France whenever a woman dies on stage, it must be like *La Dame aux Camélias*. . . . People cannot admit that one can die discreetly.[22]

Composing his opera, Debussy saved the second act, as a titbit, considering it a pleasant relaxation. Its realization, however, was not at all easy. He described his problems with it to Bonheur on 9 August 1895: 'I had believed that the second act of *Pelléas* would be child's play for me, and it is pure hell! Really, music permits hardly anything resembling conversation, and he who finds out how to carry on an "Interview in Music" will be worthy of the highest reward' (1980, p. 74).

Finally, on 17 August 1895: 'Good heavens! yes, my dear Lerolle, I find myself confronting the sad necessity of finishing *Pelléas* while you are so far away from me!' He goes on: 'this has not been without some agitation; the scene between Golaud and Mélisande in particular! For it is there that

---

[19] Robert, *La Musique à Paris* (*1895–1896*), p. 57.

[20] Peer Gynt, *La Critique*, 20 Oct. 1895.

[21] Grieg's opinion, in 1906–7, is odd: 'Extravagant music, but very full of talent, and it is ten times more pleasing to me than the "plum-pudding" of the young Germans.'

[22] Denis, *Henri Lerolle et ses amis*, p. 32.

one begins to anticipate the catastrophes. . . .'[23] Nearly a year earlier, in his letter of 22 September 1894 to Ysaÿe, he had also expressed how dark were his uncertainties: 'this pursuit for that dreamed-of expression, that a mere nothing makes evaporate, and also the voluntary suppression of all loquacity ends up by wearing me out like a stone over which carriages have passed.'[24]

During the summer of 1895, *Pelléas et Mélisande* was completed in what is known as its 'first version', after two full years of work, of thought, and of joy. Debussy was so confident, so full of illusions about the fate awaiting his work, that he questioned Maeterlinck about it once more without delay. The poet answered him on 17 October 1895: 'As for *Pelléas*, it goes without saying that it belongs entirely to you and that you can have it performed where or when you want.'*

Already, in fact, Debussy was considering working on *La Grande Bretèche*, after Balzac's story. He mentioned it in his letter to Lerolle of 23 September 1895. Unfortunately, it is not precisely known what hopes he fostered then for the performance of *Pelléas*. Léon Vallas claims:

As early as the month of December 1895, Debussy had foreseen the possibility of having *Pelléas et Mélisande* produced by the Théâtre de l'Œuvre, where, forty months earlier, he had seen Maeterlinck's play performed. For the principal feminine role he had thought of Julia Robert, who at this time had sung *La Damoiselle élue*. This project did not come about.†

In fact, six years later, at a hearing of the Commission of the Société des Auteurs on 14 February 1902, Debussy declared that in 1895 Lugné-Poe had planned to revive *Pelléas*, but without music, and, learning that an opera had been composed on the subject, had abandoned his project.

Then Debussy turned to Ysaÿe, who in 1896 agreed to try an approach to the Théâtre de la Monnaie in Brussels, but the results were negative. As

---

[23] Ibid.

[24] A. Ysaÿe, *Eugène Ysaÿe, sa vie, son œuvre, son influence* (Brussels, 1947), p. 342.

* [Grayson, *The Genesis of Debussy's 'Pelléas et Mélisande'*, p. 42.]

† [Vallas, *Claude Debussy et son temps*, p. 219. That in 1895 Debussy did not seriously consider the Opéra-Comique, where *Pelléas* would receive its première in 1902, may be explained by the fact that the director of that theatre at that time was Léon Carvalho (1825–97), a man notorious for inserting his ideas into new works he presented, as he had done with Bizet's *Les Pêcheurs de perles* at the Théâtre Lyrique in 1863, his inveterate meddling earning him from Gounod the nickname of the 'Zouave of directors' (see M. Curtiss, *Bizet and his World* (New York, 1974), 135). After Carvalho's death, the journalist Jules Huret sent a letter to a number of composers, among them Debussy, requesting their suggestions for the path the Opéra-Comique should take under a new director. Debussy's reply, dated 19 Jan. 1898, clearly reveals his disillusionment with the state-supported Paris theatres at that time (1980, p. 89).]

a last resource, he hoped to have one or two performances of his work given at the Pavillon des Muses, the elegant property of Robert de Montesquiou. Having played the score for Camille Mauclair, Debussy said: 'I would very much like to find a place for it, but you know that I am badly received everywhere. Finally, I hope that Robert de Montesquiou will be willing to give two performances at his Pavillon des Muses.'[25]

Just at the moment when he nurtured this hope, Debussy asked Catherine Stevens to marry him. He offered her all his published works, even dedicating 'En sourdine' to her in May 1892: 'In homage and to indicate a little of my joy in being her affectionate and devoted Claude Debussy.' In her *Notes* she has described the happy hours that she spent with him and the friends who then visited the Stevens family.

Ponchon loved to dress up . . . , to sing the songs of Béranger, *La Fille à papa, La Belle Bourbonnaise* . . . Debussy would go to the piano; we would sing in chorus the operettas of Hervé and Offenbach. . . . When we were alone, we would play four-hands. He made me hum his music and he played from his *Pelléas*. He arranged and rearranged it incessantly, transforming it. . . . On arrival, he would say: I have made a change there . . . or there. In spite of the problems of his life, he was usually cheerful, at our house at least. He did not put on airs, he knew how to be agreeable.

Now this request for marriage coincides with grave reversals in the Stevens family: illness, falling out of favour artistically, and (mark well) financial downfall. It did not matter; with *Pelléas* finished, Debussy believed that he could have his work performed, if not in Paris, at least in Brussels or in Ghent, and that he would become rich and be admitted *de facto* into the Stevens family circle. Nevertheless Catherine refused him, on the grounds that, 'Once *Pelléas* is performed, we will talk about it again!', as she said in her *Notes*.[26] Certainly, her affections were else-where.[27] Her answer shows us, and this we should not forget, that Debussy, in certain social circles, then cut the figure of a Bohemian, of a glutton, of 'an eccentric', of a 'man without a penny' (all these expres-sions occur in Catherine Stevens's *Notes*); furthermore, his liaison with Gaby was held against him. If one adds to this portrait of the 'social' Debussy, his strange head, which Ricardo Viñes himself found 'a little bit frightening', one can understand that at the end of this century that made

[25] C. Mauclair, 'Claude Debussy et les poètes', in *Festival Claude Debussy: Programme et Livre d'or des souscripteurs* (Paris, 17 June 1932).

[26] This brusque answer would explain the 'revenge' of the composer, who dedicated 'En sourdine' to Mme Robert Godet, when it had earlier been offered to Catherine Stevens.

[27] In 1898 she married a physician of high moral and professional character, Dr Henry Vivier, who died of tuberculosis in 1911; she died without issue in 1942.

such a virtue of propriety, prudery, and conventionality, young girls and their relatives were unable seriously to imagine being married to such a man.

Above all, one must try to understand how Debussy felt. The blow must have been keen, for, although opinion on the whole was hardly in his favour, he himself had great expectations. He was aware of his value and, doubtless, of his superiority. He had just had his *Prélude à 'L'Après-midi d'un faune'* applauded, and he had spent two years upon a work whose success and profits seemed assured. 'When *Pelléas* is performed, I will be rich. . . .' He thought he had sufficient claim to be admitted to 'bourgeois' circles. And, finally, the sentimental disappointment prompted by Catherine Stevens's rejection followed on the heels of two or three others. We can believe that his pride as a man and as an artist had been bruised. We can be certain that little by little he would become hardened, as he, unconsciously or not, anticipated some compensation, some revenge sooner or later arising from some chance event.[28]

This period of Debussy's life, that of finishing *Pelléas et Mélisande*, is therefore one of the most moving. Not for us alone, who congratulate ourselves upon the fortunate revision of his opera, and not for the pleasure that we might naïvely believe an artist should feel on the completion of his great work. This period was moving for Debussy, as well, for the denial that opposed harsh reality to his dreams, and for the deep wound that the disappointment of his most cherished hopes inflicted upon him.

For if to complete a work is 'a little like the death of someone one loves', as he had said in January 1895, Debussy could console himself to the extent that he was certain that his work opened a new life: that of the characters with whom he had lived, that of the music he had created, the material realization of his dream in the guise of a performance in the theatre. The palpable joy felt in August 1895 at the prospect of a production of *Pelléas* inspired in him the desire, conscious or not, for complete happiness. He asked the hand of Catherine Stevens in marriage. He was a 'maniac about happiness,' as he wrote to Poniatowski;[29] he wanted to be happy 'in a certain way and by using completely personal means and admittedly for a very lofty goal . . .'.

---

[28] It is moving to observe that during his first marriage, to a model (1899–1904), Debussy became more settled, but he still wore a broad-brimmed soft hat. After 1904, when he was finally admitted to the 'bourgeois' world, he also became a bourgeois: his dress became more elegant; he enjoyed feeling the fine material of his napkin; he wore a derby ('wearing a derby', perceptively observed André Schaeffner, 'was one of a number of rituals that strengthened his feeling of respectability').

[29] Letter of Feb. 1893 in Poniatowski, *D'un siècle à l'autre*, p. 307.

Now everything collapsed all at once, both his artistic projects and his matrimonial ventures. *Pelléas* would be given in neither Paris nor Brussels, nor anywhere else for quite a while, as will be seen. Debussy would find himself confronting the void, the awful void, worsened by the absence of Chausson and Lerolle and of Poniatowski, who was travelling overseas; by the continuing silence of Ysaÿe, by Pierre Louÿs's departure for Spain, by the rupture with the Stevens family, and by Hocquet's marriage. Perhaps even Debussy's parents reproached him, suggesting how unwise he had been to antagonize Catulle Mendès by his abandonment of *Rodrigue et Chimène*. A painful and inhibiting void, which is demonstrated by the absence of creative work in 1896 and the first months of 1897, which Poniatowski described as 'the torture of these ten years of waiting'. If not ten, Debussy certainly had to endure three or four very uncomfortable years.

He would seek and find a consolation with *Pelléas*. In a letter to Lerolle of 28 August 1894, he quoted Mélisande: 'Keep your dreams for my hair, for you well know that no affection can equal ours.'[30] In his bitter but deeply felt solitude, he decided to transform the opera little by little. He would live with Mélisande, with Pelléas, with all the characters whose friendship had meant much to him and whom he would find again. This would be the condensation of his masterpiece, the continual search for expression: 'to arrive at the naked flesh of emotion'. So he described the refining of the drama of love humanized and made authentic by the experience and imagination of the composer. This is the dualism that endows *Pelléas et Mélisande* with its profound truth, its intense poetry, and its unforgettable accents.[31]

[30] Denis, *Henri Lerolle et ses amis*, p. 29.

[31] D'Estrade-Guerra, who was perfectly familiar with the manuscripts and score of *Pelléas*, has given us an idea of how Debussy worked: 'It seems that Debussy, after having taken notes, had to *think through* the entire scene and after that set his first sketch to paper; then he would come back to it more or less frequently, according to how he judged that it worthily suited his purpose, and finally he would fill in the details' ('Les Manuscrits de *Pelléas et Mélisande*', *ReM* (Carnet Critique), 235 (1957), 22).

I 2

'La Mort des amants'

———◆———

No evidence has surfaced that Debussy worked on *Pelléas et Mélisande* between 1896 and 1900* In his known correspondence, unquestionably he refers to *Pelléas*, but only to its performance, or to playing it for friends on the piano.[1] There is no manuscript bearing a date later than 1895 and earlier than 1900.[2] In a letter from June 1896 addressed to Dukas, Debussy confines himself to writing that *Pelléas* 'has come back from the bindery'. In another letter from the same month, this one to Gustave Doret, he confirms that *Pelléas* is complete.† In a note written in 1902 to Georges Ricou, Debussy states: '*Pelléas* was finished a first time in 1895. Since then I have taken it up again, revised it....' He did not say any more. Three letters give a more precise account. One from 25 July 1907, to Laloy: 'I see that in May 1901 I rewrote the last scene of the fourth act' (*RdM*, 1962, p. 26). His letter of 2 September 1901, to Louÿs: 'For a long time I walked beside this little neurasthenic Mélisande' (1945, p. 165). Finally, in January 1902, once again to Louÿs: 'I am working to repair the gears of the *Pelléas et Mélisande* machine. Without seeming to, it devours my days and nights' (1945, p. 169). This work then was confined to 1901 and 1902.

There is some justification for believing that Debussy did not really rework and revise his opera before the day (3 May 1901) when he was assured that it would be performed 'the following season'. Certainly,

---

[1] Three such occasions are known: on 19 Apr. 1897, for Godet, Jules de Brayer, Edouard Rist, and Francis de Pressensé; on 2 Feb. 1899, at Arthur Fontaine's; and in 1900, for Maurice Ravel, Raoul Bardac, and Lucien Garban.
[2] The rough draft [in a private collection] bears at the conclusion of Act IV the dates: Sept.–Oct. 1893, May 1895, Jan. 1900, and Sept. 1901.

---

* [Grayson says, however: 'Although this revision [of Jan. 1900] represents the first datable recomposition of any part of the opera since August 1895, there were surely intervening retouchings' (*The Genesis of Debussy's 'Pelléas et Mélisande'*, p. 51).]

† [Dated 5 June 1896, in *Lettres romandes* (Geneva), Nov. 1934.]

['La Mort des amants', *Cinq Poèmes de Charles Baudelaire*, No. 5.]

Pelléas was accepted 'in principal' by the Opéra-Comique in May 1898.[3] It is clear that Debussy then worked on it, since there is a rough draft of the fourth act that bears the date of January 1900. Almost certainly he retouched it now and again, especially when he performed it at the houses of his friends. If he did no work upon his opera between 1896 and 1901, after having done so much between 1893 and 1895, it was because *Pelléas* was then truly finished; the colours of each scene were set, and the score had been played and replayed to all the composer's friends, so that it had no more need of exposition. In the period of its gestation, Debussy wrote letters to those friends he did not see later—Chausson, Lerolle, Ysaÿe, Stevens—or less frequently Godet, Dukas, Bonheur; most of the known letters written by Debussy between 1896 and 1900 are addressed to Pierre Louÿs, who was too occupied by his literary activities to encourage the composer to confide in him the modifications of detail that he was introducing into his work. A wounded modesty, a very understandable reaction, further prevented Debussy from enlarging upon a *Pelléas*, that no impresario wanted.[4]

A performance had been considered in vain at the Pavillon des Muses of Robert de Montesquiou, as has been mentioned. A more serious prospect was the possibility of *Pelléas* in Brussels or in Ghent, with Ysaÿe's support, but the violinist could not elicit a favourable decision and proposed as recompense a performance of excerpts at one of the symphonic concerts that he conducted. Debussy opposed it, on 13 October 1896, with discreet firmness: 'If this work has some merit, it is above all in the relationship between the scenic movement and the musical motion. . . . The simplicity of means used cannot reasonably have its proper significance except upon the stage.'[5]

To Ysaÿe, who insisted, Debussy confirmed his position on 17 November:

[3] As Louÿs wrote to Debussy on 21 May 1898: 'There you are played at the Place Boieldieu' [the location of the Opéra-Comique] (1945, p. 113). This audition was due to Messager, who on 14 Jan. 1898 had been named the theatre's musical director. Albert Carré had been named manager at the beginning of the same year.

[4] When, much later, Debussy publicly stated that he had taken ten years to compose *Pelléas*, he wanted to indicate his disapproval for works that were insufficiently thought through or revised: in fact, he implied that he had *thought* about his opera during a ten-year period. And if he declared it specifically to Robert de Flers in 1902 (absent-mindedly adding two years), it was to point out the culpable flippancy of his critics who had not hesitated to flay a work that cost ten years of effort ('Now, Monsieur, for twelve years I have had Pelléas and Mélisande as daily companions'). In reality, as we have shown, Debussy *lived* ten years with his opera; the gestation and orchestration of *Pelléas* had required three years at the most.

[5] Ysaÿe, *Eugène Ysaÿe, sa vie, son œuvre, son influence*, p. 344.

I believe that it must not be performed like that, and even if you, in your generosity, understand in spite of everything, the public will not understand, and you will cause yourself problems for nothing. ... I am very proud of your concern for me, and some day we shall see that everything will be all right.

At the beginning of October 1896, however, Ysaÿe had officially announced that some 'fragments' of *Pelléas* would be played at the one of his symphonic concerts. Apparently the composer's refusal disappointed Ysaÿe, because he did not write again. Therefore at the close of 1896 Debussy had lost all hope of having *Pelléas et Mélisande* performed in the near future.[6]

The year was a barren one for Debussy. He vainly took up a project with Louÿs for a ballet to be called *Daphnis et Chloé*. He completed only a single task: the orchestration of two *Gymnopédies* of Erik Satie, given their first performance on 20 February 1897. It was the first of Debussy's bitter years; 1897 would be no better, and 1898 worse. 'I am feeling out of sorts', and he wrote to Louÿs of 'the forlorn plant that my life represents at this moment'. He stared into the abyss; inhibitions arose and upheavals. His creative inactivity produced an emotional reaction, perhaps also a physical one. We will see it later on.

René Peter wrote: 'At this time a sort of hiatus occurred in the sentimental life of the man, a sort of stumbling; it was as if, let us admit it, he felt a passing incapacity to "conquer".' And then he adds:

A certain woman in society who knew how to flirt amusingly, and who, seeing him ready to adapt himself to the part of *cavalier servant*, was happy to draw out the episode as far as it would go, was flattered to become in some people's eyes— and perhaps even to believe herself—'the muse of the great man of the future'. However, with her refined sense of practical life, she was far from the dreamy Bilitis, whose songs Claude was then setting to music.[7]

This 'heroine' can easily be identified as Alice, the wife of Michel Peter, then to all intents separated from him. To her is dedicated the second of the *Chansons de Bilitis*, 'La Chevelure', which *L'Image* published in its issue of October 1897. So far no one has identified the 'heroine' of the sharp letter of 9 February 1897 that Debussy wrote to Louÿs:

---

[6] The question has been raised whether Debussy wanted to dedicate *Pelléas* to Ysaÿe. In his letter of 13 Nov. 1893, Debussy spoke principally of his Quartet, dedicated to the Ysaÿe Quartet, who were doubtless informed of this tribute. But, because of an error in syntax, routine with Debussy, it seems, in the sentence that it is *Pelléas* which becomes the object of the dedication; hence the confusion. It seems unlikely that Debussy would dedicate two compositions at the same time to the same person.

[7] Peter, *Claude Debussy*, pp. 38–9.

Gaby with her eyes of steel found a letter in my pocket that left no doubt about the development, sufficiently advanced, of a love with all that is most romantic to move the most hardened heart. Thereupon ... drama ... tears ... a real revolver ... and *Le Petit Journal* tells the story. ... This poor little Gaby has just lost her father, and this encounter with death has temporarily caused these little ludicrous tales. Nevertheless, I have been upset. ... (1945, p. 87)

Apparently Gaby had tried to kill herself, and doubtless there really was a gunshot, since a newspaper got hold of the story.[8] But Gaby, if she had wounded herself, which has not been established, could not have been very badly hurt, for we find her again smiling, with Debussy, one month later. 'Gaby thanks you and sends you her best smile,' he wrote to Louÿs on 9 March. However, Chausson, then Ysaÿe, had taken in the desperate woman for several days. Once again his friends took positions for and against Debussy, and more against than for, because this event marked the definite break with Chausson, Lerolle, and Ysaÿe, but not with Gaby herself, unexpected as that might seem. Debussy suffered from these defections. We find the proof of it in a letter of 27 December 1897 to Louÿs: 'You are the only one ... but the others, the sinister others ...' (1945, p. 107).

On 22 June 1897 he finished the first of the three *Chansons de Bilitis*, the most delicate one, 'La Flûte de Pan'. The second, 'La Chevelure', completed at the end of July, is dedicated to Mme A. Peter. One gets a precise idea of the passion this woman inspired in him, listening to the melody that is dense, voluptuous, and perfect, and which closes with heartrending tenderness. These five bars reveal Debussy's sensitivity.

In 'Le Tombeau des naïades', completed in March 1898, there are traces of a betrayed love, an unrealizable dream, for at this very time Debussy was deeply depressed, and he suffered from it so much that he thought of suicide. He wrote to Louÿs on 27 March 1898: 'I have been very unhappy since your departure, unhappy in the most passionate manner and I have wept a lot ...' (1945, p. 109). And then in April:

I feel alone and depressed. Nothing has changed in the darkness that underlies my life, and I scarcely know where I am going, perhaps towards suicide, a stupid outcome to something which perhaps deserved better, and that above all through the fatigue of struggling against imbecilic impossibilities, which moreover are despicable. (1945, pp. 110–11)

[8] Nevertheless, neither *Le Petit Journal*, nor *Le Journal*, nor *Le Petit Parisien* seem to have referred to it between Sept. 1896 and 9 Feb. 1897. And, as the log-book of the Commissary of Police of the relevant neighbourhood was not added to the archives of the Préfecture de Police, one is reduced to hypotheses.

At this point Alice Peter does not seem to have been the cause of Debussy's low spirits. It seems rather that it was Gaby, who had just abandoned Debussy to live with Comte Victor de Balbiani, the same person whom Debussy was going to dismiss coldly when he proposed that he compose incidental music to his *La Fille de Pasiphaé*. In fact, the last time Debussy mentions Gaby to Louÿs is in his letter of 27 December 1897. The separation was apparently carried out without disturbance, but it happened in a period of discouragement and despair. The year 1898 was perhaps the most terrible one for Debussy. Still without hope for *Pelléas*, abandoned by Gaby and by his former friends, separated from Louÿs, who took Zohra* back to her native Algeria, and having bade farewell for ever—without being aware of it—to one of his most devoted friends, Étienne Dupin,[9] Debussy was completely wretched. 'I need something to love, to which I can cling,' he wrote to Louÿs on 27 March. That is what shows us perhaps that *Pelléas et Mélisande* was sleeping soundly, that Debussy had scarcely turned his hand to it since 1895. And doubtless he also needed someone to love.

The acceptance in principle of *Pelléas* by the Opéra-Comique in mid-May 1898 seemed to him a very distant prospect. He fruitlessly sought a singer to perform the *Chansons de Bilitis*; one year later Jeanne Raunay would refuse them. In April, for Lucien Fontaine's chorus, he finished two of the *Trois Chansons de Charles d'Orléans*, for four voices. To these he would add a third ten years later. It might also have been about this time that Catulle Mendès suggested a performance of *La Damoiselle élue*.[10]

He tried to concentrate upon the *Nocturnes*, but with difficulty. He had taken them up again several months before, at the end of 1897. The differences between the three versions will probably never be known: 1892, *Trois Scènes au crépuscule*; 1894, *Nocturnes* with solo violin; 1897-9,

---

[9] Curious to see new horizons, Dupin sailed for Mexico with his wife, the sister of Alice Peter. Death awaited them there. He was assassinated on 18 Sept. 1899 on a hill near the village of Oxtutla, without witnesses, and when his body was identified two months later, his wife, desperate, killed herself.

[10] Apparently, Mendès chose to ignore Debussy's renunciation of *Rodrigues et Chimène*.

My dear master, thank you for your kind thought about the performance of *La Damoiselle élue*. 1) I have no one at hand to sing *La Damoiselle*. 2) I fear that a performance with piano would be cold and inconspicuous, particularly in a big hall like the Ambigu (Hartmann is also entirely of my opinion). 3) *La Damoiselle élue* having been given with orchestra, I am surely not such a legendary classic to run the risk of having it mutilated in a performance with piano ... (letter of Debussy to Mendès, undated, but surely between 1894 and 1898)

---

* [Louÿs had imported Zohra ben Brahim to Paris in 1897; she has been described as 'the inspiration of his poems to Bilitis'.]

Trois Nocturnes. But it could well be that the atmosphere of 'Fêtes' had been determined during the summer of 1894. In his letter of 28 August 1894, in which he announced to Lerolle that he was composing the *Nocturnes*, Debussy added that he 'often strolls in the Bois de Boulogne', in these woods, which by his own avowal, had inspired 'Fêtes'.

It is the Bois de Boulogne. A retreat with torches, evening, in the woods. ... I have seen from afar, through the trees, lights approaching, and the crowd running towards the path where the procession is going to pass. Then ... the horsemen of the Garde Républicaine, resplendent, their arms and helmets lit by the torches, and the bugles sounding their fanfare. At last, all that fades and grows distant....*

It was not by chance that Debussy placed 'Nuages' at the beginning of his trilogy and, at the end, 'Sirènes'. 'Nuages' is contemplation; 'Fêtes', action; 'Sirènes', intoxication. All three end in stillness, that is in hope; stillness prolongs the colloquy. The subject of 'Nuages':

It is night on the pont de Solférino, very late at night. A great stillness. I was leaning on the railing of the bridge. The Seine, without a ripple, like a tarnished mirror. Some clouds slowly pass through a moonless sky, a number of clouds, not too heavy, not too light: some clouds. That is all.

Yes, that particular night, sometime between 1894 and 1898 without a doubt, Debussy looked at the great city sleeping. He saw his life passing in the clouds, his melancholy, terrible life, so loved and so intensely lived. Like the clouds, time advances implacably. Debussy may have felt himself transported by the breath of a prodigious stillness. There is something tragic in 'Nuages', and this admirable tone-poem is breathless with it.

In contrast, 'Fêtes' resounds with the rhythmic gaiety of public celebrations. But every festival has its conclusion. It is the descending arc that describes the last part of 'Fêtes'. The noisier the ambience, the more heavily weighs the ensuing stillness. Nothing seems to remain but the dust left by the boots of the procession; the stillness insists on new fanfares. And suddenly, the 'Sirènes' emerge from the water, mingling their voices with the dancing foam. Forgetfulness can come only from them, and Debussy dreams of the sounds and the broad expanse of the sea. Later, this dream would be realized.

* ['Programme du Festival du 17 juin 1932, No. 2 *Nocturnes*', in *Festival Claude Debussy: Programme et Livre d'or des souscripteurs* (Paris).]

13

Fleur des blés

———◆———

ALTHOUGH eighteen months were to elapse between the first encounter and the marriage, it was in April or May 1898 that René Peter, a witness to his friend's distress, without any ulterior motive, brought about a meeting that proved beneficial. It was then that Debussy saw for the first time the woman who would become his wife: Rosalie Texier, Lilly, Lilo, the first Mme Claude Debussy. At twenty-five she was a model in a dressmaking establishment, the Sœurs Callot in the rue Taitbout. She was living with 'a nice fellow who dabbled in stocks'. Her father was a telegraph inspector for the railway at Montereau; her mother was dead. Although Lilly was pretty, blonde, and elegant, she did not immediately captivate Debussy. He found her a little 'lackadaisical'. She came too soon after Alice Peter. From the first, he was well aware that she could not be everything to him. He valued her for her 'unaggressive aesthetic'; that is to say, she seemed to satisfy the bourgeois side of his character. Besides she prepared tea surpassingly well.

It appears, however, that Gaby had not definitely left Debussy, because Lilly met her, and a friendship sprang up between them, but there was as yet no relationship between Debussy and Lilly. Considering that Debussy moved from the rue Gustave-Doré only in September 1898, one cannot help wondering whether Gaby, who had left for Orbec at the start of the year, had already completely broken with him before he settled into the fifth floor flat at 58 rue Cardinet.

The penultimate year of the century, 1899, was a turning-point in Debussy's life, the farewell to a period important to his soul, but it would take a little time before he could appreciate that. He suspected it, however, when, on 15 May 1899, Pierre Louÿs announced his own marriage. Debussy promised him a *Marche nuptiale*,* two hundred bars long, and, moved by the change that this marriage would bring to their close relationship, the change which he foresaw and which would be only

* [If Debussy kept his promise, no trace of it is known.]

[*Fleur des blés* is a song composed about 1880. Dietschy quotes some lines of André Girod's text as an epigraph to this chapter: *un bouquet* | *Mets-le vite à ton corsage* | *Il est fait à ton image* ('A bouquet | Put it quickly in your bodice, | It was made in your image').]

too real, Debussy asked him for a memento of their friendship. In return, Louÿs wrote to him this fine letter, full of emotion: 'My dear Claude. Here is the inkstand used for all my first books. You have moved me greatly in asking me for it. I am very happy to give it to you and to embrace you. Your friendship has filled my bachelor life. It still holds long hours for us, does it not? I love you much. Pierre' (1945, pp. 130–1).

Two weeks earlier, he had insisted that Debussy accept a dinner invitation from Chausson. There is a chance that these two musicians, whom *La Damoiselle élue* had brought together, met one final time, before death separated them on 10 June 1899, when Chausson was killed in a bicycle accident at his home at Limay. Debussy was thus deprived of an affection that perhaps would have flourished again. With Dupin gone, Ysaÿe angry, Louÿs married, Godet in Bavaria, Bonheur too seldom in Paris, Dukas invisible, Debussy was glad to turn again to René Peter, who succeeded Louÿs in the forthright comradeship which all three knew how to foster. Peter and Debussy considered several collaborative projects: *Frères en art* notably, and that curious farce, *Esther et la maison de fous*, neither of which came to anything.[1] He played *Pelléas et Mélisande* at Arthur Fontaine's on 2 February 1899, but there is no evidence that he was working upon it; in fact, he was unaware that his opera had been accepted at the Opéra-Comique. But he was not deceiving himself, because it would be two years before the agreement in principle was actually drawn up.

Then Debussy made a decision, one could say a desperate decision, for at heart that is what it was. He determined to marry Lilly Texier. As we have seen, when he first met her in 1898 he was fully aware that she was not the woman he needed. Then he had lost sight of her, later finding her again, probably in May 1899. ('My little friend is ill,' he wrote to Louÿs on about 15 June.) They had tried living together, but 'it did not work out happily and they separated', as Léon Vallas puts it. This is confirmed by Debussy in a letter to Hartmann of 24 September 1899. 'I have been rather unhappy this summer, with some tender compensations, and I must warn you of my marriage with the aforesaid compensations . . . that will take place soon without foolish display and without bad music. There

---

[1] 'Esther had always been devoted to the public's pleasure, as her first phase of being a courtesan would show. . . . However, one day when her last lover had described a little harshly the slackening of her breasts, she uttered this phrase, which would henceforth be historic: "Farewell, cash-books! It's all over!" Afterwards she became the Lady in Black and would devote the earnings of her nightly labours to the purchase of a lunatic asylum at Bécon-les-Bruyères. . . . From there issued most of the famous madmen . . . Prince Hamlet . . . Roderick Usher. . . .' (four sheets, undated, in Debussy's hand) [in a private collection].

is really no need to upset the universe for such a personal event!' (*ReM*, 1964, p. 114). Vallas adds:

Then suddenly love was violently born in Debussy's heart. He wanted to marry his friend whom he had known for several weeks. On the advice and from the experience of Gaby Lhéry, who had remained friendly with the two new lovers, Lilly-Lilo refused to live with him again. Debussy threatened to kill himself if she would not marry him.[2]

That earlier he had had some resistance to the idea of marriage is demonstrated by his letter of 16 May to Louÿs: 'my old liaison with Music prevents me from becoming a bridegroom' (1945, p. 130). But he was so afraid of losing Lilly, and of finding himself alone again, all the more after Pierre Louÿs's marriage, that he wrote her a beautiful and moving letter, which Vallas mentions. Upset and also no doubt feeling complimented in her soul, which was that of a 'good girl' and dressmaker, Lilly finally accepted his proposal, and in September Debussy was able to announce the coming marriage to his friends. Lilly was ill, however, and Debussy had to alert Dr Abel Desjardins, writing to him on 4 September 1899: 'Besides being adorable, she is a very brave person, and if her case is serious, do not hesitate to tell her; only, do not hurt her for my sake, I beg you' (1980, p. 99).

In addition, Debussy's financial position was always in a state of crisis. On 13 June he had written to Hartmann: 'Before you leave for Bohemia, would you be kind enough to leave me 200 francs? I have almost no lessons, and summer is a propitious time only for cicadas....' It was extraordinary, and it should not be overlooked, that on the day of his wedding, Debussy had to give a piano lesson to Mlle de Romilly (who would marry General Gérard), in order to pay for his wedding breakfast. On 19 October 1899, in fact, with Louÿs, Satie, and Lucien Fontaine as witnesses, Claude Debussy married Lilly Texier. There was no religious ceremony. Their honeymoon was a visit to the zoo at the Jardin des Plantes. He thought gratefully of Gaby and offered her the particell of the *Prélude à 'L'Après-midi d'un faune'*, inscribed 'to my dear and very good little Gaby, with the sincere affection of her devoted Claude Debussy, October 1899'.

Debussy's marriage is touching because of these circumstances and because of all it signifies. If he had no illusions about his wife's origins, if his parents were dismayed by this union with an ordinary girl without education, talent, or dowry, it would be a mistake to think that Debussy did not appreciate her simplicity, her firmness, her kindness, her lively

---

[2] Vallas, *Claude Debussy et son temps*, p. 200.

and slightly earthy wit, her elegance, and her lithe body, that Mary Garden thought 'admirable'. Protector and lover, Debussy was not displeased to discover in her something of the little girl she would remain. Pierre Louÿs's marriage had certainly been an incentive to his own, and his offered him a social foundation, important to him after his two or three earlier unsuccessful attempts. Here was a legal union for which no one could criticize him. Still, one cannot ignore the questions of what he had to offer a wife or to promise her. Thanks to Lilly, he would experience three years of happiness, in spite of financial pinches and artistic difficulties. The victory of *Pelléas* would irradiate the third year. His letters to Louÿs show his unsophisticated joy in being, at least in a legal sense, the equal of his friend. He would be proud for himself and for Lilly that Louÿs inscribed a copy of the texts of his *Chansons de Bilitis* to 'Madame Claude Debussy'. Later he would speak of his 'home'. 'The news of your home vexes me a little; in my home things are improving.' Little things like that speak of Debussy's uncomplicated soul.[3]

The new century opened with the successful première of Gustave Charpentier's *Louise*, which Debussy described to Louÿs on 6 February 1900, as serving 'too well the need for cheap beauty and imbecile art which so many people demand . . .' (1945, p. 137). As early as February 1893, he had expressed his low opinion of *Louise* to Poniatowski: 'It smells like a pipe and there is something like whiskers over the music.'*

On 17 March 1900 Blanche Marot sang the *Chansons de Bilitis* at their first public performance.† On 22 April, his publisher Hartmann died, leaving Debussy, 'the terrible man', as Hartmann used to call him, helpless.[4] On 5 August 1900 *Le Ménestrel* announced *Pelléas et Mélisande* for the coming season at the Opéra-Comique, and Debussy played it at his home for Ravel, Raoul Bardac, and Lucien Garban. That same month *La*

---

[3] On 6 May 1903, having returned from London, Debussy wrote to Messager: 'Here I am back at my house. . . . It is neither very big nor very attractive. The comforts of life are reduced to the leanest. . . . But it is the house where my heart resides, as the Greeks have said' (1938, p. 57).

[4] This was a blow to Debussy, who had for several years been receiving a monthly stipend of 500 fr. from Hartmann. The situation deteriorated later, when General Bourjat, Hartmann's nephew and heir, demanded that Debussy repay the sums he had received as advances. Naturally that occurred just when *Pelléas* had its success. Happily Fromont was there, and on 5 July 1902 he replied to the General's attack by buying back from him all of Debussy's compositions, manuscripts, and printed copies, for 8,000 fr. Hartmann himself had bought them in 1895 for 1,410 fr. from Choudens (except for the *Chansons de Bilitis* and the *Nocturnes*, which had not been composed at that time).

* [Poniatowski, *D'un siècle à l'autre*, p. 308.]

† [Accompanied by the composer.]

Damoiselle élue was performed at an official concert at the Trocadéro, held in conjunction with the Exposition of that year. And on 9 December 'Nuages' and 'Fêtes' were successfully presented by the Concerts Lamoureux.[5]

But the Debussys' return to Paris, after a three weeks' holiday in the Yonne with Lilly's family, was bitter. They had lost the child they had hoped for, and Lilly had had to spend ten days in a clinic, the Maison Dubois, from 14 to 23 August 1900, where Doctor Potherat treated her.

---

[5] 'None among the young composers, nor among the older, is endowed with a melodic inventiveness that is more enticing, more supple, more discriminating. And particularly none of them uses harmonies that are more original, more refined or more subtle...' wrote Pierre Lalo in *Le Temps* for 28 Aug. 1900. In *Le Figaro* Alfred Bruneau found *La Damoiselle élue* too exquisite, soft, and insipid. 'I want a virile art...', that is to say, conforming to his aesthetic: art that was realistic, violent, without poetry, in the manner of Zola, who was Bruneau's intimate friend.

14

A Dream come True

DEBUSSY's financial situation was so precarious that he accepted a commission to write some pages of incidental music for a single mimed performance of the *Chansons de Bilitis* at the Salle des Fêtes of *Le Journal* on 7 February 1901. He also agreed to write a musical column for the *Revue blanche*, where his first article appeared in April 1901. This same April the fate of *Pelléas et Mélisande* ceased to be problematic. At Messager's instigation, Debussy played it again, at 58 rue Cardinet, for Albert Carré, the director of the Opéra-Comique. Finally, on 5 May, excited and happy, he could inform Pierre Louÿs: '*I have the written promise* of M. A. Carré that he will stage *Pelléas et Mélisande* next season' (1945, p. 160).[1]

So Debussy took up his opera, which he had neglected for almost six years, and once more began to work seriously upon it. In his letters of this period, as in those written between 1893 and 1895, he started to mention it again. This was the last phase of work upon it, and he was in no doubt that his labours would be hellish. At first, the most taxing chore was to write out the orchestral score, which had only been sketched, and to have the parts copied. Later, he decided to re-orchestrate it, and, at the last moment, there arose the problem of lengthening the interludes to serve as a continuous musical link between the scenes while the sets were being changed.[2]

In his excitement over Carré's acceptance of his opera, Debussy's first idea was to modify the opening of the last scene of the fourth act, the episode with which he had begun his work on the project and which he

---

[1] *Pelléas et Mélisande* had been registered at the Société des Auteurs by a bulletin antedated 3 May 1901, although it was deposited on 30 Dec.

[2] Debussy had foreseen using interludes between the scenes. At the rehearsals they proved to be too short for the time required to change the sets, and therefore he had to develop them. The first edition of the piano–vocal score of *Pelléas* (1902) gives them in their original form. In collating it with the complete edition of 1907 one sees that Debussy had done this:

In the first act: between scenes 1 and 2: 33 bars added to the original 15; between scenes 2 and 3: 18 bars added to the original 10. In the second act: between scenes 1 and 2: 37 bars added to the original 9; between scenes 2 and 3: 15 bars added to the original 19. In the third act: no change. In the fourth act: between scenes 2 and 3: 45 bars added to the original 15; otherwise the interludes unchanged. The total number of bars added: 148.

2. Victorine Manoury Debussy

1. Manuel-Achille Debussy as a private
in the Marine Light Infantry, 1858

4. Alfred Debussy

3. Adèle Debussy

6. Mme Mauté de Fleurville, his piano teacher in 1871–2

5. Clémentine Debussy, his aunt and godmother

8. Mme von Meck, with whom he spent the summers of 1880, 1881, and 1882

7. Achille-Claude Debussy at the Conservatoire, c.1874

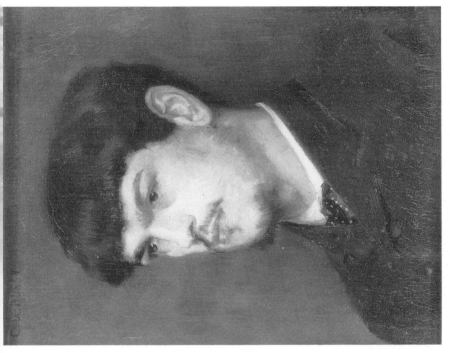

10. Achille Debussy at the Villa Medici, 1885
(portrait by Marcel Baschet)

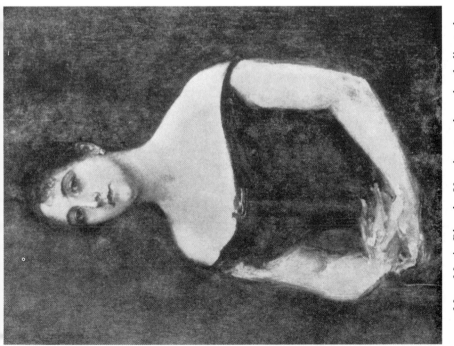

9. Mme Marie-Blanche Vasnier to whom he dedicated
twenty-six songs (oil painting by Paul Baudry, 1885)

12. René Peter, a friend from 1890 to 1904

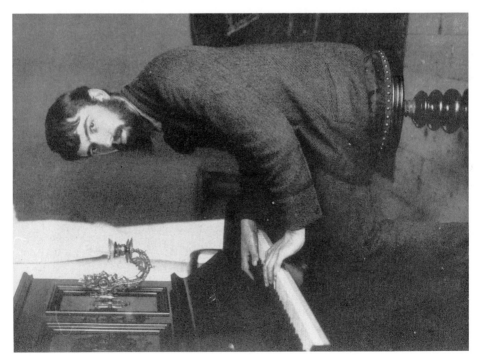

11. Robert Godet, a lifelong friend from 1888

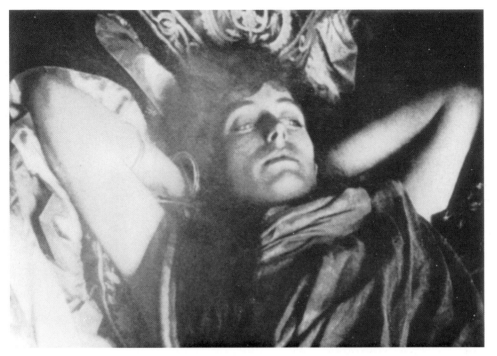

13. Gabrielle Dupont, 1893, his faithful mistress from 1890 to 1898

14. Pierre Louÿs, a close
friend from 1893 to 1904

15. Ernest Chausson, a
good friend

PLATE 16

16. Raymond Bonheur and Debussy at Luzancy, 1893. Bonheur was a
friend at the Conservatoire

17. Claude and Lilly Debussy at the time of *Pelléas*

18. Jacques Durand, his friend and
exclusive publisher from 1905

20. André Messager who conducted the première of *Pelléas*, 1902

19. Mary Garden as Mélisande, 1902

21. Paul Dukas, *c.*1895, a lifelong friend from the Conservatoire

22. Debussy in a photo taken by Dukas in his library at Eragny,
11 May 1902

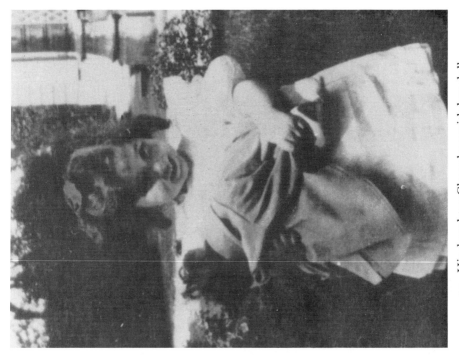

24. His daughter Chouchou with her doll

23. Emma Bardac at Pourville, 1904

25. Debussy and his parents at the avenue du Bois, 1906

26. Louis Laloy and Debussy, friends from 1902

28. Paul-Jean Toulet, a friend from 1899

27. Gabriel Mourey, a friend and would-be collaborator from 1907

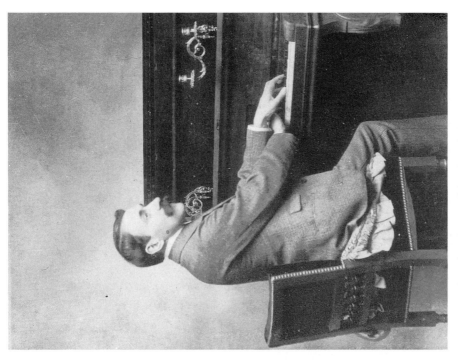

30. Ricardo Viñes, a friend and pianist who gave many first performances of Debussy's works

29. André Caplet and Debussy, c.1910. Caplet conducted many of Debussy's works and orchestrated several of them

PLATE 31

31. Debussy, 1909

had not touched since 6 September 1893. His impulsive gesture was not one of practicalities; to transpose from his head on to paper the monumental orchestration worried him less and was less important to him than the crucial dialogue: *C'est le dernier soir . . . le dernier soir . . . il faut que tout finisse . . . ('It is the last evening . . . the last evening . . . everything must end . . .').

Notified by Debussy, Maeterlinck told him, at the end of May 1901, that he would visit him to discuss 'our *Pelléas*' with him. The purpose of this visit was certainly not to discuss the cuts made in the text by the composer with the assent and even the advice of the poet, in 1894, although a year later he dared to reproach Debussy with them in his furious letter to *Le Figaro*. It could only have been about the distribution of the roles. Georgette Leblanc has vainly stated in her *Souvenirs* that the question did not come up until the end of 1901, for Maeterlinck later affirmed to the Société des Auteurs that as early as that spring he had notified Debussy that he insisted on Georgette Leblanc, his mistress, for the role of Mélisande*

As to Debussy's reaction, the singer claimed that he was 'enchanted', but she reduced the credibility of her tale when she added: '[Debussy] told me that, having seen me so violent in *Carmen*, he had at first doubted my suitability.' The truth is that Debussy said neither yes nor no; his statements agree with those of Maeterlinck.[3] At that time he was perhaps quite indifferent to the question of who the performers would be, but he scarcely appreciated Georgette Leblanc and did not think her appropriate for the part she wanted.[4]

Carré must have been notified of Maeterlinck's demand. For a while the matter rested there. Debussy went to spend the month of August and the first ten days of September at Bichain. It is not clear whether he had

---

[3] Debussy's deposition: 'We shall see.' Maeterlinck's deposition: 'M. Debussy did not reject this demand, but was of the opinion that M. Carré must not be offended, and that it was better to wait.' (Extracts from the official report of the hearings of 7 and 14 Feb. 1902 at the Société des Auteurs.)

[4] Here is Lugné-Poe's opinion: 'What is Mme Leblanc? . . . a so-so singer . . . she did not seem to me to have any standing in the musical world' (*Sous les étoiles* (Paris, 1933), 49). For his part, Camille Mauclair in the *Revue universelle* of June 1902 wrote: 'In order to interpret Mélisande one needs a slender young woman, without the domineering demeanour of an actress, an excellent musician, but having nothing of the hateful manner of a "*chanteuse*". Mlle Garden seems to me to embody these qualities.'

---

* [Georgette Leblanc was already a member of the Opéra-Comique, having made her début in 1893. She sang Carmen in the new production of 8 Dec. 1898, which was staged by Albert Carré. On 10 May 1907 she created Ariane in the world première of Dukas's *Ariane et Barbe-bleue*, to a text by Maeterlinck.]

already played his work to the poet or if he did so upon his return from holiday. We know only that the poet dozed during the performance. We also know that his mistress felt impelled to write to Debussy about her passion for this novel music, stressing her humility in the face of the role of Mélisande. Even if the four or five study sessions that Georgette Leblanc claimed to have had with Debussy did take place, they cannot have been sufficiently conclusive to evoke from the composer the deep conviction that he spontaneously lavished upon Mary Garden after having heard her: 'This is she ... This is my Mélisande!'

Carré and Messager, however, had delayed the casting of the opera; they discussed it with Debussy at the Café Weber, and left the final decision to him after he had auditioned the singers. Undoubtedly this took place before the end of 1901, for *Le Ménestrel* on 29 December announced that Mary Garden would create the role of Mélisande. Having seen her and heard her, Debussy could not even conceive of anyone else in the role. Then a furious Maeterlinck, seeing red and brandishing his cane, ran to Debussy's home to 'teach him how to behave'. When he came away without having taught him anything, the playwright was determined to find the surest method of destroying Debussy, even if it meant destroying *Pelléas* as well.

Taken up with rehearsals of the *Nocturnes*, 'very jostled ... by life', Debussy secretly determined in November 1901 to revise the instrumentation of his opera. 'I have set my mind on re-orchestrating *Pelléas* (not a word of it to anyone),' he wrote to Louÿs (1945, p. 167). When he added, in January 1902, that he was working 'to repair the gears of the *Pelléas et Mélisande* machine' (1945, p. 169), he must have thought that he had allowed it to sleep too long. This time, it 'devours' his days and nights. Time was pressing, for on 13 January the first partial rehearsals began. He had already given up his rather vague projects of collaborating with Peter and Louÿs, but he entertained Viñes, on 30 November and 14 December, when he played the suite *Pour le piano*, prior to its first public performance on 11 January 1902.

At the Opéra-Comique the enthusiasm of the singers, who had been involved with the work since the beginning, increased from week to week,* in spite of its difficulties, in spite of the lack of big arias, in spite of the composer's demands. Maeterlinck had not given up. He was still making a fine uproar in the wings, without ever succeeding in having his way about Georgette Leblanc. Carré gave sufficient support for Debussy

* ['The *Pelléas* rehearsals, which began on 13 Jan. 1902, took place nearly every afternoon, except on Sundays, until the première' (Grayson, *The Genesis of Debussy's 'Pelléas et Mélisande'*, p. 71).]

to be able to send a victorious note to René Peter on Monday, 27 January 1902: 'Maeterlink is in the bag, and Carré shares my opinion that his case is pathological. But there are still mental hospitals in France.'[5]

As René Dumesnil reported, there was nevertheless a campaign of disparagement that dates from this time: 'False news items in small newspapers, insinuating rumours spread around by word of mouth; it seemed as though there was a conspiracy, as in fact there was.'[6] Secretly annoyed, Maeterlinck did not give in. On 7 February he submitted his complaint to the Société des Auteurs. The cases were presented on 14 February. On the 21st, not very sure of himself, he refused arbitration and threatened to take his case to court, but the lawyers he consulted dissuaded him. Once again, he was in the bag.[7]

On 4 March Henri Busser rehearsed the off-stage chorus, 'Ohé, Hisse hoé'. On the 21st the first reading by the orchestra took place. 'So many mistakes! Messager was furious, and let his irritation show.'[*] Then the atmosphere of the Opéra-Comique became electric. The musicians, already put off by the strange and incomprehensible music, could only take out their exasperation on their instrumental parts, which were strewn with mistakes. Responsible because of his choice of an inexperienced copyist—his neighbour in the rue Cardinet—Debussy had to face the storm without protest. That same day he notified Godet, who, with a fine show of devotion, immediately assumed the task of correcting the errors. It took him three sessions to make everything right. As Busser remembered it: 'Messager was willing to give me the task of reading through all the string parts, while Debussy took charge of the wind parts. There were innumerable mistakes and, in spite of our joint efforts, more kept cropping up at each rehearsal, and this infuriated Messager.'

On 26 March the orchestra rehearsed the score from beginning to end.

[5] Peter, 'Ce que fut la "Générale" de *Pelléas et Mélisande*', p. 6.

[6] R. Dumesnil, *Le Monde*, 9 Apr. 1952.

[7] To tell the truth, Debussy found himself confronted with a painful problem. He had wanted to antagonize neither Maeterlinck, who had given him complete liberty with *Pelléas*, nor Albert Carré, who had accepted the work of the Opéra-Comique. For it was a personal question—and an emotional one: Georgette Leblanc set the poet and the director up against one another. For the composer the question was simply that the singer was absolutely inconceivable in the role she demanded; moreover, after six years of waiting, Debussy could not risk seeing the longed-for performance deferred or turned down by the all-powerful Carré, and therefore felt obliged to take his side, and so put himself against Maeterlinck—it was the only decision in the best interests of *Pelléas et Mélisande*.

[*] [H. Busser, *De Pelléas aux Indes galantes* (Paris, 1955), 110. For Busser's further recollections of the *Pelléas* rehearsals, see his 'Souvenirs de jeunesse sur Claude Debussy' in A. Martin (ed.), *Catalogue de l'Exposition Debussy, 1942* (Paris, 1942), pp. vi–viii. Grayson characterizes Busser's recollections as sometimes unreliable.]

The majority of the musicians remained hostile, worn out by the lengthy repetition of details, by the interpretative demands of the composer. Controlling himself during the rehearsals, Debussy was beside himself by the end of the sessions. One day, in a fit of nerves, he withdrew his score, telling only René Peter and asking for secrecy. Later, however, everything seemed to fall into place. Apparently the orchestra gradually became more docile, more respectful, and ended up being convinced by the work. Busser reported: 'One of Debussy's most frequent comments was: "Piano, piano, less loud, I beg you."'

Then on 1 April Messager asked for an addition of seventy-five bars to the second act. He threatened to give it all up, if the interludes were not developed rapidly. Debussy confronted this new outbreak with outward serenity.[8] The following day, the first dress rehearsal was held with all the artists present. From then on, the atmosphere grew calm once more during the sessions. On 12 April Massenet came to hear the last two scenes, without saying one word, except at the end of the rehearsal, because of 'the great emotion he experienced confronted with this work that was so new, so unexpected'.[9]

For Debussy there were going to be other clouds. On 13 April 1902 the première of *Pelléas* was announced for the 23rd. On the 14th, Maeterlinck's foolish letter to *Le Figaro* burst like a bomb. It is not beside the point to reproduce it here at length:

The management of the Opéra-Comique announces the coming performance of *Pelléas et Mélisande*. This performance will take place in spite of me, for MM. Carré and Debussy have failed to recognize my most legitimate rights. I would have settled the quarrel in the courts, which, once again, would probably have declared that the poem belongs to the poet, if a particular circumstance had not altered the 'nature' of the case, as they say at the Palais de Justice.

In effect, M. Debussy, after having been in agreement with me about the choice of the interpreter whom I thought to be the only one capable of creating the role of Mélisande, according to my intent and wishes, and in the face of the unjustified resistance with which M. Carré opposed this choice, decided to deny me the right to intervene in the selection of the artists, by taking advantage of a letter I had written him too confidently nearly six years ago. To this crude gesture

[8] Henri Busser wrote that, to Carré's request about the interludes, Debussy responded: 'It is impossible for me . . . I cannot "produce" on demand. I will add them during my holiday' (Busser, *De Pelléas aux Indes galantes*, pp. 112–15, 119, 123–4).

[Grayson, *The Genesis of Debussy's 'Pelléas et Mélisande'* (pp. 77–8), examines the conflicting evidence and demonstrates that the expanded interludes 'were part of the first performance'. He also describes the cramped conditions backstage that made the scene-shifting 'time-consuming' (p. 76).]

[9] Busser, *De Pelléas aux Indes galantes*, p. 112.

strange actions were added, such as is demonstrated by the receipt of registration, manifestly pre-dated to try to establish that our protests had been lodged too late. Thus they were successful in excluding me from my work, and since then it has been dealt with as though it were conquered territory. They have imposed arbitrary and absurd cuts which make it incomprehensible. They retained what I had the intention of deleting or improving, as I have done for the booklet which is going to appear, where one can see how much the text used by the Opéra-Comique varies from the authentic one. In a word, the *Pelléas* at issue is a piece that has become a stranger to me, almost an enemy. And, deprived of all control over my work, I am reduced to hoping that its failure will be prompt and resounding.

It is known that the 'particular circumstance' that had 'altered the "nature" of the case' was not Maeterlinck's marriage to Georgette Leblanc, which had never taken place although it was said to have occurred, but their liaison, which was well known.* The dramatist's account of the facts is accurate, with the exception, as we have seen, of the 'arbitrary and absurd cuts', accepted and even suggested by the poet at the end of 1893, and which are far from making the work incomprehensible. Finally, Maeterlinck's purpose appears very clearly to have been to harm Albert Carré in particular, for the original text, 'adopted by the Opéra-Comique', that is to say the version of 1892, happily shortened by Debussy and Maeterlinck, remains at least as authentic as the play as revised by the poet.[10]

Very upset by this inflammatory letter and by the harm it threatened to wreak upon his opera, Debussy asked Godet to prepare a reply, a move which the latter discouraged absolutely. On 17 April Messager and Debussy were 'in a foul humour'.[11] The following day the postponement of *Pelléas* to the 29th was announced. On the 22nd, it was set back to the 30th. Finally, on the 25th, there was the first dress rehearsal for the personnel of the Comique. Carré was convinced that the opera would be a success. Debussy was probably aware that people were talking about him, that a nucleus of fervent admirers existed, and that his music had penetrated into intellectual circles of all persuasions, that *Pelléas* itself,

---

[10] In later editions of his play, those of 1902 on, Maeterlinck notably rectified several mistakes in French committed in the first one. In particular, he no longer wrote 'Pélléas' but 'Pelléas,' a mistake that had been put down to Debussy's uncertain grasp of orthography.

[11] Busser, *De Pelléas aux Indes galantes*, p. 112.

* [Georgette Leblanc's irregular status put her in a position to exert pressure and caused Maeterlinck to give in to her.]

before its first performance, had been admitted to the salon of Mme de Saint-Marceaux.[12]

And then came Monday, 28 April 1902. The Press gave the results of the general elections held the day before. It also announced modestly, amid the usual fever of political discussions—irony of fate—the dress rehearsal of *Pelléas*, set for 1 p.m. Someone was there to help bring about 'the prompt and resounding failure' he had wished for. Maeterlinck, truly beside himself, was caught up in a plan of disparagement which only he could have conceived, perhaps in collaboration with Georgette Leblanc. This poisonous plan, tragic in its madness, was to arouse hilarity in the house, which could well have provoked a catastrophe; it is astonishing that no one thought to suppress it immediately.

So the great day had arrived, after six years of waiting, coming after so many disillusionments, so much frustration, and so much patience. Seven years earlier, on 17 August 1895, Debussy had written to Lerolle: 'Now my worries begin. How is the world going to behave towards these two poor little creatures?'[13] Without illusions even then, he hurried on to unburden himself. 'I hate crowds, the vote for everybody, and the patriotic phrases.' On 28 April 1902 Debussy wore his bitter forced grin.[14] He had invited Godet, Louÿs, Bonheur and his sister, Valéry, Léon Blum, Paul Robert, Toulet, Jacques de Montesquieu, Curnonsky, Castéra, Henri de Régnier, André Lebey, d'Indy, René Peter, Bréville—the theatre was completely full. Debussy was going to hear, as he put it, 'the beautiful falsehood' [*le beau mensonge*] in which he had lived for such a long time with the characters of the drama. He was going to watch them live before his eyes through the interpretation of the singers, 'and the tender voice of Mélisande, secretly overheard . . .'. He would find it above all in the fifth act, with an astonishment which he could not express for emotion. Then Messager imposed silence upon the orchestra in the auditorium.*

---

[12] At one of the Wednesdays of Mme de Saint-Marceaux, Colette saw

entering one evening the score of *Pelléas et Mélisande*. It arrived in the arms of Messager, clutched to his heart as though he had stolen it. He began to read it at the piano, to sing it, with passion in a voice like rusty zinc. He stopped, started again: 'And that! . . . And that! . . .' And when he sang the role of Mélisande, he almost shut his eyes. (Colette, *Journal à rebours* (Paris, 1941), 109–10.)

[13] Denis, *Henri Lerolle et ses amis*, p. 32.

[14] It is advisable to specify that the dress rehearsal of *Pelléas* took place on Monday, 28 Apr. 1902 and not on the 27th, as most of the biographies have stated.

---

* [Thirteen paragraphs are omitted here; they contain Dietschy's conjectures of Debussy's reactions to the performances.]

The dress rehearsal of *Pelléas* produced no scandal, no intervention by the police, no interruption of the orchestra. There was some laughter, certainly, which prompted some protests, and the protests increased the laughter. There were some sarcastic remarks, some catcalls. Surrounded like a doe at bay and trembling, Mary Garden confronted mocking faces. Her Scottish accent was humorous only to those who had decided to enjoy themselves and who had been encouraged by the plan. 'Ah, je ne suis pas heujeûse!' and 'Je n'ai pas de khürage!' Yniold was harshly treated as well; his references to Golaud as 'petit père' were found hilarious. Debussy had shut himself up in Carré's office. Carré was much astonished by the public's behaviour; everything had seemed propitious. Having celebrated the triumph of *Louise* two years earlier, he had fully expected he would be given the chance to celebrate that of *Pelléas et Mélisande*.[15] The day following the dress rehearsal *Le Figaro* reported: 'Enthusiastic partisans and bitter adversaries disputed with taste and animation. . . . A humorist whom someone asked about the fate of the new work, answered: it is up for a vote.'

After a beautiful day, respite following a dark, rainy week, the evening of 30 April saw the première of *Pelléas et Mélisande*. Present were: André Suarès, Maurice Ravel, Maurice Delage, Léon-Paul Fargue, Pasteur Vallery-Radot, Robert Kemp, René Dumesnil, Claude-Roger Marx, Robert de Montesquiou, and in the box of Mme and Mlle de Romilly were Debussy's parents. Ravel, Delage, Fargue, and the painter Paul Sordes were among others who did not miss one of the first thirty performances of the opera.

The atmosphere of the first performance was not the same as that of the dress rehearsal. Then in the theatre there had been above all a willingness to disparage, the public disporting itself. On the evening of the première, however, it was a struggle to the death: passionate and unrestrained partisans, unrelenting and furious adversaries. The première was stormy. There were 'mocking laughter . . . and violent arguments. . . . The tower scene almost unleashed a tempest . . . in the theatre people insulted each other. . . . Finally, after Mélisande's death, there was a thunder of applause—ours—in the midst of a storm of shouting . . .'[16]

[15] Arthur Pougin, in *Le Ménestrel* of 4 May 1902, wrote, alluding to Debussy and his *Pelléas*: 'I guarantee you that if, in the midst of your pretentious and empty intellectualizing, a simple phrase of *Le Postillon de Lonjumeau* was heard, you would see the public heave a great sigh of relief . . .' Among the other detractors (during the intermissions), Henri Busser observed Georges Hüe, Xavier Leroux, and the Hillemacher brothers.

[16] R. Dumesnil, *Le Monde*, 9 Apr. 1952.
[But Grayson, *Genesis of Debussy's 'Pelléas et Mélisande'*, p. 87, and Orledge, *Debussy and the Theatre*, p. 64, give convincing evidence that the première, unlike the dress rehearsal, was ultimately a success.]

Another reaction appeared in *Le Figaro* on 1 May 1902, expressing the viewpoint of 'Un Monsieur de l'orchestre':

Many musicians were present. They belonged to two schools: the makers of avant-garde music and the old, bearded musical reactionaries. There were some fabricators of operettas and of oratorios. . . . There were also some fabricators, in short.
There were also some important critics who explained why it was beautiful.
All the musical points of view of Paris were represented: all the subtle ears . . . all the habitués of the major concerts and the lesser auditoriums were present. . . . There were some passionate people, some lukewarm ones, some fanatics, some indifferent ones, some who did not give a damn. There were even some deaf people. . . .
Everyone gesticulated . . . or shrugged. Some said that it was a musical event of the highest importance. . . . Others said disrespectfully that it was a joke.[17]

It was necessary no longer to be faithful to earlier music to recognize the vast novelty of *Pelléas*. And it is necessary to make an effort to imagine, more than half a century later, how much Debussy's masterpiece could and must have rightfully aroused so many false judgements which were undoubtedly sincere. Among them, there is one which, through the author's personality and his unusual musical sensitivity, can serve as a yardstick to measure the Debussyste revolution. Then thirty-five years old, curious about all music, an enthusiast for Beethoven ('the true God') and for Wagner ('the complete Artist'), one who became a master of French prose and thought, one who twenty years later offered Debussy a resplendent acknowledgement, André Suarès wrote about *Pelléas* the day after the première.[18] His article was published in *La République*, 2 May 1902, where he used the pseudonym of 'Litte'.[19]

---

[17] Debussy immediately sent a copy of the score to Mary Garden with the following inscription: 'To Mademoiselle M. Garden. In the future others will sing Mélisande. You alone will remain forever the woman and the artist that I had hardly dared hope for. Your grateful Claude Debussy. May 1902.'

[18] Also twenty years later, Dukas acknowledged Suarès's admirable *Debussy*:

I have just reread your fervent poem to Debussy. . . . And if my admiration for you rekindles my love for him, that is the essential thing. Whatever is said, your book will remain a very beautiful and rewarding one. I am happy that you have written it. He lacked a really strong voice in the admiring chorus. Here is one that loudly dominates all the others, and it is the voice of a man, at last. 'He' would have been happy to the bottom of his heart, I assure you, with this change of resonance. (Dukas's letter to Suarès, 19 Feb. 1923, in the collection of Mme André Suarès [in 1962]).

[19] Suarès's intimate friend, Maurice Pottecher, wrote the official music column for the journal. The extracts that follow are taken from the original draft, not published *in extenso* (collection of Mme André Suarès [in 1962]).

Debussy, a sculptor of rare harmonies, a very refined artist, is one who seems to hate nothing so much as passion, strength, the high sentiments of heroic souls, the simple, basic forces of life and action. . . . An orchestra treated in shades of grey: all the tone colours are muted, all the insights are veiled, a host of exquisite details pass unnoticed. . . . The orchestra plays dissonances of which the resolution and the writing are evidence of a surprising ability, but one would not believe what boredom, what fatigue they produce. The ear does not know for sure where it is being led . . . Debussy is the most subtle, the most exceptional of harmonists, but it seems that music in itself means absolutely nothing to him. . . . One can see in this music the most bizarre contrast between Wagner and the classics. One asks oneself, then, is this what might well be a music contrary to what music was to Beethoven and to Wagner. . . . The abuse of chromaticism to the point of nervous tension; the absence of all framework, a work without muscles, without bones, all comprised of cartilage; a slowness, a monotony, a morbid languor, these are some of the characteristics of this musical Medusa, of this sonorous polyp. . . . Nevertheless, this declamation is absurd and perfect at the same time . . . the unity of the whole work . . . its cohesiveness is a virtue in Debussy. He has his own personality, he has a talent which is great. And finally, his mistake is perhaps to have believed that he was a composer; but one cannot deny that Debussy is an artist.

Suarès's extraordinary opinion is still permeated with the musical atmosphere of the classics; he disapproved of *Pelléas* in the name of the established order; he denounced as blemishes or inadequacies what would come to seem the rarest virtues, and, at first, he rejected what troubled him in his heart and his instinct for harmony. A remarkable judgement, when one thinks that twenty years later, when he was fifty-five, at an age when most men have set minds, he revealed a surprising ability for renewal, a pure passion which made the musical idols of his youth grow pale. His is an opinion that inspires indulgence for all the other ones spewed forth about *Pelléas* by critics who were so old or so set in their ways that they had to remain faithful to the prevailing harmonic practices of their twenties. The judgement is further remarkable because at that time Suarès did not own a score of *Pelléas*.

Suarès was so upset that he immediately asked Dukas to intervene with Debussy so that he might obtain a score. In his reply of 5 May 1902, Dukas told him that Debussy had promised to send it to him. Dukas went on to hope that 'besides the impression that you have received at first, and which is correct in part, you will find something better and more solid that also exists in it and that you seem not to have been aware of at all'.[20] But Debussy did not send the score. Later Suarès got a copy of the 1907 edition, and with it began his understanding of Debussy's art, and by about 1914 he had arrived at a deep commitment to it.

[20] Collection of Mme André Suarès [in 1962].

Dukas had another conversion to make: that of Pierre Lalo, who, however, had admired the *Nocturnes*. Assisted by Doret and Poujaud, it took him three weeks and an eloquent act of persuasion to convert this 'important critic', for he was then judged to be one—because of his connections and his culture; it led him to confer in *Le Temps* of 20 May an unrestrained eulogy, a penetrating and remarkable evaluation of *Pelléas*. D'Indy's article was a friendly musical review: one is keenly aware that the author had to constrain himself not to say that his own truth was of a superior order and sacred, but he was deeply honest, and two years later he would repeat that 'M. Debussy is something like a Monteverdi to us'.[21]

There were three particularly abusive articles. In *Le Figaro* on 1 May Eugène d'Harcourt treated Debussy as an unscrupulously ambitious novice. In the *Revue des deux mondes* Camille Bellaigue spotted in *Pelléas* 'germs of decadence and death'. Henry Roujon, director of the Beaux-Arts, declared that the arrival of *Pelléas* at the Opéra-Comique was 'a national disgrace'.[22]

Two articles were unusual because of their prophetic and decisive character: that of Henry Bauër, in the same *Figaro*,[23] and that of Gaston Carraud, in *La Liberté*, who affirmed and developed his first opinion in two other reviews that praised Debussy's classicism with rare wisdom. As early as 3 May *Le Figaro* could say:

Those who desire the return of the stormy and sensational periods of musical art can declare themselves satisfied. M. Debussy's work leads us in fact to heroic days. . . . It has aroused passionate curiosity, some zealous polemics, some bitter criticisms; it has experienced the fate of contested works, and I imagine that therein lies, for a composer of M. Debussy's value, the noblest success that he could have desired.[24]

Debussy had ceased hoping for this noble success. It gave him an unsullied joy, and the admirable photograph—the best perhaps—taken at Eragny on 11 May 1902 by Paul Dukas reveals this 'Debussy *aux fleurs*',

---

[21] *Revue bleue*, 26 Mar. 1904.

[22] Roujon and Debussy are buried not far from one another in the cemetery at Passy. The former was placed beneath an official bust, the prerogative of a director of the Beaux-Arts; the latter lies under the bluish marble of a tomb simply marked: Claude Debussy, Musicien Français, 22 août 1862–25 mars 1918.

[23] On 7 May 1902 Debussy wrote to Henry Bauër: 'Thank you for your fine article on *Pelléas*. You will never know what a powerful consolation it has been to me amid so many hateful stupidities . . .' (1980, p. 114). Georges Ricou reported that Debussy had said to him after the first several performances: 'They will come to it. Perhaps in twenty years, but they will come. It takes time for them to understand.'

[24] Camille Mauclair in the *Revue universelle* wrote: 'M. Debussy is a symphonist of the first rank. For me, he is a man of genius . . .'

this 'Vuillard', as Auguste Martin has justly observed,[25] taken by a verascope, which gives the projection a relief, a modelling, a sense of life, that show him to us filled with happiness, sitting beside the first hawthorns of this unforgettable May of 1902.

The increasingly favourable reception of *Pelléas* can be measured from two later reviews in *Le Figaro*. The first of these was in the issue of 21 May 1902: 'The seventh performance of *Pelléas et Mélisande*, yesterday, affirmed the success of M. Debussy's work. . . . Each evening it wins a new victory with the public, and it is applauded by the most famous composers.' The second appeared on 22 June: 'It has been a long time since a dramatic work has been so passionately discussed as *Pelléas*. . . . Such a production will remain like a date in the history of dramatic music.'

Nevertheless, some stubborn people continued quite openly to attempt to disparage the new opera. The praises granted to Debussy irritated the older composers to the very quick. Lisping with mean-spirited pleasure, Saint-Saëns declared to Pierre Lalo in July that he had not left for his usual holiday: 'I am staying in town to speak ill of *Pelléas*.'[26] Théodore Dubois forbade his students at the Conservatoire to attend performances of it.[27]

Happily there were young people and unprejudiced music lovers who welcomed *Pelléas* so warmly that they attended every performance and fell under the spell of Debussy's art. In his *Études* Jacques Rivière reported:

Perhaps one cannot imagine just what *Pelléas* meant to the young people who took it to their hearts at its first appearance, to those who were between sixteen and twenty. A marvellous world, a cherishable paradise where we could escape from our problems . . . It is quite literally that I say: *Pelléas* was for us a special

---

[25] A. Martin, 'Commentaire sur un visage', *Inédits sur Claude Debussy*, p. 22.

[26] Mentioned by Pierre Lalo in *Le Temps*, 10 Sept. 1941. Over a period of thirty years, from 1884 (when he opposed Debussy for the Grand Prix de Rome) to 1914 (when he opposed Debussy's election to the Académie), in the meantime condemning *Printemps* and waging open warfare against *Pelléas*, Saint-Saëns had harboured a kind of hatred against Debussy. It is ironical then that the youthful Debussy had made transcriptions of Saint-Saëns's compositions for Durand.

[27] The directors of the Beaux-Arts, after the dress rehearsal, had insisted on condemning fifteen bars at the end of the third act, for the purpose of suppressing an improper dialogue of twenty-five words between Golaud and Yniold. ['And the bed? Are they near the bed?'] This move was quite justifiable; the implications inevitably suggested by this passage could only undercut the tragic sense of the scene, particularly at the end of an act like this one. It is astonishing that Maeterlinck had been able to conceive it in a drama in which he had purposefully renounced the explicitly physical.

forest and a special region and a terrace at the shore of a special sea. We escaped there, knowing the secret door, and the world no longer existed for us.[28]

René Peter also emphasized the springtime freshness of the score which found its natural allies among young people.

Each of us young people, shaking friendly hands during the intervals, felt that he was defending something other than the work of one of us. Each of us had the feeling that he fought for his own sake. For when a melodic idea was released in the air, when a chord had filled the house with unusual vibrations, we experienced the feeling that for a little while all of us participated in the spiritual world of the performance.[29]

Messager left for London after the third performance;* his replacement at the Opéra-Comique was Henri Busser. Deeply moved, Busser did not achieve right away the 'marvellous atmosphere' of the opera, as he had been allowed to rehearse only two scenes. Debussy described him to Messager in London in these terms, writing on 9 May 1902: 'Busser arrives looking like someone who is going to take a cold bath and who does not enjoy the prospect ... (The orchestra is admirable, supporting him and whispering nuances to him ...) He does not bother at all with singers and only throws them some perfunctory chords' (1938, p. 16).[30]

This judgement was probably slightly exaggerated. Debussy had approved the replacement of Messager by Busser and did not want any other conductor. After his departure, Debussy addressed Messager as though he were his only friend, his confidant, his comrade in arms, he who had realized *Pelléas*, had conducted the première and defended it.[31] On 12 July 1902 Debussy saw Messager again in London, where he stayed for several days, and from there on 16 July 1902 he wrote a soothing letter to Lilly, back in Paris:

My very dear little wife, Your letter did me immense good—if you knew how alone I feel in spite of everything; no longer hearing your imperious voice calling 'Mî-Mî' leaves me as melancholy as a guitar. I loved your lack of courage very much. You see, it is very nice to be the strong little wife, but there are times when

[28] J. Rivière, *Études* (2nd edn., Paris, 1944), 127.

[29] Peter, 'Ce que fut la "Générale" de *Pelléas et Mélisande*', p. 3.

[30] Busser soon mastered the score, and on 9 May (the same day this letter was written) he received a score of *Pelléas* inscribed with the 'grateful friendship of Claude Debussy'.

[31] On 22 July 1902 Debussy wrote to Messager: 'With you I experience a feeling of absolute confidence and that is quite exceptional for me who am for the most part very reserved [*fermé à double tour*], because I am so afraid of my colleagues' (1938, p. 41).

* [In 1901 he had been appointed director of Covent Garden for the principal season, a position he held until 1905. The 1902 season opened on 8 May. Mary Garden made her Covent Garden début that year, as Manon on 3 July.]

the strong little wife must have her weaknesses. That adds an extra charm to her graciousness. . . . Would you believe that it is impossible to get a cup of good tea? That makes me think of my rue Cardinet and the dear little wife, who, among other gifts, possesses that of making tea! Ah! in England there are no such wives as that; here they are wives for horseguards with their complexions of raw ham and their movements like those of a young animal . . . Indeed, there probably are some necessary trips which serve only to prove that it would have been better not to have left home. Besides, did I need the harsh experience of absence in order to understand that I could not get along without you? It is logical; and the moral surgery has proved profitless . . . (1980, pp. 119–20).[32]

He returned to Paris to find her in the grips of a crisis of kidney stones. If he had 'too many reasons for being worried', it was also because of the financial difficulties confronting the household. As he wrote to Messager on 22 July 1902: 'Truly, the ironic and cruel God who directs our fates makes us pay dearly for the most innocent pleasures' (1938, p. 41).

After 28 July he could enjoy some peace in the country, at Bichain in the Yonne, where his father-in-law had retired on his pension in 1901. There there was complete rest, no sounds of music; there were walks in the Burgundian countryside of his ancestors, where he loitered watching flocks of sheep and the village boys making an old carousel turn to the sound of a barrel-organ. Already, however, he was thinking about a new work to follow *Pelléas*. He had got to know Paul-Jean Toulet in 1899, but they did not become at once 'as thick as thieves'. With *As You Like It*, Toulet awakened in Debussy's soul a former love: Rosalind, she who had been his favourite heroine when he came back from Rome. Once more Debussy found the subject to his taste, but, because Toulet left for Tonkin at the end of October 1902, staying at Dien-Bien-Phu, the project was not revived until 1917, when it was too late. Rosalind could have been another dream.

He describes his uncertainty about how to proceed after *Pelléas* in a letter to Messager, dated 8 September 1902: 'I have not written one note. . . . In order to do what I want I must go off in a completely new direction. To begin a new work appears to me like a perilous leap, and one risks breaking one's back' (1938, p. 54).

He was also considering *Le Roi Lear*, which André Antoine was putting on, and, through the intervention of René Peter, Debussy asked to supply the incidental music. Of seven pieces that he named, he made orchestral sketches of only the first two: 'Fanfare (d'ouverture)' and 'Le Sommeil de

---

[32] The tone of this letter, with its affection and slightly forced humour, shows that there was nothing very deep joining these two.

Lear'. These were published in 1926 and rated as 'two little pieces of slight significance' by Vallas.[33]

Debussy and his wife returned to Paris on 15 September 1902, their arms filled with flowers from the country. The autumn was mild and slightly overcast. *Pelléas* had triumphed. Certainly, there was still the matter of revising the work, of inserting the modifications of details, and God knew how many of them there would be over the years! But *Pelléas* was born, it lived, it flourished.

Afterwards another idea would have to ripen, another dream would have to develop.[34]

[33] Vallas, *Claude Debussy et son temps*, p. 360. There also survive four bars of the 'Prélude', which was inscribed to Jean-Aubry in July 1908; these are reproduced in *Plaisir de France*, Christmas 1941.

[34] In Dec. 1902 Gabriel Fauré wrote to Albert Carré: 'I remain opposed to Debussy's procedures, but I do not applaud his work any the less for it, for it has given me at more than one place a true shiver, some palpable emotions that I have enjoyed full-heartedly and unrestrainedly.'

15

Le Diable and *La Mer*

LILLY DEBUSSY did not have the least comprehension of Debussy's search to express himself. At first Debussy was amused by the songs she hummed, by verses 'of an aesthetic that was scarcely self-assertive'. He was also amused to hear her call him 'Mî-Mî', and he liked her generous, faithful heart, her need for his presence, the firmness of this brave little woman. She had not given him a child, however much they might have wanted one. One cannot help wondering how much a child might have changed both their lives.

She was pretty and stylish, compared with the wives of Debussy's friends, although by 1903 she was already beginning to develop jowls. Her eyes had come to take on the slow, moist motion of those of a doe. Poor Lilly, at thirty she was losing her undeniable physical charms that had been her chief ornament.

She neither inspired nor exalted Debussy. Since he had got to know her, he had composed little, except the unimportant *Lindaraja* for two pianos, four-hands, which stems from April 1901, which he never dedicated to anybody, and which he never turned over for publication. Besides, there was that 'Nuit blanche', incomplete, unpublished, started at Bichain in July 1900. As for the interludes for *Pelléas*, those stemmed from 'ancient dreams' in which Lilly had no place. It is significant that he did not dedicate to her the music he was composing during these years. For instance, there were the three *Nocturnes*, published in 1900. He did not even consider her;* Hartmann received those dedications. Then there was the suite *Pour le piano*, which he completed in 1901, and of which he had composed an early version of the first piece in 1894, under the influence of Yvonne Lerolle, now settled, married, she to whom he had dedicated the 'Sarabande'. He offered the 'Prélude' to Mlle de Romilly and the

---

* [Here Dietschy is in error. The particell of the *Nocturnes* bears the following inscription: 'This manuscript belongs to my little Lilly-Lilo, all rights reserved. It is also a token of my deep and passionate joy in being her husband. Claude Debussy. January 1901.']

'Toccata' to Nicolas Coronio, two of his pupils. In July 1903, however, he completed, the *Estampes*, basing it upon earlier work, drawing notably for 'Jardins sous la pluie' upon the third of the *Images (oubliées)*, which had been offered to Yvonne Lerolle in 1894. He might have dedicated at least one of the three pieces of this collection to his wife, but he did not even do that. He presented the collection as a token of gratitude to the man who had just finished painting his official portrait, Jacques-Émile Blanche.[1]

At the end of 1902 he had been obliged to agree to contribute to *Gil Blas*, but he it was with little pleasure that he sent an article to *La Renaissance latine*.[2] He had sworn by all the gods that he would never accept the ribbon of the Legion of Honour; yet when Laloy, at the beginning of 1903, told him of his nomination, he was dumbfounded. He was thinking not of himself, but of his parents, who were so susceptible to patriotic sentiments [*phrases tricolores*]. Ex-Captain de Bussy wept with emotion when he heard the news. And the new *chevalier* thanked Laloy on 4 January 1903 for his support and for the joy 'he had been able to give his aged parents' (*RdM*, 1962, p. 6).

On 17 June 1903 Debussy wrote to Louÿs that he felt 'sickened by age', a phrase which suggested to André Gauthier that his illness had already begun to take effect.[3] However, this had not happened yet, although it would start six years later without his being aware of it. Something must have been wrong. On 8 September 1902 Debussy had written to Messager: 'for a long time I had been like a squeezed lemon, and my poor brain did not want to learn anything any more' (1938, p. 54). The creation of *Pelléas*, the events that had preceded it, the uproar that had followed it, had caused him such a deep resentment that he hid it, disguised it with irony.

In June 1903 he busied himself with an American commission, paid for in advance—the *Rapsodie* for saxophone—which he took very seriously. Then, doubtless under the strong impression he had received from *La Guirlande*, a ballet by Rameau, which he heard at the Schola Cantorum on 22 June, he decided to pay the composer the compliment of a piano piece, entitled, 'Hommage à Rameau'. Debussy very quickly became aware that, having become famous, he was somewhat a prisoner of opinion, and

---

[1] Blanche, who was notorious for his inventions, has passed on an anecdote, which is perhaps not entirely false, that 'Jardins sous la pluie' was inspired in 1903 by an afternoon storm in the painter's garden at Auteuil. In fact, if the musical sketch itself derives from someone or something else from an earlier time, the title of the composition could well stem from the shower in Blanche's garden. For another account of its origin, see Ch. 11, n. 13 above.

[2] Letter of Debussy to M. Périvier, *Le Figaro*, 22 Dec. 1902 (Archives de la Seine, Paris).

[3] A. Gauthier, *Debussy: Documents iconographiques* (Geneva, 1952), plate 104–5.

that he had to find a direction that would be 'post-*Pelléas*', a way of escaping from the pigeonhole in which his critics had filed him. His next step must be to prove that *Pelléas* was a unique work and not his unvarying manner as a composer.

On holiday at Bichain, where he had been from the beginning of July 1903, he completed the *Estampes* and then returned to one of his projects from 1889, to the libretto of *Le Diable dans le beffroi*; he completed one musical episode and almost all the text. At the same time he was haunted by the sea, by its immensity, by its ceaseless advancing and retreating. On the one hand, there was the devil—not the evil spirit, he wrote to Messager, but that of contradiction, this devil to whom Poe had assigned the function of 'changing the good old order of things'. On the other hand, there was the sea. The sea had always had an extraordinary effect upon him; it was as if he had an intimate relationship with it. In the peaceful region of the Yonne, he remembered the sea's harsh, unknowable moments. They grew in his memory like bubbles in boiling water. He did not try to stop them, he allowed them to keep bubbling, in the more and more giddy undertaking, in the still unrealized desire for the surge that would overturn his life. Then, he could say, 'I am—as so often happens to me—at a dangerous turning-point in my life.[4]

At Bichain in July 1903, he had no idea that exactly twelve months later the turning-point would be reached. A ground swell would wash away all the past. He was preparing himself for it involuntarily; he hoped for it without knowing it.

Debussy's letter to Messager of 12 September 1903 contained an important announcement. At Bichain, where 'the Ocean does not precisely wash the hills of Burgundy', Debussy sketched the three symphonic movements entitled *La Mer*. He believed that his 'countless recollections' were worth more than 'a reality whose charm generally weighs too heavily' (1938, p. 74). His countless recollections were of Cannes, Arcachon, Fiumicino, Dieppe, Cancale. Poor Lilly is nowhere in this work that he was drafting. Nor was anyone else. Debussy was not in love. He half-confessed it to Toulet on 28 August: 'My life is uneventful' (1929, p. 22). He was then more firmly determined than ever to renew himself, in spite of the fact that certain people claimed, as he said in his letter to Messager of 12 September 1903, that he 'could not escape from the style of *Pelléas*'. He defied his critics, saying that, if he could not move beyond *Pelléas*, 'I would immediately set myself to growing pineapples in my room, considering that really the most irksome thing is having "to start over again"' (1938, p. 74).

[4] As he would write to Caplet on 23 Mar. 1910, in a similar situation (1957*a*, p. 47).

He knew his critics so well, and so clear was his thinking, that he continued this letter: 'Besides, it is probable that these same people will find it scandalous that I have deserted the shade of Mélisande for the ironical pirouette of the *Diable* . . .' (1938, p. 75). This is in fact what would happen: not with *Le Diable dans le beffroi*, which would never see the light of day, but with *La Mer*.

Undoubtedly, this was the origin of *La Mer*. It is both a reaction against *Pelléas* and the premonition of the personal events that would follow it, but Debussy's falling out of love had evoked no siren. Hearing the eternal rumble of the sea as it broke upon the shore, he saw from a distance the purplish waves charging like buffaloes. 'The sea is not happy', as Pelléas observes in the grotto of lies; nor was it so in 1903 in Debussy's imagination. He does not summon its soul, as in 'Sirénes', but he sees the huge, fundamental vastness of sea and sky and wind. He feels their power, the intimate relationship of water, air, and space, in a chaos that is at once mysterious, poetic, and visionary: menacing waves, the inky sky, the wind that surges madly.[5]

It is odd that Debussy, during this summer of 1903, enjoyed Bichain and its neighbourhood so deeply. He would not enjoy it in the future, but he scarcely suspected that. He considered buying some land there, nor did he weary of taking walks. 'Here we are far from the empty noise of the big cities, and Bastille Day takes place here, as if muted.'[6]

The house that he rented, situated along the main road 'above the little village', was a former inn, overlooking the narrow valley of the Poule and a spinney of acacias and poplars which no longer exists. He spoke to his friends of the trees of Bichain as though they were his only companions. It was as if Lilly scarcely existed any more. In his last letter to Messager from this holiday, he calls her politely 'my little wife'. The term was affectionate enough, but he did not expect a miracle from her.[7]

[5] Debussy informed Durand on 12 Sept. 1903, the same day he described *La Mer* to Messager, that the wind had whistled wildly at Bichain for the past two days. 'Do you find this weather nasty enough! Hasn't the wind, which causes the sea to dance, damaged the trees of Bel-Ébat?' (1927, p. 14).

[6] Debussy's letter of July 1903 to Fromont, in a private collection.

[7] His daily conversation with Lilly was dreary. The photographs of the two together have a glum aspect. Debussy appears not only indifferent towards, but also deeply bored with, his wife. In contrast, so great was his affection for Messager that he could write to him on 22 July 1902: 'There are things that I have spoken of only to you, and that is what makes your friendship precious to me to a point that I am incapable of expressing . . . The feeling that I mention is perhaps something above love' (1938, pp. 41–2).

16

L'Isle joyeuse

---◆---

RETURNING to Paris on 1 October 1903, Debussy was at once busy with new rehearsals of *Pelléas*. It was at this same time that his pupil Raoul Bardac invited him with Lilly to dinner at his mother's. Then he met for the first time the woman who would become the second Mme Claude Debussy, this Emma Bardac whom Fauré had admired, loved, and immortalized before him, and who would gradually appear to him as the Woman, not as his dream woman, for there was nothing of Mélisande about her, but the woman of his earthly happiness. She seemed to unite all the aspects needed to satisfy the desires that had been forming themselves within him for a long time.*

She was from Bordeaux, her maiden name was Moyse. At seventeen, she had married the banker Sigismond Bardac, to whom she had given first a son Raoul and then a daughter Hélène, always known as Dolly. Unbeknownst to him, Debussy had already charmed her for a year or two before their first meeting by means of his songs, which she sang to the accompaniment of Charles Koechlin, who has described the eager understanding she displayed towards this music and her feverish curiosity when she asked him to tell her about the composer and the man.

Small, stylish, youthful in appearance, open to all emotions, simple, forthright, but also able to cajole, she exuded an insinuating charm to which all sorts of men were responsive. She could not have been more feminine. She had turned many heads, but she was fascinated only by uncommon men. Her approach was reserved, because she knew herself to be impulsive. With one glance she established both her sympathies and her antipathies.

Cultivated, intelligent, a fine musician, she had an attractive profile, whose charm resulted perhaps from the contradiction between the

---

* [Dietschy's account of Debussy's second marriage should be treated with some caution. Some of the composer's letters to his closest friends reveal that there were occasional problems. As long as Emma's daughter Dolly de Tinan, née Bardac, lived (until 1985), she tried to prevent any overt or implied criticism of her mother to appear in print.]

[*L'Isle joyeuse* is the title of a piano solo, first drafted about June 1903 in Paris and extensively revised at Saint-Hélier on the isle of Jersey in July and Aug. 1904.]

expression of her eyes and of her mouth. She had her feet on the ground, but she knew how to lose herself in a dream. Above all, she was unsurpassed at revealing the shortcoming of her peers; sometimes she got off barbed phrases that evoked laughter. One was never bored in her company.

She was forty-one when her portrait was painted by Bonnat in 1903, and she seemed to be only thirty-five, the age that Lilly looked, although she was only twenty-nine, in her photograph of 1902. Bonnat, however, has not tried at all to make Emma appear youthful, for she is even more beautiful in a photograph of 1904, which shows her under the brim of a charming shepherdess's hat. Her questioning lips disagree with the mystery attached to her happy glance, fixed upon the sea.

It is evident that, beside her, poor Lilly grated terribly. Her taciturnity, her constrained passivity aroused pity, but it is obvious that the poor dear lacked vitality and accomplishment. Debussy had a way of referring to her as 'my poor wife'. Gradually he was detaching himself from her. By 1904 she meant nothing to him any more.

Other dinners followed the first. Although aroused from the start, Debussy did not permit himself to yield to the seductions of Emma Bardac straight away. He did not want to make another mistake. It was only gradually that he got carried away, became hooked.

On 9 January 1904 Ricardo Viñes played the *Estampes* for the first time in public and had to give an encore of 'Jardin sous la pluie'. On the 22nd, in *Le Journal*, Jean Lorrain set a match to the gunpowder by attacking the 'Pelléastres' and, through them, Debussy himself. Lorrain thus launched the first offensive in a war that had simmered since 1902 and would cease only with the outbreak of that of 1914. One could believe that Debussy was reaping there what he had sown: in his letters and in his reviews that appeared in the *Revue blanche* and *Gil Blas* between April 1901 and July 1903, he had not minced words in order to say what he thought about his lesser colleagues.[1] He inflicted clawmarks on musicians of more ample reputations: Meyerbeer, Mendelssohn, Schubert, Grieg, and Saint-Saëns. He had claimed the liberty of asserting that neither Beethoven nor Wagner were sacrosanct gods, and he had eviscerated Gluck. But far from being a blow returned, the attack by Jean Lorrain, who was in his sixties and at the end of his life, summed up all the senile annoyance of those whom age or inadequate comprehension made impervious to the delights of novelty.

---

[1] He wrote to Laloy on 17 Apr. 1904: 'Rest assured that the Sonata of Sérieyx is too much for your ailing condition' (*RdM*, 1962, p. 10).

A year earlier, at the end of January 1903, Debussy, with the eager encouragement of Laloy, had accepted to go to hear his Quartet in a fashionable environment where music was honoured—the salon of the Princesse Cystria.[2] He went back there in December, and he returned at the beginning of January 1904, and once again at the end of the same month. The princess was generous and that caused 'a regular gold mine to flow into my banks', as he wrote to Laloy. He went once to the salon of Comtesse Greffhule. In February 1904 he accompanied Mary Garden, who recorded three of the *Ariettes oubliées* for The Gramophone Company, and he had dedicated all six songs to her.* Was it then that Debussy declared his love for Mary Garden, as she reported in her memoirs, which are not completely reliable?[3] Apparently, Mélisande's voice had not ceased to work a species of 'tyranny' upon him and the dedication suggests that Debussy was weary of his wife, and that he was at the end of his tether, and in a hurry to find a woman with whom he felt better 'matched'.

He sketched his *Danses* for harp and string orchestra, which he would dedicate to Gustave Lyon, and finished them in the brisk April of 1904 which foreboded a stormy summer, as it would prove to be.[4] At least, he had finished a piano piece, published in February 1904, entitled *D'un cahier d'esquisses*, the final product of these earlier seeds.[5]

Poor Lilly! She was down with bronchitis and had to follow a cure. She knew the attractive hostess, but she barely noticed the ability of a great artist—whom she believed to be permanently attached by a monosyllabic

[2] Without acknowledging his source, Vallas wrote that from early on Debussy had ceased to like his Quartet. This is scarcely believable, for one sees that the composer participated actively in the performance of his work, both in private and in public, between 1894 and 1904, notably with Crickboom, Hayot, and Luquin. Debussy wrote to Laloy, 17 Apr. 1904: 'I would very much like to hear my Quartet in your salon . . .' (*RdM*, 1962, p. 10).

[3] M. Garden and L. Biancolli, *Mary Garden's Story* (New York, 1951), 78.

[4] Debussy's *Deux Danses* contrast the sacred and the profane, both in the title and in the music, a continual dualism. Because of that, and from the rocking of the rhythm, from the sudden impetuosities, by the ebb and flow of the harp, by the abrupt conclusion, Debussy unconsciously expressed his unease in them. In their sensuality these *Danses* seem like an anticipation.

[5] In the *Revue bleue* of 2 Apr. 1904 (repr., *RdM*, 1962 pp. 45–6), Paul Landormy, who had interviewed Debussy, ascribed to him some strange opinions on several composers, expressed in biting terms. Annoyed, Debussy wrote to Laloy the following day: 'It is extraordinary how incorrectly this so-called musician [Landormy] hears!' (*RdM*, 1962, p. 9).

* [The dedication of 1903, which still appears in the current edition, reads: 'For Miss Mary Garden, unforgettable Mélisande, this music (already somewhat old-fashioned) in affectionate and grateful homage.']

contract—to make comparisons. So she made the rash mistake of urging her husband to go more often to Mme Bardac's, whose association could only serve to increase the notoriety of the composer of *Pelléas*. But he did not want to go. He struggled while he waited. And when Mary Garden asked him the reason behind his resistance, he answered: 'I do not know.' He knew only too well.

He ended up by going there, and Emma sang for him, for she possessed, in addition, the gift of a pleasing voice, which was a change from the imperious cries of 'Mî-Mî' in the rue Cardinet. He dedicated to Emma the *Trois Chansons de France*: the two 'Rondels'* of Charles d'Orléans and 'La Grotte' of Tristan Lhermite, which he had just composed, and which were published in May. He must already have discarded his role of husband to have dared to dedicate this work to a woman other than his own wife; moreover, he left the domestic hearth, but he returned to it, as though seized by remorse. He hesitated in this way several times, going one day as far as Arcachon and drawing curses round his head when he returned. Lilly hoped to win him back to her with arguments of rights of property, but the more she stormed the more he grew apart from her. The smaller the cause, the angrier the defeat of love, and the more public.

He had secretly decided to leave, at least by 12 June 1904. That day he wrote to his old friend, Pierre Louÿs, two simple sentences, filled with unhappy meaning. He was worn out with climbing up to the fifth floor, and he had discovered his first grey hairs. He saw the years flying by, his youth was all but over. His fine hopes had become disillusioned; two years after the creation of *Pelléas*, Debussy was as poor as before and as alone, if not more so. A topic for malicious discussion, he was not leading the easy life that he had obviously sought for himself and that he also desired for his parents. He did not have a suitable wife.

A heatwave seized Paris during the latter half of June. In a letter dated 6 June 1904, he acknowledged receiving some flowers from Emma Bardac:

How kind of you and how good they smell! But above all, I am made profoundly happy by your thought. That entered my heart and remains there, and it is for such things as these that you are unforgettable and charming ... Forgive me if I have kissed all these flowers as though they formed a human mouth. Perhaps it is crazy ... (1957*b*, p. 27).

She gave him what no one had given him before: she pleased him, she spoiled him, she respected him. He felt himself seized by a great eagerness to live. His inspiration returning, he composed the second series of *Fêtes*

---

* ['Le temps a laissié son manteau' and 'Pour ce que Plaisance est morte'.]

galantes, which he dedicated: 'to thank the month of June 1904: A.l.p.M.' (*A la petite Mienne*: 'for my own little dear'). In an entirely natural way an understanding was formed between them. They had decided to unite their lives and, by escaping, to hasten the dissolution of their two impossible marriages. In this intoxicating time, *Le Ménestrel* misleadingly announced a *Dionysos* by Joachim Gasquet and Claude Debussy, but another potion excited the composer. On 23 June he accompanied at the piano a performance of the *Ariettes oubliées* and of the *Fêtes galantes*, at the last musical Thursday of Mme Édouard Colonne. Then, a final thought for Pierre Louÿs: he sent him, as though it were a medal commemorating their friendship, a copy of *Estampes*.[6]

Then, on Friday, 1 July 1904, Debussy sent a telegram inviting Laloy, almost threateningly, to come to lunch the following day. 'Don't think, and come.' Arriving a bit intrigued, Laloy found a Debussy and a Lilly as usual: 'I was their only guest, and both laughing made me admire their faïence plates that they had caused to crackle in the frying pan in order to imitate the real stoneware.'[7] That day Debussy wore a mask. He knew that this time he was leaving home permanently; doubtless, he had even set the day of his departure. It was a necessary pretence, perhaps, lest he lacked the courage to go away; and lest, without 'this horrible tearing apart', life would become unendurable for both of them. The extraordinary thing is that it was exactly at this time that he completed *Masques*, which was to have been the first of a series of *Images* for piano. Jeering masks, fantastic ones, frightening in their blank impassivity, disguising and crushing an altered conscience. Debussy told Laloy that he was about to leave for the country with Lilly, as usual. Perhaps they went there, we do not know, and, if it were true, it was probably the following week.

On 14 July 1904, on what was said to be a stormy evening, Debussy left his wife and went to Emma Bardac, whom 'the extended absences' of her husband had left alone. With her he embarked for Jersey, for the 'îsle joyeuse' far from their world, to a shelter protected by the sea. After their furtive departure, they arrived at the Grand Hôtel at Saint-Hélier for an unforgettable stay.

Voluble, passionate joy runs through *L'Isle joyeuse*, like a flock of birds

[6] June 1904 is the date of the longest flight of the two lovers. They went to Pourville, where the two famous photographs of Debussy, relaxed and open, were taken. In that in which he looks hypnotically at his cigarette, one sees something like a clowning whimsy; in the other (that with his arm raised to his brow) can be read a candour so anachronistic in a man of forty-two, such an acutely liberating pleasure, that Debussy seems to pretend to be a young fellow, unable to disguise his laughter in his false beard. These two unusual pictures confirm Lilly's bitter opinion: 'She had hooked him!' [*Elle l'a eu par la geule!*]

[7] Laloy, *La Musique retrouvée*, p. 140.

dazzled by the dawn and drunk on the freshness of the morning.* The past was buried when Debussy finished this piece with its strong and flexible muscles. *L'Isle joyeuse* is vastly different from Watteau's *The Embarkation for Cytherea*, where one danced the minuet; rather it resembles the ecstatic *Île heureuse* of Besnard, exhibited in the Salon of 1902. *L'Isle joyeuse* is in every regard the isle of Jersey, an isolated place and a place of uninhibited joy—the composition proves it overwhelmingly.[8]

By 7 August the two lovers were at Dieppe, where the following month Debussy received from his publisher the works born of his passion: *Fêtes galantes*, *Masques*, and *L'Isle joyeuse*. As the days passed, he 'dreaded to return to this damned Paris' (1927, p. 21). In spite of his happiness, he was so apprehensive and his conscience so little at ease that on 19 September he answered a letter from Messager, who was unaware of what had occurred, to give him a constrained account of the previous months:

These past months my life has been singularly strange, much more so than one could possibly wish. It is not convenient to explain in detail, which I would find rather embarrassing. It would be better for the two of us to talk over some good whisky.

I have worked ... not as I would have wanted ... Is it too much uneasiness or perhaps I have wanted to climb too high? No matter! I have often fallen ... There are lots of reasons that I will tell you one day ... if I have the courage to do it, for they are particularly sad reasons ... I miss the Claude Debussy who worked so happily upon *Pelléas* for, between ourselves, I cannot find him any more, and that is one cause of my wretchedness, among many others ... (1938, pp. 77–8).

He was unable to work on *Le Roi Lear*. It had been he who, about 1903, had returned to the project in collaboration with Antoine.[9] A year later,

---

[8] One should notice that *L'Isle joyeuse* and *Masques* are Debussy's longest piano pieces. Their almost unbridled dash—one would not dare to say their romanticism—clearly reveals that both were created during the conflagration of 1903–4. They do not possess the understated eloquence of the earlier and later piano works, and that is why they testify to Debussy's uncontrollable feeling for Emma Bardac.

[9] In an unpublished letter that bears no date, Debussy queried: 'Nothing more is heard about *Le Roi Lear*. Precisely, I have just found the copy.... I would very much like to know if I should keep it so as to be able to continue to work it or whether to send it back to you.' As far as this work is concerned, Debussy discussed it with Durand, 24 Aug. 1906: 'Colonne is asking for *Le Roi Lear* back...' (1927, p. 45)—apparently, in its incomplete orchestral form, of which, as we have observed, only two scenes have been published. [These fragments are the 'Fanfare (d'ouverture)' and 'Le Sommeil de Lear' of *Musique pour Le Roi Lear*.]

---

* [It should be noted, however, that an earlier version of *L'Isle joyeuse* existed in June 1903, when Debussy played it to Viñes. Then the composer was considering it as a potential part of the *Suite bergamasque*. See 'Le Journal inédit de Ricardo Viñes', *RIMF*, 1980/2, p. 226.]

he was surprised by an announcement of the play's première on 1 October. But it was *pro forma* that he asked, on 20 September, for a week's delay, and, in order to discourage the project, demanded an orchestra of thirty. His spirit was too preoccupied. Above all, he dreaded coming back to Paris, where he would be exposed to public opinion; yet he had to return, and on 25 September he moved alone into a flat at 10 avenue Alphand, buying some furniture and works of art on credit.

Then his problems began, those which always pursue a happiness founded upon a thing destroyed. The holidays were over. Little by little Paris filled up. It is not known whether Lilly, back in the rue Cardinet, saw her husband again then, or if a third party mediated, but she was so certain that no reconciliation was possible that on 13 October in desperation she shot herself beneath the breast. Taken to a clinic in the rue Blomet, cared for by Dr Abel Desjardins and Sister Marie de Salles, she escaped death and kept the bullet, which had been lodged in a vertebra.[10] If Mary Garden is to be believed, this attempt at suicide was Lilly's final gesture to try to separate Debussy from Emma Bardac. These facts were confirmed by the suit that the unfortunate Lilly brought against her husband. Her law suit revealed her resentment in her violent abuse of the man who had abandoned her. The event, of which only a few had been aware, became public knowledge on 4 November 1904.[11]

Two days later the *Danses* for harp were first heard, at the Concerts Colonne. Gabriel Fauré judged the music as that composed by a man guilty of having involved in a scandal the woman to whom he, Fauré, had dedicated his *La Bonne chanson*. 'One finds in [the *Danses*] . . . a great many of those same harmonic idiosyncrasies that are at times unusual and attractive and at other times merely unpleasant'.[12]

From then on Debussy could be judged only severely by his friends;

---

[10] Pierre Louÿs wrote to his brother:

I went out yesterday to go to see poor Mme Debussy, who wounded herself in the chest with a revolver, on 13 October, after having been deserted by her husband. The bullet penetrated her stomach twice . . . The operation, however, has been very successful and the unhappy women seems to be out of danger . . . (H. P. Clive, *Pierre Louÿs (1870–1925): A Biography* (Oxford, 1978), 181.

[11] On that date *Le Figaro* published this report:

Mme D., a very pretty young woman, married to a very distinguished composer, acknowledged as the leader of the young school, and one whose opera had been much applauded recently in a subsidized theatre, tried to kill herself a few days ago . . . The disconsolate woman wanted to die when she became aware that her husband had been unfaithful to her. The composer has not been reconciled, so it seems, to his young wife, and their impending divorce has been announced. M. D. will be remarried to Mme B., the young divorced wife of a well-known financier.

[12] *Le Figaro*, 7 Nov. 1904.

people in general saw him as a famous and impecunious artist who had left his wife in strained circumstances to run off with the rich and fawned-upon wife of a banker, who was Jewish besides. The Dreyfus Affair was not yet over. It is undeniable that at first glance this situation was bound to cause gossip; but perhaps it ought to be acknowledged that from then on Lilly imposed upon friends for assistance because of her lack of money, and that their judgement upon an unfaithful husband was bound to become more severe the more they felt themselves involved with the abandoned wife. They would rather have acknowledged an unfaithful husband who was being kept but who lived at home. Further, the whole situation deteriorated when the abandoned wife shot herself. After that they bore an irreconcilable grudge against the man guilty of bothering their lives, even more so since he, consistent with his attitude, had evidently not been able to foresee the attempted suicide of the wife whom he had deserted, so it seemed, for the arms of a woman of the world, and all the while remained impervious to the storm he had raised. As he would be hard up until his divorce, he could do little to help his wife financially.

Seen from Debussy's point of view, the situation was entirely different. He was aware of his artistic value, and he felt unrewarded by his daily life, having awaited stoically some recompense that he surely expected by the time he was forty, and seeing himself denied the profits that others, less scrupulous or better favoured, were enjoying to the full. He was a Debussy on his way up, distressed at leaving by the wayside an innocent wife, but one who had remained a shopgirl, who had given him neither children nor inspiration of any kind and with whom all deep understanding was precluded, a wife who had been accepted with a grimace by Debussy's parents. Here was a Debussy who had finally met his 'ideal' woman, pretty, stylish, intellectual, outgoing, cultured, a musician and singer, affectionate, rich, and separated from her husband. This was a situation that no one can attempt to judge; rather it must be recorded as an inevitable occurrence, for it must be remembered that an 'artist of that importance perhaps has rights to certain prerogatives', as Louis Laloy has tactfully put it.[13]

The event could bring joy only to those who resented Debussy's reputation. It made such an uproar that it created at first a vacant space

[13] In Laloy, *La Musique retrouvée*, p. 142. As a moral issue, this situation would be hereafter quite troublesome for Debussy, and one which rubbed his susceptibilities raw. He had not been deceived about it. According to the unpublished notes he had taken of his conversations with Laloy in 1935, Edward Lockspeiser has told us what Debussy said of the first period of his liaison with Mme Bardac, she who, according to the set plan, had the 'incovenience'—if one dare say it—of being rich: 'You know what that makes me look like.'

around the man guilty of having produced it and who suffered more from it than was then suspected. 'I have seen such desertions take place around me! Enough to be discouraged for ever . . .', he wrote to Laloy on 14 April 1905 (*RdM*, 1962, p. 12). Besides, *Le Figaro*, on 3 January 1905, reported that Lilly had tried to end her life another time and that there was little hope of saving her, but this was a false report. Pierre Louÿs told his brother: 'You must have read in the papers that Mme Debussy has tried to commit suicide again. That is untrue, there was neither an accident nor a drama. On the contrary, everything seems settled.'

Some friends, trying to be helpful, proposed a reconciliation between Lilly and her husband. Edouard Rist, in particular, hurried to the avenue Alphand and begged Debussy to return to his domestic hearth. Hunched over the manuscript of *La Mer*, where he hoped to hide himself as at the bottom of the sombre, sadly ebbing sea, Debussy refused. The following month Emma Bardac informed him that she would give birth before the end of the year.[14]

On 14 April he received the first signs of loyalty, from Laloy, whose 'clear-sighted sympathy prevented him from trampling' carelessly on a man's life. Little by little the other friends followed, for life goes on and forgetfulness buries everything. But he would be afraid of Lilly for years. When it was seen that Emma's fortune was not as considerable as has been claimed or that she herself had expected, the spiteful ones were glad of it as though it were a rightful punishment for the wish for money that they scented in Debussy.[15] In time the censure expressed by certain people would be softened by extenuating circumstances. Those who remained faithful were: Laloy, Dukas, Godet, Durand, Satie, Viñes, Koechlin, Curnonsky, Toulet, and Coronio.

It was in total isolation and amid harsh moral anguish that Debussy carried on, as early as 1 January 1905, the composition of *La Mer*. He took it up again at the end of the 'Jeux de vagues'. On 5 March the vast symphonic fresco was completed. *La Mer* was dedicated to Jacques Durand,* who opened wide to Debussy the doors of his publishing firm,

[14] To dispel a fable, it is necessary to specify here that it is known from an impartial friend of Debussy's, Lucien Monod, who became, after the attempted suicide, a defender, a neighbour, and a close friend to Lilly, that the musician did not try to see his first wife again, nor would he ever see her again.

[15] It seems that Emma Bardac hoped for an inheritance from her wealthy uncle, the banker Osiris, but when he died, he bequeathed 25,000,000 fr. to the Pasteur Institute and a surprising 50,000 fr. for the construction in Lausanne of a chapel dedicated to William Tell (*Le Figaro*, 4 Feb. 1907).

* [The draft of *La Mer*, which is dated 'Sunday 5 March at six o'clock in the evening', bears an almost invisible inscription: 'for my own little dear whose eyes laugh in the shadows' [*pour la p.m. dont les yeux rient dans l'ombre*].]

for Durand bought the rights to *Pelléas et Mélisande*, guaranteeing to his friend a yearly income of 12,000 francs, in exchange for the rights to his future works. Debussy was grateful for this sign of confidence and favour. He was not yet aware that this contract would make him a prisoner. On 24 May 1905 he wrote to Durand: 'The other day, I did not know how to tell you all my gratitude. I was very moved to find you both so spontaneously generous to your poor Claude, who was so helpless' (1927, p. 28).

He felt constrained to accept this offer, because his financial troubles, owing to Emma's expectation of living in high style and to Lilly's demands, began again and would get worse. He explained them tersely to Fromont: 'I don't have the first sou ... I am overcome by regret and worries.' He mentioned them in three letters to Laloy. On 17 April 1905: 'I am having meetings with some very tiresome people, but which are determining my poor fate.' Again, on 2 May: 'worn out by worries of every description, to such an extent that soon I will no longer have the strength to laugh at them—which is what one should do.' And on 20 May: 'I am weighed down by meetings, by discussions, and so far nothing is settled' (*RdM*, 1962, pp. 12–14).

If, on 4 May 1905, Emma Bardac had obtained a favourable divorce, Debussy had to wait until 2 August to be legally free, but the judgement was decided against him.[16] On the following day it was announced in the newspapers. The hearing took place on 21 July; on the 24th, Debussy, impatient and beset by nerves, took Emma to Eastbourne, a place he found 'peaceful and charming'. For him the first days were 'an almost animal relaxation'. Three weeks later his 'thinking machine is recovering bit by bit', and he transformed the 'Reflets dans l'eau' drastically, a task which delayed sending the first series of *Images* for piano to the publisher. If *La Mer* can be said to contain the sentimental storm that then beset Debussy, 'Reflets dans l'eau' can be said to mark its conclusion.

Other *Images* suggested themselves to Debussy when he got back from Eastbourne at the beginning of September, to move for two weeks into the Hôtel de la Feuilleraie, in Bellevue, Seine-et-Oise. He thought of a second series, for two pianos; the first two, 'Gigues tristes' and 'Ibéria', were eventually developed,* but the third, 'Valse', never saw the light of day† In October he moved into a private house on the avenue du Bois de

---

[16] The only complaint that Debussy brought up against Lilly, and this no doubt was suggested by his lawyer, was that 'she closed doors too noisily'!

* ['Gigues tristes' and 'Ibéria' became *Images pour orchestre*, Nos. 1 and 2, respectively.]

† [The only references to these *Images* are found in letters to Durand of May and Sept. 1905 (1927, pp. 28, 33, 34).]

Boulogne, where he would live for the rest of his life. Besides, he had the kind idea of moving his aged parents to 35 *bis* rue La Fontaine, where they would be closer to him. They had retired to Levallois-Perret, and at last to some degree the son was able to see to their well-being.

Hardly settled, Debussy was in the throes of the rehearsals of *La Mer*, which had its first performance at the Concerts Lamoureux on 15 October 1905.* The sky was very overcast that day, fine rain fell incessantly, which should have reminded the critics that drizzle makes the sea dark and sad. Debussy had foreseen that the critics would be completely lost and that they would reproach him for not being at all faithful to himself. Those who had spoken most favourably of *Pelléas* were confused or hostile when confronted with *La Mer*. Pierre Lalo, as though to get even for having had his hand forced in 1902, wrote that 'Debussy had wanted to feel, but instead he has not truly, deeply and naturally felt'. This article touched Debussy to the quick, and on 25 October 1905 he sent Lalo a dignified letter of protest (1980, pp. 145–6). To Laloy on 13 September and 17 October 1905 he complained about Gaston Carraud, such a prophet as far as *Pelléas* went, for adding to the many 'belittling remarks and foolish squibs' put forth by his colleagues who did not appreciate the novelty of *La Mer*: 'about which it seems to me they have been particularly mistaken ... M. G. Carraud accuses me of working for America. Another, whose name I cannot remember, defines me as a composer of the "impalpable". Does he take music to be a colonial commodity?' (*RdM*, 1962, pp. 15, 16).

Assuredly, nearly all agreed in recognizing the 'prodigious orchestration' of *La Mer*, but it was the 'craftsmanship' that they praised. The outcome, however, was that orchestras competed to perform Debussy's earlier compositions: *La Damoiselle élue*, the *Nocturnes*, the *Prélude à 'L'Après-midi d'un faune'*. It could be said that *La Mer* washed up these shells and, as it withdrew, it revealed them.[17]

This lack of understanding and this opposition affected Debussy more than can easily be described, particularly because they seemed to him to be inspired in part by the upheaval in his private life. It could be thought that the composition immediately following, 'Serenade for the Doll', was an ironical gesture towards the public; it was, however, prompted by a

[17] On 17 Dec. 1905, eleven years after its creation, the *Prélude à 'L'Après-midi d'un faune'* was given by the Concerts du Conservatoire, the first of Debussy's works admitted to that venerable institution. In a letter to Jules Ecorcheville, written some six years later, Debussy recalled the performance in the 'gratuitously uncomfortable' little hall, 'where the memories of the old masters are increased by the musty and unattractive aroma'.

* [Conducted by Camille Chevillard.]

great emotion. On 30 October 1905 Emma gave him a daughter, Claude-Emma (nicknamed Chouchou), who was so much a part of them both that she carried both their first names. He found in her a joy mixed with a little worry, as in some delicate miracle whose mechanism he scarcely understood.

He announced the good news to Laloy on 4 November: 'Several days ago I became the father of a little girl. The joy of it has overwhelmed me a bit and still frightens me' (*RdM*, 1962, p. 17).

At least as far as the marriage went, it was Chouchou who sealed the union of Claude and Emma. She did much to create the happy and deeply felt intimacy of the lovers of the *L'Isle joyeuse*. The masks had fallen, the *colloque sentimental* would continue.

17

'Brouillards'

IT was as though Debussy's life from then on was shrouded in wisps of mist. As early as 1906, he was living in it. Everything had changed since he had slipped off to Jersey in July 1904. He had acquired a daughter, a stepdaughter, a stepson, a new wife, a private house, two servants, and Kim, his dog, who had taken the place of Line, the cat who had lived at rue Cardinet. The majority of his former companions, the moral sticklers and the bourgeois, did not come round any more. Furthermore, one of them who wrote of a 'desertion that harms the conjugal hearth' demonstrated that yielding to the impulses of the heart bothered not only artists. Certainly, Debussy retained some comrades, some friends, and he acquired some new ones: Jean Marnold, Laloy, Roger-Ducasse, Lacerda, Bardac, Séverac, Viñes, Victor Segalen, Jean-Aubry, André Caplet, Pasteur Vallery-Radot, d'Annunzio, Inghelbrecht, and Walter Rummel. The faithful ones returned little by little: Henri de Régnier, Satie, Doret, Coronio, Koechlin, Dukas, Godet, Mourey, and Curnonsky; but they were not there yet, only Laloy and Toulet had already come back. With Peter and Hocquet, a page had turned; they wrote to each other at long intervals, but they did not see one another again. There was no break with Pierre Louÿs, as has been said; they did see each other again.[1]

In spite of its comforts and its elegant surroundings, the house in the Bois de Boulogne was still a little strange to him. At that point Debussy had hardly had time to feel at home in it. 'You are in an old house which has been your friend from early childhood' (*RdM*, 1962, p. 21), he sadly informed Laloy on 10 September 1906—Laloy was spending the summer in his old family place at Rahon in the Jura. Debussy himself had never stopped moving from one place to another. He had not acquired a sense of permanence in a friendly atmosphere over the fleeting years. His

---

[1] The contact with Édouard Rist was not re-established. They did meet one day, and both gave a gesture of greeting, but neither encouraged it. With Coronio, who was younger, peace was made at a concert conducted by Debussy. The pupil threw himself impetuously into his master's arms. Uneasily, Debussy exclaimed, like an actor on the stage: 'But enough now of this excessive emotion!' and a burst of laughter followed.

['Brouillards', *Préludes*, Book II, No. 1.]

family did not count. He felt profoundly alone, in spite of Emma and Chouchou. It would require the affectionate care of the one and the chatter of the other for him unconsciously to discover an atmosphere dear to his soul.[2]

In 1906 he produced a single composition: 'Serenade for the Doll'. From 1907 come the second series of *Images* for piano. In fact, 1906 and 1907 were the only two years of comfort and the last years of good health that Debussy enjoyed.

A great weariness engulfed him—a sense of comfort, too—during the first six months of 1906. He did nothing, except play bridge with Laloy and chat with Toulet. It was of this period that Pierro Lalo wrote in *Le Temps*, of 21 February 1906:

At the time of the first performances of *Pelléas et Mélisande*, a small public opposed Debussy's art with apathy, or were hostile and sarcastic. But who then would have thought that two or three years would transform that hostility into approval and that just the name of M. Debussy would attract an enthusiastic, almost fanatical, crowd? Yet that is what has happened today . . . The Debussyste religion has supplanted the Wagnerian variety. I remember that one day in a foul mood I described M. Debussy as an evil magician. I am removing the word 'evil'. Seeing the faces of his faithful admirers, who could doubt that he has enchanted them and that he rules their souls by elegance and by sorcery?

Certainly, Debussy read, as he always had; he saw most of the exhibitions, particularly those of painting. His name is found among the subscribers to de luxe books and reviews.[3] Perhaps he was feeling himself a prisoner of his fame and of the commitments he had made: on the one hand, to compose in accordance with his ambition to climb 'always upward' [*toujours plus haut*], as his youthful motto put it; on the other hand, to produce music to merit the income he received from his publisher. He had gone beyond *Pelléas* with *La Mer*; now he would have to go beyond *La Mer*.

Debussy told Maurice Leclerq in an interview in *L'Éclair* of February 1908: 'the composer (or the artist of today) who has achieved great

---

[2] In spite of his patriotism, which would become from year to year more touchy, he was responsive to British influences. On a card decorated with coloured flowers, he had Emma send this sentiment [written in English] to their friends: 'All kind thoughts at Christmastide and sincere wishes for your happiness throughout the coming year. From Mr and Mrs Claude Debussy.' One of his regrets, Vuillermoz wrote, was that of not being able to speak English.

[3] On 13 Jan. 1907 André Saurès wrote to his friend Latil, speaking of *Voici l'homme*. 'I have been told that as of last week there are only five subscribers, but among them are Rodin, the painter Claude Monet, and the musician Debussy. In their three arts, those are the best in France and perhaps in Europe' (collection of Mme Suarès [in 1962]).

notoriety has only one concern; to produce personal works, works as original as possible.' He sought but could not find a text that inspired him.

To Laloy, whom he had left without news, he excused himself, on 2 January 1906: 'All my problems result from my need to write music that I must extract laboriously from a stony brain . . . My appearance then is pained, a bit like an idiot, someone who seems to be hearing voices' (*RdM*, 1962, p. 17).

In May 1905 Laloy had started a review, in collaboration with Jean Marnold, calling it *Le Mercure musical*, and he asked for the participation of Debussy, who had immediately conceived a series of *Entretiens avec Monsieur Croche*. But Debussy's divorce suit was then causing him too much concern—and would continue to do so until his death. On 13 September he was scarcely more inclined to participate because he distrusted those who had gathered around the magazine. He found them

sinister . . . frighteningly informed. I really do not see what this poor *M. Croche* would be able to do amid so many exigent experts. I would very much like to inform you of his death in these terms: *M. Croche, antidilletante*, justifiably discouraged by the musical manners of this age, has died quietly amid general indifference!' (*RdM*, 1962, p. 16)

To Laloy, who insisted in a friendly way, Debussy repeated on 10 March 1906 that he wished to hold himself aloof from the fray. Furthermore, he was told of an inopportune quip dropped by Maurice Ravel—the cause of the coolness between the two composers, who were soon going to find themselves arrayed one against the other, due to the competitive wishes of Ravel's supporters. Debussy wrote:

why express opinions to people who do not listen! Music is at present divided into a group of little republics where each one exerts himself to make more noise than his neighbour . . . all that produces so much unworthy music that the taste for 'the other music' threatens to be lost. . . . Don't you believe that it would be better to hold to a more wary attitude and preserve a little of this 'mystery'; otherwise we shall end up making music unmysterious because of the loose talk and gossip which the artists countenance as though they were old actors? There are certainly some things that should be said, but to whom? For whom? For those people who shilly-shally from Beethoven to Maurice Ravel? Finally, it is fortunate that no one in our day possesses talent, because it seems to me that that would be the most vexatious or the most ridiculous position imaginable in the world. (*RdM*, 1962, pp. 18–19)

Little by little he turned towards his daughter, towards Chouchou, who was the image of her father and who had inherited his singular intelligence. He wrote to Laloy on 10 March 1906: 'I have been rather worried about the health of my little Claude recently. It is so difficult to know what is going on in these little creatures, that it is so easy quickly to lose one's head' (*RdM*, 1962, p. 18). She was the only one who inspired him in 1906; she gave him the quality of feeling to which we owe the *Children's Corner* of 1908; however, it was in 1906 that he wrote and had printed the third piece of that collection, 'Serenade for the Doll',* for already, at the foot of the cradle, was the doll, the first illusion. With its tenderly awkward melancholy the music seeks to hold on to the most moving moment in the life of a woman, the charming frankness of a baby with her own baby, for the baby will soon grow, but the outgrown doll will remain as it was that first day, eternally content with the single, instinctive love that it prompted.

In April 1906 an admirer came to visit Debussy. This was Victor Segalen, who showed him on the 27th a first, incomplete sketch of his Buddhist play, *Siddhartha*. Debussy was interested by it, but he did not take it up. On 18 April he had written to Durand: 'The fact of being unable to think with the same freedom is somewhat idiotic: imagine a blind intellect' (1927, p. 41).

In June he seemed to pull himself together. 'I am working to get over a long bad spell.' Then, on 7 July: 'I am beginning to work with that eagerness mixed with nervous tension which is usual with me.' He reported that he was working on 'Ibéria' and on *Le Diable dans le beffroi* and was counting on completing the orchestral *Images*. From 6 August until the beginning of September he took a holiday at the Grand Hôtel in Puys, six kilometres from Dieppe, where travel was by means of a horse-drawn vehicle, the 'Omnibus'.

On 8 August 1906 he reported to Durand, who was tormenting him:[4] 'Here I am again with my old friend the sea ... It is truly the thing in nature which best puts one back in one's place' (1927, p. 44). But the beach was impossible, the hotel uncomfortable, and he could not find again the feeling he had experienced when confronted by the ocean the year before. He was in a hurry to return to Paris, after having complained that he had been forced to remain there. He was nervous about the cast of *Pelléas*, that was due to be revived in the autumn, and on 26 October 1906 he excused himself to Hector Dufranne:

I hope that you will forgive the nervousness that I have brought to the rehearsals of *Pelléas*, which caused me to go farther than I really meant to. You and Vieuille

[4] Without let-up, in Debussy's view. He wrote to his publisher in 1906: 'You are too much of an artist not to understand scruples and uncertainties ...' (1927, p. 46). Once he cheerily addressed him as 'Durfils', the telegraph address for Durand's firm.

* [The English titles in the *Children's Corner* may well be connected with the fact that Chouchou had an English governess.]

are almost the only ones who have preserved any understanding of the art that I tried to produce in *Pelléas*. This is why I ask you to continue to protect this work, which other people do not seem to love as much. In the fifth act, it seems to me that the movements are a bit languid. Then, I beg you, exaggerate more the sad and touching grief of Golaud . . . Convey well the impression of all that he regrets not having said, not having done . . . and of all the happiness that eludes him for ever (1980, pp. 154–5).*

By the end of 1906 he seemed to have recovered his composure. Emma had set aside for him his ivory tower, a fine bright study, which she filled with flowers summer and winter. Chouchou had begun to take her first steps. 'Each person's happiness', he wrote to Laloy at Christmas 1906, is comprised 'of jealously guarded intimacy' (*RdM*, 1962, p. 23).

In 1907, however, his morale was scarcely improved. Short periods of exhilaration were followed by bouts of depression. 'I am working between alternatives of joy and sadness.' His weariness ran deep, prompted by financial concerns, the loss of former friends, a lack of promising projects, and the slow working out of the orchestral *Images*. The only compositions he completed were the second series of *Images* for piano. He complained for the first time of 'unbearable intestinal discomforts'. Above all he grew irritated with the 'opposition' that was aroused around him; the 'republics' made too much noise; he was being compared continually to Ravel, 'who will go much farther than Debussy'.[5] Emile Vuillermoz did not think twice before writing, on 27 February 1907, in *La Nouvelle presse*: 'The author of *Pelléas* will come to see that all the young parasitical generation that is developing around his work writes Debussy better than he does.'

In this bullfight, where lances were waved and banderillas raised, Vuillermoz was followed by Pierre Lalo, and then there was 'the Cocteau gang', who incited the quarrel between Debussy and Satie. For it was a real conspiracy, doubtless wilfully and knowingly prosecuted, which grew still more heated in 1908 over *Boris Godunov*. It is impossible to stress enough just how much Debussy was aware of it and how deeply he was affected by it. Here is some additional evidence. Having written an account for his review *S.I.M.* (15 February 1907) of the first performance

[5] As early as 30 Dec. 1904 Romain Rolland informed André Suarès: 'I have got to know various musicians. One, among others, who is more Debussyan than Debussy, Ravel' (collection of Mme. Suarès [in 1962]).

---

* [Dufranne and Félix Vieuille were the original Golaud and Arkël, respectively. Garden and Jean Perier still held the two title roles; the Geneviève was now Suzanne Brohly (in the place of Jeanne Gerville-Réache) and Yniold was now sung by Jeanne de Poumayrac, instead of 'le petit Blondin'. This season the opera was conducted by François Ruhlmann, and the fiftieth performance of the work after its introduction at the Opéra-Comique was celebrated on 23 Dec. 1906.]

of Ravel's *Histoires naturelles*, a work that produced scandals, Laloy saw himself suspected of betrayal. Debussy advised him to leave to others the task of sacrificing 'deliberately the innocent and instinctive masterpiece which is Mussorgsky's song-cycle *The Nursery* to the modish Americanism of *Histoires naturelles*', which 'can be only an example of music that has lost its way' (*RdM*, 1962, p. 24). On 8 March 1907 he apologized for this indiscretion:

Nervous people are intolerable ... But, between ourselves, do you sincerely believe in 'humoristic' music? First of all, it does not exist in itself. It always requires some occasion, either a text or a situation. Two chords, feet up in the air, or in whatever other preposterous position, are never necessarily humorous, and could become so only empirically.

I agree with you in recognizing that Ravel is undeniably gifted, but what irritates me is his attitude of a clown or, better, of a fakir who makes flowers grow around a chair.... Unfortunately, a surprise must be prepared, and it can be astonishing only once! ...

Now, I ask nothing better than that it should be entertaining—that would even be a very pretty excuse for music, which so many people torture and harrow ... an art whose only concern is to make us smile. (*RdM*, 1962, p. 25).[6]

On 9 January 1907 *Pelléas et Mélisande* received its Brussels première, and Debussy travelled there without much expectation. Two days earlier he had written to Durand: 'It is better to play the part of being a famous dead person, with whom people can do as they like' (1980, p. 156). Of the orchestra, he reported to Laloy on 23 January: 'Some heavy, shrill woodwinds; by contrast, some brasses [that sound] as though [they are] wrapped in absorbent cotton ... a disconcerting habit of distorting the most common rhythm. In sum, a constant struggle ... to reach something that is remotely possible' (*RdM*, 1962, p. 24).

On 20 March 1907 Segalen sent him some notes on Maori music, entitled *Voix mortes*, which Debussy considered:

It is extremely odd; no essay of this type has interested me so much. With those who trouble themselves to write about such a subject, all too often it seems that they have never seen the colour of what they seek to describe ... Such works are too often heavy and in them one breathes only the disconsolate odour of the document.[7]

---

[6] What Ravel said later about Debussy illustrates the incompatibility of the two composers: 'Debussy is an admirable musician, but how sad it is that he orchestrates ineptly!' (E. Vuillermoz, *Maurice Ravel* (Paris, 1939), 14).

[7] A. Joly-Segalen and A. Schaeffner, *Segalen et Debussy* (Monaco, 1961), 58–9. The relationship of Debussy with Segalen has also been studied by Jean-Aubry in *Cahiers du Sud* (1st quarter, 1948).

His chief concern seemed to be to try to escape from his lethargy.[8] In order to appease Durand's 'editorial appetite', he had to revise the instrumentation of *L'Enfant prodigue*. He set himself to orchestrate 'Le Jet d'eau'. He engaged Busser to perform a similar function for the *Petite Suite*. Furthermore, he accepted an engagement to conduct concerts in London and in Italy, where he planned to offer 'the first performance of the *Images*'.*

In July 1907 Gabriel Mourey submitted to him a large project, *L'Histoire de Tristan*, after the narrative of Joseph Bédier. Debussy accepted it enthusiastically. The idea seemed to fit so well the path he wanted to follow, that while on holiday at Pourville from the beginning of August, he admitted to Durand on the 5th: 'I almost dread the moment when I receive the libretto, for this adventure seems to me both beautiful and alluring' (1927, p. 52). At the same time, Segalen sought to re-arouse his interest in *Siddhartha*. Debussy was wary, but still receptive to an original idea. He answered the writer on 26 August 1907:

It is nothing more than a prodigious dream! However, in its present form, I do not know any music able to penetrate this abyss! It could merely serve to underline certain gestures or to give specific connotations to certain scenic effects... Notice that I do not claim to do the impossible; very simply ... the project frightens me.[9]

Debussy proposed an alternative idea to Segalen. 'Don't you think that there might be something worthwhile to make of the myth of Orpheus?' And Segalen applied himself to *Orphée-Roi*, but his ideas were not inspiring.[10]

When he got back to Paris, Debussy saw Mourey again, on 23 September, to talk about *Tristan*. On the 25th Debussy reported to

[8] According to J.-É. Blanche, Debussy spoke insistently about a very hazy project, even begging me to furnish him with a canvas. He imagined a cosmic drama, with neither words nor action, in which the singers, invisible chorus and solo voices, hymned onomatopoetically, while lighting effects shifted across the stage. The performers, hidden behind the scenery, would personify and symbolize clouds, winds, and the sea.' ('Souvenirs sur Manet et Debussy', *Le Figaro*, 22 June 1932).

[9] Joly-Segalen and Schaeffner, *Segalen et Debussy*, p. 66.

[10] In spite of the sympathy he held for him, Debussy never believed that a productive collaboration with Segalen would be possible. Having been directly involved in their planning sessions, Laloy goes so far as to say that Debussy lost a lot of time on this intractable *Orphée-Roi* (Laloy, *La Musique retrouvée*, p. 175).

* [These conducting tours, even those when his health was deteriorating, were probably undertaken by Debussy in order to earn the money needed to maintain the standard of living which Emma enjoyed.]

Durand: 'We have worked, argued, revised, but I believe that we have got hold of something quite promising' (1927, p. 56). A month later, he grew uneasy with Mourey's careless speed and he complained about it to Laloy on 15 October 1907: '*L'Histoire de Tristan* moves ahead ... it is even moving too fast for my taste ... I have never understood the drive to work on the cheap, without wanting to look behind you, drawn on, moreover, only by the thought of an utterly hazardous success...' (*RdM*, 1962, p. 27).

The Press, however, as early as 5 August 1907, mentioned rumours of the Debussy–Mourey project, but then everything turned sour. In 1900, immersed in the *Tristan* of the troubadour Thomas, Bédier had written and published as a diversion his tale of *Tristan et Iseult*, which enjoyed an amazing popularity that surprised this writer who was indifferent to success. Bédier's friend and cousin Louis Artus had soon grasped its possibilities, for he reshaped it as a scenario and obtained from the author all rights for adapting it for the stage. When he learned that Mourey, 'an obscure man of letters', had stolen his property, he asserted the priority of his rights. At the Société des Auteurs, Artus made known both to Mourey and to Debussy his eagerness to write the libretto of *Tristan* himself in a spirit of harmonious teamwork, but Debussy took the matter haughtily and avowed that he would go ahead with Mourey, in spite of all the legal objections. Then Artus threatened to sue if Debussy persisted in poaching on this protected turf.

Truly, as much as Artus flattered himself offering his co-operation to the celebrated composer of *La Mer*, to the same extent Debussy could not conceive working with a writer of vaudevilles, the author of *La Culotte*. With every reason, Debussy came to object humorously on 19 February 1908, in *Comœdia*, which had accused him of lending his hand to the 'insubstantial music' of Paul Delmet.* Already, in 1897, Pierre Louÿs had been unable to persuade Debussy to write the music for a ballet drawn from *Aphrodite*, because its performance would have taken place at the Olympia, which was a gathering place for whores. Aware of or guessing Debussy's feelings towards him, Artus set up a protective wall around this *Tristan*, which Bédier would have ceded very willingly to the composer if he had not already made a gift of it to his cousin. Debussy was stymied; as the project was too close to his heart, he went to see Bédier. Laloy later wrote: 'two characters, equally noble, cautious and perceptive, were able to understand one another with a hint and without even a word spoken.'[11]

---

[11] Laloy, *La Musique retrouvée*, p. 175.

* [Debussy wrote in *Comœdia*: 'I would be entirely obliged to you to leave the glory of Paul Delmet intact. I assure you that he has never done me the honour of requesting any collaboration whatever with me.']

Laloy had arranged the meeting. Checkmated by Louis Artus and disillusioned by Gabriel Mourey, Debussy seriously considered that perhaps the beautiful prose of Joseph Bédier might serve him better than the adaptation of a vaudevilliste, however lyrical it might be, or the hasty text of an 'obscure man of letters'. Hope was reborn in Debussy, and he wrote to Laloy on 2 April 1909: 'The gods are with us ... If truly "Joseph" [Bédier] could sacrifice "Louis" [Artus], I would offer him "Gabriel" [Mourey] as a burnt-offering' (*RdM*, 1962, p. 31).

But Artus short-circuited him with Bédier, and the latter, caught between two fires—and, moreover, deaf to all music—could not of course go back on his word. Artus triumphed, and then Mourey made other suggestions to Debussy: *Huon de Bordeaux*, *Le Chat botté*, and *Le Marchand de rêves*. Yet a hope for *Tristan* lingered on for another year, as may be seen from Debussy's letter to Laloy of 15 May 1910: 'I regret that you have been unable to see Bédier. That would have helped a great deal in settling everyting in place, both people and feelings (*RdM*, 1962, p. 38).

At this point Artus had written none of the play that he would later publish. Obstinate because of an unlucky promise, he kept a tight hand on *Tristan*. The attitude of Artus played a significant role in depriving French music of a new opera about Tristan, but one cannot deny Debussy's enduring interest in the *Tristan* of Bédier, nor the failure through circumstances beyond his control of other projects preceding *Tristan*. Nor can one deny the reservations, concealed or overt, that he made to those who later suggested projects to him, up to and including *Khamma* and *Le Martyre de Saint Sébastien*.

Nor can one deny any longer that Debussy was relatively inexperienced in literary and dramatic matters. This did not help the composition of the two operas based upon Poe: *Le Diable dans le beffroi* and *La Chute de la Maison Usher*. Finally, although Debussy accepted *Khamma*, it was for reasons that had nothing to do with music. Rather, as we shall learn, although he foresaw the failure and mistake that *Le Martyre* would turn out to be, he none the less gave his agreement to d'Annunzio, without knowing anything of the work, even pretending—tactfully—'a sort of fever' that he was far from feeling, when, in reality, as he wrote to his wife: 'To me this tale says nothing worthwhile' (1980, p. 199). His almost frantic haste proved how impatient Debussy was to 'immerse himself' in a large-scale theatrical work that demanded his best.

Now the best of himself that he put into a *Martyre de Saint Sébastien*, a work that promised to be a failure as well as an error of theatrical judgement, might have been better put instead into *Tristan*. The collaboration of Bédier and Debussy, without any intervening librettist, would have joined the far-seeking poet of a unique love and the only composer capable of realizing it, and might plausibly have produced a masterpiece in which the soul of France, in the harmony of its most virile and most tender aspects, would have found sovereign expression.[12]

October 1907 is the date of the second series of *Images* for piano, but Debussy worked on them until January 1908. 'Poissons d'or' may have been inspired by a black lacquer panel embellished with gold and mother of pearl which hung in his study. The scales glint and pass like lightning in bubbling water, resembling the thoughts of a restless mind. Ricardo Viñes remembered how this composition was dedicated to him, on 26 November 1907:

I saw him nervous, ill at ease, making signs to his wife. He was a discriminating friend, but his moods could be difficult. I was expecting a friendly insult and asked myself what was going to happen to me. Debussy sat down at the piano and played 'Poissons d'or' in his flexible, velvety manner. Then he showed me the dedication, laughing. I thanked him for it, deeply moved and uneasy . . .

'Cloches à travers les feuilles', dedicated to the sculptor Alexandre Charpentier, referred to a local custom of the Jura region, as Laloy described it in a letter to Debussy: 'the tolling that sounds between vespers on All Souls Day and the mass for the dead, passing from village to village, through the yellowing forests in the silence of the evening.'[13] Yet it is 'Et la lune descend sur le temple qui fut', which was dedicated to Laloy. The point of the title, 'a faultless Alexandrine' written by Debussy himself, was doubtless influenced by some travel accounts or by some oriental tales, for the East was then in vogue. Segalen, Toulet, and Laloy indulged in chinoiseries. In 1910 the Pavillon de Marsan held an exhibition of Chinese art that delighted Debussy.

The period between October 1907 and January 1908 was that of the second series of *Images* for piano. It must be stressed that these four months were particularly significant, when the daily married life of Debussy weighed heavily, as will be seen. The collection opens with 'Cloches à travers les feuilles' and ends with 'Poissons d'or'. This order is essential to the balance of the three pieces upon a recital programme. In chronological fact, Debussy composed 'Poissons d'or' first, which expresses in rapid zigzags independent fancies, flight, then 'Cloches à travers les feuilles', which is filled with bitter regret, and finally 'Et la lune descend sur le temple qui fut', which is an evocation of nothingness, the icy, pale reflection of stellar spaces, where all pain is numbed.

[12] Artus wrote his dramatization of *Tristan* about 1914, but it had to wait fifteen years to enjoy what was no more than an indifferent success in Nice, on 30 Jan. 1929. It was also performed in Paris, at the Théâtre Sarah-Bernhardt, on 19 Mar. 1929.

[13] Laloy, *Debussy*, p. 95.

During this same October of 1907, alone in his bright study, without the will to work on the orchestral *Images* that he had begun, worried about this *Tristan* that was evolving too insubstantially, Debussy questioned himself about his inactivity, confronting grave uncertainties which he confided to Laloy on the 15th:

An ordinary rain is falling on Paris, but I do not see its purpose very well ... peace does not dwell in my soul. Is it the fault of the landscape of this corner of Paris? Or is it that I am clearly not made to put up with domestic life? So many questions, which I cannot find the strength to answer. (*RdM*, 1962, p. 27)

The radiant year of 1904 was really only yesterday, and yet it already seemed so distant to him! The rapture of Jersey had gradually died down; the reality of daily routine had taken its place, and it weighed upon him in proportion to the troubles of every sort that accumulated. He was aging; the dream which had nurtured him for so long had evaporated. These years had covered the image with a fine film, across which the Damoiselle or Mélisande of earlier days appeared to him now as nothing more than blurred silhouettes.

The years had passed; middle age took the place of youth and Debussy turned forty-five. He had gradually been overtaken by the comfort of his home, he had become a bourgeois, it was his 'family that hindered him and blocked his way ...'. Seeking to shake off the languour that filled him, he asked himself if he was again 'at a dangerous turning-point' in his life—a healthy reaction, as far as his work was concerned, and which led him to a decision on another level. On the afternoon of 20 January 1908, at the town hall of the XVIth Arrondissement, he got married again. Emma understood then that she had known how to possess him definitely, by creating around him this atmosphere of considerate ease, of discretion, of discriminating intimacy, and of passionate tenderness that he needed, that he had looked for for a long time, perhaps without truly recognizing it. There he spent the last ten years of his life, and they were irradiated with happiness.*

* [Once again Dietschy described Debussy's marriage to Emma as Dolly de Tinan insisted it be.]

18

'L'ombre des arbres'

————◆————

In 1908 and 1909, six and seven years after the première of *Pelléas*, Debussy was still being heatedly discussed. Certainly, *Pelléas* no longer aroused opposition in the theatre, but the opera elicited controversy in the Press and at the hands of the critics. Those who came late to understand and enjoy it were similarly tardy in their appreciation of Debussy's later works. If on 19 January 1908 *La Mer* aroused a noisy demonstration that it had not caused at its first performance more than two years earlier, it did so then because feelings had been conscientiously heated by certain musical journals. The work's adherents and opponents met in open conflict.

Debussy was particularly hurt by the comparison that was then made between *Boris Godunov* and *Pelléas et Mélisande*. The two works were being given in Paris almost simultaneously in 1908: the first from 19 May, the second from 12 June. Some newspaper reviews tried to show that *Pelléas* could not have been conceived without *Boris*, to which it owed everything. It was on this occasion that Charles Bordes insinuated that *Boris* was the 'grand-papa of *Pelléas*'. Writing in *Le Mercure de France*, Jean Marnold went one better: 'the musical genius who created *Pelléas* had visibly absorbed [*Boris*] like a sponge.'[1]

Then Pierre Lalo in *Le Temps* took up Debussy's defence. He analysed the dominant characteristics of both *Boris* and *Pelléas*, deciding that there were only 'very superficial analogies' between the two works. He denounced the pointlessness of the controversy, because, before *Pelléas*, 'before the enchantment of this music, everything else is silence'. Grateful, Debussy wrote to Lalo that same day (23 June 1908):

To have shed a little light upon the debate between *Boris Godunov* and *Pelléas et Mélisande* is a fine gesture on your part, all the more so because, since a certain number of imbeciles have intervened, the matter has threatened to take on nearly diplomatic proportions. Do you not think that it would be a pity to look for

[1] In his letter of 2 Aug. 1909 to Laloy, Debussy drew the following sketch of Jean Marnold: 'He has preserved his erudite and embalmed air of an Assyrian king for the Théâtre des Gobelins' (*RdM*, 1962, p. 36).

['L'ombre des arbres', *Ariettes oubliées*, No. 3.]

examples from the Russians—indeed even from Mussorgsky; I can attest that during a trip I made to Russia twenty years ago no one mentioned his name? It was only in France that I began to make his acquaintance—this must be the case with many of the Russian composers. On this point, we are not very dissimilar, for it is remarkable how little we like to admit that one of ours has found whatever it might be... And that aptitude we use to uncover—it makes no matter where—a resemblance! Will we take pride only in our modistes' hats? But here I am insisting, when I want simply to assure you of my friendly appreciation. (1980, p. 172)

This letter is admirable for all that it expresses of Debussy's wounded pride and rumpled national feeling. But Pierre Lalo, although he remained loyal to *Pelléas*, would soon separate himself permanently from Debussy's art. At this time, Pietro Mascagni, 'the *verismo* composer from Leghorn', emboldened by the financial success of *Cavalleria rusticana*, unburdened himself publicly about *Pelléas*: 'Modern music will not last. *Salomé* and *Pelléas*? They will soon disappear. The music of *Pelléas* makes me think of those who accompany films, who modestly and timidly play their little tunes while the most extraordinary events unroll on the screen.'[2]

As early as 1907, however, *Pelléas* started to make its way across the Western world: Brussels, Frankfurt, Lyons, Milan, New York, Cologne, Budapest, Prague, Berlin, Munich, Rome, and London. Even if its reception was scarcely different from what it had been in Paris, Debussy became everywhere a celebrity.* Nothing shows this better than an article by Raphaël Cor, entitled *M. Claude Debussy et le snobisme contemporain*, a masterpiece of deep misunderstanding, published in October 1909 by the *Revue du temps présent* and followed by a memorable questionnaire. A hundred people were interviewed. Seventy of the most notable refused to state their position publicly. Of twenty-nine published replies, five were favourable to Debussy, among them those of Ansermet, Albert Carré, and Fernand Gregh; five were ferociously hostile, notably those of Camille Bellaigue and Sâr Péladan; six were of a prudent neutrality; three

---

[2] *L'Éventail*, Brussels, July 1908.

* [In New York, H. E. Krehbiel (1854–1923) wrote in the *Daily Tribune*, 20 Feb. 1908:

No one should be ashamed to proclaim his pleasure in four hours of uninterrupted, musically inflected speech, over a substratum of shifting harmonies, each with its individual tang and instrumental color, but neither should anybody be afraid to say that nine-tenths of the music is dreary monotony because of the absence of what to him stands for musical thought.

But another critic wrote: 'For me from now on, this is the only music.']

were disdainful; seven avoided the questions asked, and three were antipathetic, among them that of Romain Rolland.[3]

In 1908, in order to have a third song to go with the two *Chansons de Charles d'Orléans*, composed ten years earlier, Debussy reread the rondeaux of the royal poet. He felt himself drawn to 'Quant j'ai ouy le tabourin', and on 16 June 1908 he wrote to Laloy asking him to clarify certain Old French words:

I find this little poem so full of sweet interior music that—naturally—I cannot stop myself from 'exteriorizing' it, as our friend Victor Segalen would say. May the noble Charles d'Orléans be willing to forgive me for it. I must tell you at once that I am awaiting your reply so that I can set my colours. (*RdM*, 1962, p. 29)

To appease Jacques Durand, Debussy had to take up an older work again: orchestrating the *Marche écossaise* of 1891. He finished the *Children's Corner* in the course of that summer, and it represents an innocent, secret corner in the tangle of bread-winning labour. His soul had found an eager freshness which is distilled in this collection devoted to the life of his little daughter: the study, the zoo, the game, the day after Christmas, the holidays, the puppet show. Nothing equals the refined, deep melancholy of 'The Snow is Dancing'.

'Ibéria' was finished on Christmas Day, 1908. On 10 August 1908 he had written to Durand: 'I hear the sounds of the roads of Catalonia, and at the same time the street music of Grenada' (1927, p. 63). With the year 1909 he began 'Gigues', although he first called it 'Gigues tristes', and the first sketches that he made coincided with the first serious symptoms of his disease. As early as January 1909 he had to consult a doctor, who prescribed a diet and exercise. The following month he complained of almost daily haemorrhages, and these obliged him to resort to cocaine and morphine. He wrote to Durand, on 5 February 1909: 'I have been working a lot, moving ahead only with difficulty, in spite of the good will and the passion that I put into orchestrating these poor *Images*' (1927, p. 68).

'Poor *Images*', he said. It is true that he had had them on his desk a long time, that he worked with reluctance, and that he tortured them a little while he was torturing himself, pushing ahead to finish. He had written

[3] Rolland kept his antipathy toward Debussy. On 25 Mar. 1918 he wrote:

The death of Claude Debussy. Poor 'little Greece expiring'.... The only creator of beauty in music of our time. He drank sensual delight, and success and well-being and idleness and futility absorbed him. What will remain of him? Some carved vases, some small bas-reliefs, perfect, that will encroach upon the grass of the Appian Way. Traces of the great elegance of his ruined Athens. (*Journal des années de guerre* (Paris, 1952), 1435.)

about them to Durand on 5 August 1907: 'There remained quite a few passages that worried me . . . it was well written, but it was with this usual drudgery that one had to work to conceal and which is so tedious' (1927, p. 51). Certainly, they do not have the high quality of the earlier symphonic works. There are harshnesses here and there, and some conventional passages, but some lucky discoveries, and some beautiful parts as well. 'Ibéria' is the most accomplished. 'Rondes de printemps', completed on 10 May 1909, in spite of some breathlessness and some padding near the end, contains some gems that Maurice Ravel seems to have been one of the first to have revealed.[4] But this is not the Debussy of old. Although he remained creative, although he was faithful to his standards, his distressing life enclosed him, hemmed him in, imprisoned him. He no longer had the freedom of the shepherd playing his pipe. From here on, he was watched from all sides: the public, his colleagues, the critics, especially his publisher, were all interested in seeing him produce a continuous series of compositions.[5]

Five years earlier he had refused to become a member of the Superior Council of the Conservatoire. Now, in Feburary 1909, encouraged by Fauré, he accepted the position left vacant by Ernest Reyer's death. On 14 February 1909 Le Figaro commented upon this development: 'Make no mistake about it: this is a substantial artistic event. It has produced a downright sensation in the traditionalist seats of musical instruction. It is well known that M. Debussy cuts the figure of a revolutionary, because of his ideas and his technique.'

In that same issue of Le Figaro, by turns satirical and serious, Debussy expressed his reaction to it to an interviewer: 'I am literally dumbfounded. The best of it is that I am going to replace that poor M. Ernest Reyer. . . . I took a dozen years to write Pelléas et Mélisande, which tells you that I do not work rapidly. You see, people write too much and they never think enough.'[6]

To Laloy, he confessed more straightforwardly, on 19 November 1909: 'It seems to me that there is too much fuss about a nomination that can

---

[4] Inversely, Debussy must have noticed them in the 'Prélude à la nuit' of Ravel's *Rapsodie espagnole*, first performed on 19 Mar. 1908. Ravel perhaps was aware of this resemblance on hearing 'Les Parfums de la nuit' of 'Ibéria', which was premièred 20 Feb. 1910.

[5] At the beginning of 1909, Debussy suffered from haemorrhoidal crises. His skin took on the colour of old wax and became flabby, his eyelids heavy. It cannot be doubted that the lassitude of which he complained was due to this rectal complaint, related surely to the cancer that would be later diagnosed, and which might already have existed.

[6] C. Debussy, *Monsieur Croche et autres écrits*, ed. F. Lesure (rev. enl. edn., Paris, 1987), 287, 290.

have effect only so far as I am permitted to fill the position' (*RdM*, 1962, p. 31).

Certainly, Debussy, remembering the Chilo de Bussy of 1879, was not at all displeased in 1909 to occupy a chair at the summit of the instruction of music, but financial considerations also prompted his acceptance. For it was surely not with a high heart that he gave up the little freedom that remained to him. He made an even heavier sacrifice when he began conducting his own works. He went to London on 25 February 1909 and conducted the *Prélude à 'L'Après-midi d'un faune'* and the *Nocturnes*, and, of these last, 'Fêtes' was encored. He took up the baton at a Concerts Colonne, on 9 April 1909, presenting the first Paris performance of the *Trois Chansons de Charles d'Orléans*. On 10 May he went back to London. On 21 May Rose Féart* became the first Mélisande at Covent Garden. But when he was abroad, Debussy wanted only to return home; as he confessed to Laloy on 18 May 1909: 'Our life is a kind of Calvary comprised of rehearsals, and I work to protect *Pelléas* as well as possible. However, [Cleofonte] Campanini has been a pleasant surprise. He seems to understand. Obviously, it is a bit 'superficial', but alive and tense. The orchestra is flexible, with good strings...' (*RdM*, 1962, p. 32).

He also kept his aged parents abreast of his successes, writing to them on 23 May:

Dear Papa, dear Maman. Here are some further details about the première of *Pelléas* in London, which were reported to me, because I did not attend that ceremony. The success was marked from the first act to the very end. The singers had to take a dozen calls, and for a quarter of an hour they called for the composer, who was peacefully in his hotel, 'far from the vain noise of applause'. Then Campanini was called out twice, and the crowd finally consented to go home to bed. According to the reviews, it seems that such a reception is exceedingly rare in England, where the public's temperature usually remains below zero. . . . So *vive la France*! Long live French music! Forward with music! . . . I have had to supervise the scenery and the lighting, besides the music. . . . Your devoted old son, Claude Debussy. (1980, p. 176).

The year 1909 was one of honours, marked by the Nadar photographs—dressy, bourgeois, official. They show the change that had taken place in Debussy in the space of a few years. His eye is less lively. His hair seems thinner, his beard is heavier, and his lower lip is touched with some

---

* [Debussy had specially chosen Féart (Mélisande) and Edmond Warnery (Pelléas) to participate in the London première. His letter of 18 May 1909 to Durand (1980, p. 175) contains this observation: 'As for Mlle Féart she is unspeakably unsightly, she lacks poetry, and I continue to regret the absence of the graceful Miss Teyte,' referring to Maggie Teyte, who had sung Mélisande at the Comique in 1908.]

bitterness. The collar of his jacket rises higher in the back, and his appearance seems more casual. He appears rumpled, certainly, in his expensive suit, which is quite unlike the jacket he had worn in the photograph taken at Eragny.* His pose is conventional, but the Debussy of the Nadar photographs is definitely no longer the Debussy *aux fleurs*. Peter acknowledged it: 'Our Claude, still so young and eager, has taken on a sort of patina and no longer looks himself.'[7]

He composed an *Hommage à Haydn*,[8] and spent part of the summer pushing ahead with the scenario and sketching several scenes of *La Chute de la Maison Usher*. Twenty years had passed since Debussy had first read that unusual tale. He had since reread it many times; the landscape, the atmosphere that it summoned up, obsessed him. Doubtless he saw a bit of himself in Roderick Usher,[9] for, as Poe described that character: 'his reserve had always been excessive and habitual.... ([He possessed] a peculiar sensibility of temperament.... It was, he said, a constitutional and a family evil....'

When Poe speaks of 'that silent yet importunate and terrible influence which for centuries had molded the destinies of his family, and which made *him* what I now saw him', Debussy also felt weighing upon him the burden of an heredity that he sought to define: 'our soul is bequeathed to us by a set of completely unknown people...' (1957a, p. 57). Perhaps from the flood of ideas that nurtured his spirit as it strove for perfection came his frank awareness that he had to live outside the boundaries of conventional life. Uneasy in his ability to adjust to the present, Debussy may at least once have imagined that he suffered 'much', like Poe's tragic hero, 'from a morbid acuteness of the senses', and discovered in his own imagination the horrible fissure, this 'barely perceptible fissure', which, originating in the mind of Roderick Usher, extended 'from the roof of the building in front, made its way down the wall in a zigzag direction, until it became lost in the silent waters of the tarn'.

Debussy wrote to Caplet of his suffering. First, on 24 July 1909, he complained of his strange state of mind: 'Perhaps it is the punishment of those who love ideas too much, but who limit themselves to the pursuit of

[7] Peter, *Claude Debussy*, p. 195.

[8] It was given its first performance, 11 Mar. 1911, by the pianist Ennemond Trillat, whom Debussy described in a letter to Laloy of 11 Feb. 1914: 'He has an artist's soul, timid and sensitive; thank God, he does not have the soul of a pretentious modiste that virtuoso pianists so often have' (*RdM*, 1962, p. 40).

[9] He admitted as much to Godet on 4 Sept. 1916: 'Except that I don't have the mental disorder of Roderick Usher..., yet we are both hypersensitive' (1942, p. 156).

* [In 1902.]

a single one ... to an *idée fixe* ... the prelude to insanity (1957*a*, p. 38).[10]
Then, on 25 August of the same year: 'I have dwelt these last days within
La Maison Usher. ... There one acquires the singular fixation of hearing
the dialogue of the stones, while one waits for the fall of houses as though
it were a natural phenomenon ... Furthermore, if you press me, I will
admit to liking those people there better than ... many others' (1957*a*,
p. 38).[11]

But distractions came along to trouble him, and he allowed them to,
because once again it was a question of finances. He told Laloy, on 27 July
1909, that he had decided 'to write come what may the scenario of a
Russo-Venetian ballet' which Serge de Diaghilev had proposed to him,
and he begged Laloy to give him moral support

in the dealings that I am about to have with people who, as you so correctly say,
speak and think in Russian. I humbly confess that I have tended to behave
brusquely in what I know to be one of my faults: I get carried away in the heat of
the moment and then come to regret it. (*RdM*, 1962, p. 34).

He goes on: 'Besides, I keep in a secret corner of my heart the idea of
working with you on the *Oresteia* of Aeschylus. With that, we shall be
absolutely in charge' (*RdM*, 1962, p. 34).

The ballet took its course. On 30 July 1909 Debussy wrote to Laloy,
trying to straighten out his friend's confusion between Diaghilev's plans
and the proposed scenario. He explained that it was Diaghilev, not some
character in the ballet, who was going to Venice to meet his maître de
ballet and wanted to take along the scenario to show it to him. Debussy
believed the scenario need not be complicated:

As it is only a matter of a *divertissement*, to last fifty minutes, at the most, I find it
useless to upset the universe and you, and I am writing the said scenario with the
minimum of complication that could be used to link the dancing groups ...* I
intend to enjoy myself writing this ballet, just the frame of mind for a
divertissement ...

Debussy goes on to say that he is anxious to secure Laloy's participation in
the project. 'I would add that I do not see why the fact that I am having

---

[10] In an unpublished letter that lacks an indication of the person to whom it was
addressed, written 'at Étienne Dupin's' (about 1890), Debussy admitted: 'I am sick, and
sick in the head.' This is a Baudelairean phrase doubtless, but also, at that time, a
foreshadowing of an uncommon fate. (Communicated by Edward Lockspeiser.)

[11] Henri Busser, unaware of Debussy's restlessness at this period, reported: '5 July 1909.
Long visit with Debussy at his house on the avenue du Bois. He seems bored there' (Busser,
De Pelléas aux Indes galantes, p. 178).

* [Elsewhere in this letter Debussy explains that this ballet was proposed as a vehicle
for Nijinsky and Karsavina.]

to write the scenario myself precludes the possibility of your taking part...' (*RdM*, 1962, pp. 34–5).

Then, on 2 August, an impediment arose: 'Our mutual Russian friend fancies that the best code of behaviour with people is first to lie to them. That requires perhaps more talent than he possesses for it, and in friendships I admit that I do not play such games' (*RdM*, 1962, p. 35).

So the project was aborted, as announced to Laloy on 23 October 1909: 'Autumn is not kind to me. First, I am in bad health, and my activity can be compared only to that of a broom without a handle. As for the ballet, I have given up completely, for this year at least, to write my own' (*RdM*, 1962, p. 37).[12]

On the other hand, he had the satisfaction of giving pleasure to his parents. On 10 September the first biography of Claude Debussy in French was published.[13] He thanked its author, Laloy, with feeling:

Today I received the detailed and delightful narrative that you were pleased to write on the subject of Claude Debussy. If I am not sure of being absolutely all that you say I am, the emotion of being understood so thoroughly ('without pretence, moreover.' as the other* said!) is absolute. There is something sharp like a strong light projected in the shadow of the thought. It is like a burglary in which the victim congratulates the burglar. Finally, and more straightforwardly, I am very happy, and my wife joins me in assuring you of our affectionate friendship. (*RdM*, 1962, p. 36)

While 'the wind, the rain stir the few remaining leaves' in this December of 1909, Debussy began his *Première Rapsodie* for clarinet, and, starting his first book of piano *Préludes*, he summoned up the classic Greek chitons in the 'Danseuses de Delphes', the gentle whistling of the wind in 'Le vent dans la plaine', and the orange sails of the regatas in 'Voiles'. Another prelude, 'Les Collines d'Anacapri', as full of joy as *L'Isle joyeuse*, bears the date of 26 December 1909, that same day, Lucienne Bréval† made a triumphant impression with the *Chansons de Bilitis*. On the following day, however, Debussy composed the prelude 'Des pas sur la neige', which

---

[12] He had already written the scenario, *Masques et bergamasques*, which would be published in 1910.

[13] It is remarkable how many of the first books on Debussy and *Pelléas* were in English: in 1907, L. Gilman, *Debussy's Pelléas et Mélisande: A Guide to the Opera*, (New York); in 1908, L. Liebich, *Claude-Achille Debussy* (London); also in 1908, W. H. Daly, *Debussy: A Study in Modern Music* (Edinburgh).

---

* [Golaud to Pelléas in Act III, sc. 3.]

† [Bréval, a dramatic soprano, owned an autograph particell that contained the final half of Act IV, sc. 1, and the complete final scene of Act IV of *Pelléas*, bearing dates of 1893 and 1895, which she bequeathed to the Paris Conservatoire, but which is now in the Bibliothèque Nationale.]

seems to express the searing sadness of the artist alone with his thoughts and haunted by the fleeting footprints that symbolize the unhappy path of man across the immensity of the world.[14]

He also composed two series of songs in 1910: *Le Promenoir des deux amants* and the *Trois Ballades de François Villon*. He made a discreet but significant admission to Laloy on 16 May: he described himself as 'a little dull'. To Caplet, on 23 March, his admission was more open: 'I am—and this happens to me often—at a dangerous turning-point in my life' (1957*a*, p. 47). There was a final attachment, secret and very tender, but it led to no rupture.* *Le Promenoir des deux amants* is clearly dedicated to 'Emma Claude Debussy . . . *p.m*, son mari, Claude Debussy'—'p.m.' is an abbreviation for 'petite mienne'.

When he left for Vienna at the end of 1910, Debussy understood even better how closely he was bound to Emma. In the letters and telegrams sent to her while he was travelling,† it is touching to read what an integral part of his life his wife and daughter were. Away from them he found their absence so unbearable that he sought and found a hundred ways to bring them close in his thoughts. He clung like a child to the comfortable life she had made for him. Doubtless he felt himself a bit helpless as he travelled all alone in foreign countries. But Emma and Chouchou were truly essential parts of his life, and their house was filled with their three presences. The intimacy of his home was both dear and necessary to him above all else, and this intense attachment shows better than anything how far Debussy was in spirit from the real world. Earlier he had written to Durand, on 18 July 1908: 'The external world scarcely exists for me' (1927, p. 62).

If the opinions of Pierre Lalo, more obtuse and pretentious than ever, and the polemic in the *Revue du temps présent* had intensified Debussy's mental solitude, it should be noted that they had added much to the prestige of the composer of *Pelléas*. As early as 1910 he was truly the leading composer of his time. His compositions were played incessantly.[15]

---

[14] The two preludes, 'Les Collines d'Anacapri' and 'Des pas sur la neige' follow one another in the first book of *Préludes*, and the second is—in fact—'like a tender, mournful nostalgia' for an impossible longing. The 'emotional disturbances of middle age' showed themselves harshly in Debussy.

[15] On 20 Apr. 1910 Ravel gave the first performance of *D'un cahier d'esquisses*. The Parent Quartet played the Quartet for the sixty-second time. *Le Figaro* reproduced the music of 'La Fille aux cheveux de lin'. On 27 Apr. *La plus que lente* was given along with *L'Enfant prodigue* at one of the 'five o'clock' concerts. When Debussy wrote to Durand, on 25 Aug. 1910, that *La plus que lente* is 'for the innumerable "five o'clocks" where the beautiful listeners are encountered and of whom I have thought' (1927, p. 90), he alluded to the concert series which had been organized by *Le Figaro* several years earlier.

* [Here Dietschy seems clearly to refer to an affair with an unidentified woman.]
† [These letters can be found in 1957*b*, pp. 77–142.]

But the discussion around his name and his music, around the man and the composer, was still so dense, and his work still appeared so new to the general public, that it inspired from one year to the next the most contradictory and misleading judgements, often emanating from the same critic and in the pages of the same journal. A good example, covering a span of seventeen years, and concerning the *Prélude à 'L'Après-midi d'un faune'*, is furnished by *Le Ménestrel*, certainly a reactionary journal and wholeheartedly devoted to accessible music, opera, and salon works, the sort of thing that Suarès described as 'the joy of Naples, of Buenos Aires, of New York, and of the middle class of Paris and Berlin'. Clearly, in this case, *Le Ménestrel* being the voice of a music publisher, commercial considerations played their part in the opinions expressed about Debussy's *Prélude*. Here are some of them, spread out over the years between 1894 and 1911.

At its first performance the work is found 'interesting'. The following year 'it lacks heart and vigour'. In 1903 it possesses 'unwholesome charm'; in 1905 the *Prélude* is adjudged 'amusing, suggestive, impressionistic', then 'formless, without rhythm, without accent'. Early in 1906 it 'pleases with its smooth transitions'; in October it is described as 'childish, sickly'; in 1907 it has 'become a classic . . . its charm, its irresistible attractiveness are no longer in question'. But two weeks later the same critic complained that the *Prélude* 'is served up to us every Sunday'. In 1908 *Le Ménestrel* saw it as containing 'vice'. In 1910 Arthur Pougin prefers not to speak of it, because 'one must not offend anyone'. In 1911 the *Prélude* is declared to be 'a most successful composition . . . a prime example of descriptive music'.

The *Nocturnes* experienced a comparable fate. Between 1901 and 1912 they are judged successively as: 'lifeless and without thought'; 'Fêtes' is eccentric, 'a Bœcklin in miniature'; 'one cannot help loving them'; 'poverty of imagination, monotony'; 'insinuating and pleasing'; 'subtle and spectral'; 'amusing, puerile . . . without feeling'.

On 13 May 1910 Debussy met a Mr Blumenberg to discuss a projected trip to the United States, which he seemed to be looking forward to very much. At the end of the same month the *Trois Ballades de François Villon* were finished. According to Suarès, 'What Villon proclaimed, Debussy, perhaps unconsciously, has made plainly heard. His harmony expressed not only four centuries of music, but four hundred years of amatory culture.'[16]

The summer of 1910 was a bitter one. There was no holiday, as the lack of money was too serious and the creditors were pressing. His father was gravely ill. He experienced one day of relaxation at Laloy's house in Bellevue, where he met Stravinsky.

[16] A. Suarès, in *ReM*, May 1930, Pensée XLV.

He resumed his dialogue with Roderick Usher that had been so frequently interrupted, but this House of Usher was too gloomy under the August sky, and it intensified his deep discouragement. He revealed it to Laloy in a letter of 24 August 1910: 'I am in a hateful mood and rebellious at the thought of any kind of pleasure, except that of destroying myself each day a little bit more. . . . It is not entirely my fault, but I am quite unhappy. There is indeed a little of the Usher family . . .' (*RdM*, 1962, p. 38).

By 13 September his spirits had recovered somewhat, as he informed Durand: 'Music, after some days of nothingness, seems to want to be more lenient with me' (1927, p. 91). Then they plummeted again. On 25 September he wrote again to his publisher: 'As for me, I am in a restless period . . . I have, at the same time, the desire to go away, no matter where, and a fear of setting out' (1927, p. 92). At this time Debussy's financial problems were extreme. 'It was timely,' he wrote to Durand, who had just advanced him some money. Both Debussy and Emma were prodigal, having the habit of living beyond their means. Then he suffered a great loss; after prolonged suffering, his father died, on 28 October, without having regained consciousness.

A little later, the dancer Maud Allan commissioned a ballet, *Khamma*, from Debussy. He sketched it unenthusiastically. On 28 November he left his two 'dear ones' to travel to Vienna and Budapest. In Vienna he received a letter from Gabriele d'Annunzio, who proposed to him that they collaborate upon a 'mystery that [I] have long been thinking about'. He accepted with 'a sort of fever', but he wrote to his wife on 3 December: 'To me this tale says nothing worthwhile' (1980, p. 199). It seems strange that he did not mistrust this project from the first. On the other hand, Toulet had given up *As You Like It*; as Antoine had *Le Roi Lear*. *Siddhartha* was only a sketch, and *Tristan* was legally impossible. *Orphée* had not gone further than the stage of preliminary discussions, and *Oresteia* existed only as a name. The ballet Diaghilev intended for Nijinsky and Karsavina had been dropped. As for *Le Diable dans le beffroi* and *La Chute de la Maison Usher*, they were dragging along. And of *Le Marchand de rêves*, *Le Chat botté*, and *Huon de Bordeaux*, considered with Mourey in 1909, only the titles are known. This newest project, *Khamma*, was another ballet for another dancer. In this mishmash of projects, there were both Shakespeare and Buddha, a tale of chivalry, mythology, Greek tragedy, the Russo-Venetian scenario, Perrault's fairy tales, a chanson de geste, an American devil, and, more recently, a Canadian dancer attending the chief god of the Egyptians. Now, finally, there was a Mediterranean saint, conceived by an Italian for a Russian dancer.

Debussy's dilemma probably lies in this list. After *Pelléas* he had not found a satisfactory poet, nor, above all, a poetic text. He did not find them because he was seeking simultaneously to renew the subject matter of lyric drama and to renew himself. He had asked the painter Jacques-Émile Blanche for the plot of 'a galactic drama', beyond human passions; he wanted to penetrate the virgin forests of the physical world, of the subconscious, of human mystery, progressing 'in anguish' as far as terror and horror. Edgar Allan Poe helped him with *La Chute de la Maison Usher* and *Le Diable dans le beffroi*. Although the dissonances of *La Mer* had surprised the critics, it was a stage of his journey. *Siddhartha* would have been another, if the 'prodigious dream' of Segalen had not turned out to be an 'abyss'. Because of the great range of expressive possibilities that it offered, *Tristan* had captured Debussy's imagination.

Just as these subjects offered a contrast to the ripening of *Pelléas*, intermediaries thwarted the composition of *Tristan*. This is why Debussy only half-believed in *Orphée-Roi*, in *Le Marchand de rêves*, in *Le Chat botté*, in *Huon de Bordeaux*, in the *Oresteia* of Aeschylus. This is why he returned seriously in 1909 to *La Chute de la Maison Usher*,* serving as his own librettist. He completed without outside help the scenario for *Masques et bergamasques*. In any event, it must be said that Debussy had neither a sufficiently assured style nor the experience in the theatre to write an adequate libretto or scenario for musical setting. He abandoned *Masques et bergamasques* without music, and he laboured over the two tales of Poe. He had the grace to confess to Godet, on 6 February 1911, that he was not sorry to postpone until later 'the two tales of Poe ... because of many accents that do not please me any longer, and of an arrangement of scenes that is inadequate' (1980, pp. 204–5). It was his own text that did not please him. But he did not want, at any cost, a third party between himself and Poe. The squabbles that he had had with Maeterlinck and Artus encouraged him to keep for himself all stages of the two short operas he had upon his desk, and of which he planned to retain his rights

---

* [In the summer of 1908 Giulio Gatti-Casazza, on the eve of assuming directorship of the Metropolitan Opera in New York, went to Paris.

> I paid a visit to Debussy to pay my respects to him and to find out whether he had anything ready or in his mind. The composer received me in a very friendly manner and told me that he was really considering three compositions: *The Legend of Tristan*, *The Devil in the Belfry*, and *The Fall of the House of Usher*, the last based on the story by Edgar Allan Poe. But it was impossible for him to say when any one of these works would be ready for the theatre.... We agreed on a very small advance. (G. Gatti-Casazza, *Memories of the Opera* (New York, 1941), 157),

Surely, Gatti's visit of 1908 was no small factor in Debussy's working upon *La Chute* during the summer of 1909.]

as librettist, thereby earning a double fee. Tired of groping and urged on by Emma, he felt forced to consult with d'Annunzio, and so he allowed himself to slip into his florid wake and be given a deadline for a work of some compass: *Le Martyre de Saint Sébastien*. But he accepted *Khamma* first, and he did not conceal that it was 'for reasons of money needed at home'; later he gave up both Maud Allan and Edgar Allan Poe in order to work on Saint Sebastian.

Perhaps his idleness delayed his choice of the new subject and hindered the composition of the works in progress. This is the impression given by the 'statements' he made in June 1908 to Gatti-Casazza, director of the Metropolitan Opera, as reported by Vallas: 'Do not forget that I am a lazy composer . . .' And, later: 'What is dominant in me is not talent; it is uncertainty and idleness. I am getting old and more idle than ever.'[17]*

It would be a grave error to believe these remarks; on the contrary, Debussy gave proof of an 'energy that was deeply stoical', as Edward Lockspeiser has remarked perceptively (1957*a*, p. 25). For it was hard for him to be saddled with financial worries and to be unable, for reasons of artistic scruple, to write music 'for food', though this money would have relieved these worries; to have to accept commissions against his better judgement which he left unfinished or which, if he completed them, made small sums; to feel himself being pressed by his publisher; to have to travel to conduct his compositions; to hold his ground against the critics, and to fight the first inroads of his disease. It was a struggle worthy of Corneille that trapped this great artist, and it makes us appreciate him even more.

Of the Debussy of this period, André Suarès has drawn this excellent sketch:

I did not know him and never spoke to him, yet I heard his voice. It was a little veiled, very musical. It had something of a muted viola about it. The accursed shyness that made it difficult for me to approach men, and which comes from them more than from me, prevented me from getting to know him any better, and when the desire for it seized me, it was too late. . . .

I knew that Debussy had an opinion of my work that would have permitted me to tell him all the value that I had found in his. But he was then upon his bed of pain, and I did not dare to approach him in that condition.

. . . I see you as I saw you one single time, against a prop in the wings of the

[17] Vallas, *Claude Debussy et son temps*, p. 366.

---

* [Gatti's memories of Debussy's remarks differ somewhat. The opera director remembered him saying something to this effect: 'It is a bad piece of business you are doing. I have some remorse in taking these few dollars. Yes, because I do not believe that I will ever finish any part of this. I write for myself alone, and do not trouble myself at all about the impatience of others' (Gatti-Casazza, *Memories of Opera*, p. 157).]

theatre.... Some people were speaking to you, some friends no doubt. Perhaps you could not believe nor agree with all they wanted to say. They were talking to you, that is why I remained silent. I would have had to speak my name. I already imagined the eyes and the expressions of these enemies. Since then, they have all remained so, with one exception, Henri de Régnier, so polite, so friendly, and so free of all malevolence.

... You had a distracted manner and one entirely absorbed in a single emotion, at the same time thoughtful and sensual, sad and kind. Outwardly you seemed to be involved in all that surrounded you, but your true presence was a thousand leagues away, in some hidden depth. There was nothing ascetic about you, nor of a man who escapes from the world, but much of one who is a stranger there ...[18]

[18] Unpublished notes, written between 1910 and 1914 (collection of Mme Suarès [in 1962]).

19

The High Season

———◆———

No matter what one might have said, Debussy had no enthusiasm for Gabriele d'Annunzio's *Le Martyre de Saint Sébastien.* We have seen that he was suspicious of it before he became acquainted with it, and he had accepted it without having read a line of it, carried away by the poet 'who is a sort of irresistible whirlwind' (1957*a*, p. 50), and anxious to be involved at last in a collaboration that seemed serious with a composition that could be performed. He agreed to write it, on 10 December 1910, also because he was, as always, short of funds. He justified himself to Caplet on 14 February 1911:

first of all, it is worth the trouble of racking one's brains for it; then, again, perhaps I still have time to indulge in a folly, even indeed . . . to make a mistake. Among my good little friends whom you know, some have paid me the honour of laying bets on my small chance of succeeding with such a dangerous undertaking. (1957*a*, p. 51)

Eight days earlier he had notified Godet: 'It is much more sumptuous than the poor little Anglo-Egyptian ballet. Needless to say, the cult of Adonis is combined with that of Jesus: a very beautiful notion in my opinion . . .' (1942, p. 126).

It was probably fortunate that the poet had not yet written anything when Debussy gave his consent. The finished work turned out to be almost unreadable. What came to irritate Debussy was the spectacle itself. Conceived for a star dancer, it struck him as more like a virtuoso showpiece than a religious drama. It is remarkable that Debussy, completely irreligious as he was—and perhaps for that reason—was embarrassed by the thought of an Ida Rubinstein, in her tights, twirling on her toes, expressing the highest aspiration of faith and the suffering of the martyr.* His uneasiness appears in two letters. The first was to Emma, written on 3 December 1910: 'I will acquire the reputation of making a speciality of female dancers' (1957*b*, p. 89), the dancers in question were

* [Dietschy gives an erroneous impression here. Rubinstein was not a conventional Russian ballerina, but rather a rich amateur with considerable technical limitations, a dancer whose beauty and mimetic gifts were well received in works which were especially designed to capitalize on her strengths and minimize her weaknesses.]

Maud Allan, who commissioned *Khamma*, directly followed by Ida Rubinstein and *Le Martyre*. His second letter was addressed to Caplet: 'I have put by Monsieur E.-A. Poe's strange tales for the whirling legs of some of the most notorious dancers of our times...' (1957a, p. 50), this letter, dated 14 February 1911, was written when he was hard at work on the third act and had just received the first.

One should not be misled by Debussy's ironical flattery to d'Annunzio—as when he wrote to him, on 29 January 1911: 'What do you expect me to do when I am confronted with the rush of beauty in your double* and parallel *envoi*...' (1948, p. 64), or when he complimented d'Annunzio on 19 June on the publication of *Le Martyre*: 'What a beautiful book! and what a beautiful work, truly!' (1948, p. 77).

Coming from a man who knew so well how to turn compliments, that was an insipid one, quite neutral for a work that had enchanted Debussy! Once the drama had been admitted in principle, Debussy saw the artifice in it and retained only what was essential, and it is because of the music that *Le Martyre de Saint Sébastien* still survives. The poet was right when he wrote to the composer in March or April 1911: 'You are enclosed within your eagerness and within your dream' (1948, p. 71).

The first act reached Debussy on 9 January 1911, and he threw himself into it headlong. Three days later he wrote to Durand 'I am working like a Trojan.' On 14 February, to Caplet: 'I have very little time in which to write a great deal of music. You know how much I love that!' Then he goes on to reveal his fear of not being able to complete his score by the deadline: 'Therefore I cannot hesitate for one minute to make a choice. In mining coal, they refer to one type as the "unscreened". That describes my position, to a T' (1957a, p. 51).

Returning from Boston,† Caplet was able to lend him a ready hand with the orchestration; without his help, it is possible that *Le Martyre* would not have been completed in time. All this while, Debussy was also involved with other obligations relating to his music. Jane Bathori gave the première of *Le Promenoir des deux amants* on 14 January 1911, accompanied by Viñes. Two days later, Paul Mimart played the first public performance of the *Première Rapsodie* for clarinet. The same day Marguerite Babaïan, accompanied by A. Delacroix, introduced the *Trois Ballades de François Villon*,‡ and on 11 March Ennemond Trillat performed

---

* ['Double' because the text was in both French and Italian.]

† [Caplet had been engaged by the Boston Opera Company; there, he conducted a staged version of *L'Enfant prodigue* (first given, 16 Nov. 1910), and *Pelléas* (starting 10 Jan. 1912), when Georgette Leblanc sang Mélisande; and, on 30 Mar. 1912, a single performance of *Le Martyre*.]

‡ [Information supplied by Christian Goubault.]

a similar service for the *Hommage à Haydn*. The Opéra-Comique revived *Pelléas*.* Debussy himself, on 5 March 1911, had conducted the orchestral version of the *Trois Ballades de François Villon*, and he played four of the *Préludes*, Book I, on the 29th of that month.[1]

And besides, on a cold day at the end of March, one blurred by snow-flakes, he was at the podium to conduct the *Children's Corner*, the orchestration of that work being principally by Caplet, who had been asked and had agreed to help out with it. On 21 November 1910 Debussy had been uneasy about it: 'so sumptuously dressed. I even wonder if it [*Children's Corner*] will know how to behave in this new guise. And I would be sorry if it seemed pretentious like that . . .' (1957a, p. 49).

In April 1911 he finished in succession two parts of *Le Martyre*: one, a short prelude, which he referred to as 'The Vestibule of Paradise'; the other, 'The Lamentation of Saint Sebastian'. 'I can do no more . . .' he informed his publisher Durand. As it had been with *Pelléas*, however, it was at this point that the troubles began. At first, as Arthur Honegger has reported, 'the requirements of the sets brutally imposed a premature final chord to a composition that asked only time to work itself out'.[2] In April or May 1911 Debussy himself wrote to the impresario Gabriel Astruc: 'There are some more serious things which must not happen again at any cost—among others, an unsatisfactory relationship between stage and music' (1980, p. 208).

Six days before the première was to take place, the Archbishop of Paris denounced the work as sacrilegious. He enjoined Catholics 'to refrain from attending performances which would be offensive to their Christian consciences' and which caused the placing 'on stage and the demeaning, under the most improper circumstances, of the story of one of our most glorious martyrs'.[3] Then, on the morning of the dress rehearsal, an accident cost the life of the Minister of War at a flying field at Issy, where

[1] Notably 'Le vent dans la plaine' and 'Minstrels' (which was encored). 'The composer was also the performer, and his forthright and delicate playing may rightly be praised; he was given a loud and surpassingly long ovation' (*Le Ménestrel*).

[He also played 'Les sons et les parfums tournent dans l'air du soir' and 'Des pas sur la neige'.]

[2] A. Honegger, *Incantations aux fossiles* (Lausanne, 1948), 90.

[3] Disapproving of the fact that the archiepiscopal ban had been decreed in ignorance of d'Annunzio's text, A. Mangeot in *Le Monde musical* (30 May 1911) did not hesitate to write: 'Thus to an act of sublime faith does a Prince of the church answer with an act of bad faith.' Camille Bellaigue, however, submitted to the ban.

* [This revival took place on 18 Feb. 1911, at which time Marguerite Carré, the wife of the director of the Opéra-Comique, sang Mélisande, a role she made her exclusive property for the next decade.]

forty years earlier Captain de Bussy had tempted fate in 'a just war'. On this same day, 21 May, André Suarès sent d'Annunzio these fulsome words: 'May the noble roses of France be enwreathed this evening with your Roman laurel. And may the heart of Paris, dear Gabriel d'Annunzio, refurbish tonight your Latin fame!'

Suarès, however, foresaw failure and wrote on the same day to Latil, his intimate friend: 'D'Annunzio is running towards disaster. He has, moreover, dragged Debussy in his wake . . .' It was not a disaster, but rather a failure, a failure to the extent that the stagework would hardly ever be given again in its original form. It foiled all the hopes it had aroused and made all the work that it had required count for little. If the theatre at the first performance was filled, it was due to 'the princess of poses', Ida Rubinstein. Yet, in its way it was perhaps a glorious failure. Nor should one neglect to acknowledge d'Annunzio's role in having inspired music of such humble and touching mysticism. He gave Debussy an artistic experience of great innocence, as Émile Vuillermoz reported:

One May morning . . . a performance in Italian was organized. . . . This rendition was of unequalled quality. Debussy himself, who was to a great degree reserved in his feelings, could not maintain his usual attitude of ironical goodwill and, quite simply, he wept. That was undoubtedly a unique moment in his life as an artist . . .' (ReM, 1 Dec. 1920, pp. 156–57)

Le Martyre de Saint Sébastien bears the weight of the basic principle of d'Annunzio's aesthetic: vulgar lyricism, that is to say, perceptible inadequacy. It suffers from its ornately manufactured text and from its ambiguous relationship with dancing. Debussy's music is too true, too pure, too deeply felt not to be distorted to some extent by dancing. 'Twirling legs' are never able to express more than superficial feelings. Nothing prevails against this axiom: the highest sacrament enforces silence and immobility. In the secular order, as Debussy himself expressed it, 'A true impression of beauty can have no other effect than silence.'

In all of d'Annunzio's text it would be difficult to find anything comparable to the uneasy sense of mystery evoked by the touching lament, three times sounded by the cor anglais, in the Prelude to 'Le Laurier blessé'. This simple phrase reveals the intensity of Debussy's emotion. D'Annunzio's poor judgement and superficiality are revealed by his having chosen a religious subject for a dancer.[4]

Undoubtedly, the staging emphasized the rhetorical exaggeration of

---

[4] It should be rembered that d'Annunzio, penniless, laden with debts in Italy, was forced to earn his livelihood. He yielded to the taste of the day which he had helped form, and for that he should not be too harshly judged.

the spectacle. It relegated the music to a secondary plane, and rightly so, as far as the text goes, and perhaps even—in its way—as far as the music goes, which was too unassuming, too sincere for this showy context. It should not be forgotten, moreover, that the movements of the crowd had been conceived by the poet himself, who was not a little proud of them, for d'Annunzio was a captain in the theatre as well as one in the Italian army. On 14 February 1911 he pointed out to Astruc, as though he were offering him a favour, that 'in the four acts, the crowd has a major role' (1948, p. 68).

For d'Annunzio it was the crowd that mattered. His letters to Astruc speak of 'the grandoise, the bronze, the ebony, the bodily rhythm, the eloquent bodies, the extraordinary masks', all to exalt the poet rather than the high purpose of Sebastian. But he was too perceptive not to have felt straight away that for Debussy, on the other hand, the saint was the essential. In his letters to the composer, d'Annunzio almost succeeds in convincing us that he feels as profoundly as his collaborator. He might just have been sincere.

Le Martyre de Saint Sébastien was not so much a failure as a mistake, one that Debussy foresaw and feared from the start. It was a mistake because of the fundamental dissonance that exposes music that is too delicate to blend with the poet's paste jewellery. Debussy recognized it quite promptly,[5] but he admitted it openly only two years later, in his letter of 12 June 1913 to d'Annunzio. It was in fact an aesthetic judgement that he addressed to the poet with regard to *La Pisanelle**—and the poet accepted the reproof in silence.

You adopt, if I dare put it like this, a style that is too beautiful for the speech of actors and for the ears of the audience, a condition that the garish confusion of the settings renders even more disordered. In my opinion, it is precisely the style that must not be adopted.

Why is there so much to confuse the eyes when the ears have so much to get hold of? For several years now we have submitted to those influences in which the North combines with Byzantium in such a way as to stifle our Latin genius, which depends upon grace and clarity. (1948, p. 86)

It could be said that Claude Debussy's martyrdom began with *Le Martyre de Saint Sébastien*. The lack of success registered by the lavish spectacle had secretly wounded him. His financial woes were terrible and

---

[5] The poet as well, moreover: 'M. d'Annunzio . . . busies himself at this time, it seems, in reducing the proportions of [*Le Martyre*] and in converting it into a true lyric drama . . .' (*Le Ménestrel*, 24 June 1911).

* [*La Pisanelle*, a ballet, with plot by d'Annunzio, settings by Léon Bakst, and a musical score arranged by Ildebrando Pizzetti, was another vehicle for Ida Rubinstein.]

incurable.[6] Further, his illness, without anyone being aware of it, had taken hold. He wrote to Durand, on 13 July 1911: '*Le Martyre de Saint Sébastien* has tired me more than I myself would have believed ...' (1927, p. 97).

He was exasperated by the routine of holidays: the hotel, the food, the anonymous summer guests, the necessity of dressing properly, the communal beach. Nothing reminded him of his youth. He suffered from all this, as he confessed to Durand: 'How right you are, dear friend, to love your own house ... Everything is so provisional in life that only the charm of the house that saw you play as a child and dream as a youth should be something special, and at my age, in my melancholy, I feel the lack of it' (1927, pp. 97–8).

He also wrote to Caplet on 31 July 1911, the day before he was to leave on holiday. 'The thought of moving and renting somewhere for the summer fills me with horror—a little house in a large park, where one has been frightened as a child, that is what I need ...' (1957a, p. 54).

Perhaps he was thinking of the park in *The Fall of the House of Usher*, on the edge of 'a black and lurid tarn', where huge dark clouds passed. He had to go, if only for Mme Debussy and Chouchou. They went to Houlgate, staying in a room in the rotunda of the hotel that faced the sea. There was Chouchou, noisy, sun-tanned 'like the bronze statue of Marshal Ney'.[7] On 11 August 1911 he wrote to Durand: 'I can hardly wait for the moment when we settle back in our little house, which is so peaceful and, at the same time, so tumultuous ...' (1927, p. 100).

He finally returned home on 31 August full of regret for the holiday which had not been one at all—as shown in his letter of 6 September to Durand:

Leaving a scene that was too crowded and too observed, we discovered the Norman countryside ... houses with gardens leading down to the sea, full of flowers and genuine trees; nobody about, no casinos on the horizon ... To think that people fortunate enough to own a house in this sort of Paradise cannot wait to leave it to go looking for the international tumult of Trouville! Sad! Sad! (1927, p. 102)[8]

There is something touching and foreboding about this search for, this need of, a house especially in the light of his physical condition. The most

---

[6] He did not hesitate to offer 6,000 fr. in interest to someone [possibly Jean Marnold] who could lend him out of hand 20,000 fr. repayable 'at the end of the month of July 1912', [adding, 'My wife and I naturally will sign the note'] (*RdM*, 1962, p. 39).

[7] A postcard from Debussy to his mother, dated 1 Aug. 1911.

[8] A quarter of a century earlier, Debussy, speaking of the seashore when he saw it at Fiumicino, wrote to M. Vasnier (August 1885): 'The world and the casinos were lacking, obviously, but that is why I loved it' (*ReM*, 1 May 1926, p. 30).

productive holiday that he would spend would be that of 1915, when he stayed in a private house: the villa 'Mon Coin' at Pourville. There would be a fine harvest then, his last.

In its issue of 26 August 1911, *Le Ménestrel* had announced that Debussy would edit Rameau's *Pygmalion*, and, on 14 October of that year, the same journal discussed the repertoire of the Opéra-Comique for the current season, adding: 'Then will come, in a sequence still to be settled, other unpublished works, among them *La Chute de la Maison Usher* and *Le Diable dans le beffroi* of M. Claude Debussy.' There was also the strong possibility of a trip to Boston, where he had been asked to conduct *Pelléas*, but nothing came of it. He was very unhappy about it, above all at not being able to go.* He said so to Caplet in a letter of 22 December 1911: 'You can well believe that I have not told anyone what it cost me to give up the trip to America ... (1957*a*, p. 57).† And to Godet he admitted on 18 December 1911: 'Sometimes I am so miserably alone ... it could not be otherwise, however; and it is not the first time. Chouchou's smile helps a lot to get me through certain dark moments ...' (1942, p. 130).

The world was full of upsetting events during the years 1912 and 1913. Almost everywhere there was unrest, rearmament, mobilization, warfare. The summers were overwhelming. Paris was like an old queen intoxicated by her own party, and Debussy reacted to it in a letter to Godet, dated 9 June 1913: 'This is the moment they call "The High Season". You have no idea how this increases the crowd of fools one has the habit of meeting here. These people, not content to flay the French language, import their own aesthetics, which they believe to be novel and which already smell of death' (1980, p. 239).

Poor Debussy! The times of massive theatrical projects had passed, and the current period hardly allowed for them. Since 1909 Paris had been invaded by strangers of every type. Choreography was much in fashion then; there was constant talk of ballets, of galas, of *divertissements*. Even Toulet was thinking about a Persian ballet. Under the burden of financial necessity, Debussy had to come to terms with these 'master-builders of spectacles'.[9] He went back to the idea of *Khamma*. He

---

[9] Debussy numbered Lully among these. 'This old rogue of a Lully, who was more a shrewd master-builder of spectacles than a real musician.'

* [Apparently, Emma refused to let him go without her. Debussy's reaction to the 'arguments' appears in his letter to Caplet of Oct. 1911: 'In short, I am extremely demoralized' (1957*a*, p. 59).]

† [A letter dated 22 Oct. 1911 from Debussy to Henry Russell, impresario at Boston, explains this reference. Debussy wrote: 'I must definitely renounce going to Boston ... I make this decision, you may be certain, only with regret and because of family reasons serious enough that I could not consider going' (1957*a*, p. 75).]

compromised his precious *Prélude à 'L'Après-midi d'un faune'*.[10] And then, during a three-week period in the late summer of 1912, he composed his long neglected masterpiece, *Jeux*, and orchestrated it the following year.* He had written to Durand, on 13 January 1912: 'Personally, I am feverishly trying to find all my shortcomings, and am anxious to finish anything at all at any price' (1927, p. 107).

After *Jeux*, he completed, on 10 October 1912, the unfortunate 'Gigues', which he had begun in 1909. The same thirst to finish work made him conclude the second book of *Préludes* in December 1912, with 'La Terrasse des audiences du clair de lune'.

The November issue of *Musica* had announced a *Crimen amoris* in three scenes, by Debussy and Charles Morice, the first plan for a ballet based on a subject from Verlaine, which would be taken up again later, but without any notable result. The Opéra-Comique celebrated the hundredth performance of *Pelléas* on 27 December 1912.† Since 30 April 1902 it has been given at a rate of approximately nine times a year. A hundred guests were invited to this festive occasion, notably Paul Dukas, Xavier Leroux, Florent Schmitt, and the Under-secretary of State for the Fine Arts—who honoured Debussy with 'a lively talk', but left the rosette of the Legion of Honour in the shadows. If Sylvain Bonmariage is to be believed, Debussy had seen Pierre Louÿs again in May 1912 at Mme de Givré's. 'Spring held sway over Paris. Tea was taken in the garden, in a sort of magical closeness.' The conversation had come round to music critics, and Debussy, idly chatting, had been moved to observe:

Reyer, who knew what music is, became a self-appointed music critic. It was enough for him to be admitted to the pages of the *Débats* to write nonsense for it and to impose his opinions. Pierre Lalo, whom Toulet and I like so much, avoids criticism by saying interesting things about musical works, but he is only a scholar. A critic! I see only one of them, the only one which a musician can pay

---

[10] 'It was almost against his will that Debussy granted the authorization to use his music' (S. Lifar, *Histoire du Ballet Russe* (Paris, 1950), 213).
[The ballet, *L'Après-midi d'un faune*, was first performed at the Châtelet, 29 May 1912, with scenery and costumes by Bakst; the choreography was by Vaslav Nijinsky, who also danced the role of the Faun.]

* [*Jeux*, a one-act ballet on a contemporary theme, a tennis game, was first performed by Diaghilev's troupe at the Théâtre des Champs-Elysées, 15 May 1913, with scenery and costumes by Bakst, the choreography by Nijinsky. It was dropped after only a few performances, but it has been subsequently revived by other ballet companies. The score has entered the concert repertoire.]

† [This is the date given by Dietschy, but miscountings were not unknown at the Opéra-Comique. S. Wolff, in *Un demi-siècle d'Opéra-Comique: 1900–1950* (Paris, 1953), gives 28 Jan. 1913 as the actual date of the hundredth performance of *Pelléas*.]

attention to. That is Willy. He knows nothing of music. He does not know what a semi-quaver is, but he understands a composition and, if it is worth the trouble, is able to make it important.[11]

On 12 January 1913 he admitted to Godet: 'I am haunted by the merely average, and I am afraid.' He was much affected as well by Toulet's moving away from Paris, writing to him on 18 January: 'I am not yet accustomed to this departure of yours, which resembles a flight from everything, and everybody. I have never told you what hurt feelings it seemed to hide, what injured sensibility...' (1929, pp. 78–9).[12]

In June 1913 he agreed to collaborate with André Hellé to supply the music for a children's ballet. He turned to his daughter and asked about her dolls. He dipped into Chouchou's toy box to write this delightful, Dickensian *La Boîte à joujoux*, which is hardly ever performed and is irresistible as an orchestral suite. He finished the piano score of it in October 1913,* and in July he completed his last collection of songs: the *Trois Poèmes de Stéphane Mallarmé*. He never stopped thinking about the theatre. Georges de Feure suggested two texts to him. The first was *Le Palais du silence*, which would have its title changed to *No-ja-li*, but it never took on musical substance. The other was a scenario derived from Verlaine's *Fêtes galantes*, but here, as with *L'Histoire de Tristan*, a third party intervened, claiming priority. This was Charles Morice, whom Debussy mockingly referred to as Maurice-Oblat, and this ballet vanished like water down the drain.[13]

[11] S. Bonmariage, *Catherine et ses amis* (Gap, 1949), 162–3. It is possible to credit these remarks as very plausible, being in the vein of Monsieur Croche. Rereading the criticisms of Willy, one must agree that, in the main, Debussy was right: 'Monsieur, I do not like specialists. In my opinion, to specialize is to limit one's universe by that much...' (C. Debussy, *Monsieur Croche Antidilettante* (3rd edn., Paris, 1950), 13).

[12] It is odd to read Toulet's letters to Debussy, written after 1913, that is to say, after his 'flight'. Having withdrawn from the superficial life that he led in Paris, Toulet seemed all at once to have become aware of Debussy's greatness, though maintaining his habitual bantering tone.

[13] Of all the projects on which Debussy and Gabriel Mourey had hoped to collaborate, from 1907 on, only one single page survives, a truly delightful one, for flute, written as part of *Psyché*, but now called *Syrinx*.

---

* [Debussy began orchestrating *La Boîte à joujoux* in the spring of 1914, and on 1 Nov. 1917, in his last letter to Durand, he described the orchestration as almost finished (1927, p. 190). It was completed after Debussy's death by Caplet.]

20

'Recueillement'

———◆———

DEBUSSY's musical life continued its course. His financial problems remained as acute as ever. At the end of 1912 Debussy had agreed to contribute to the musical journal *S.I.M.* as a critic. In 1913 he had an interview with a mutual aid society formed the preceding year, entitled the Avenir du Prolétariat, to which, according to Vallas, he had given over his author's rights. What was he not obliged to do to sustain his standard of living?[1]

His travels began again. His itinerary included Moscow at the end of 1913, Rome and The Hague in February 1914, and Brussels in April 1914. These unsettling journeys wore him down but were intended 'to earn fees that did not amount to much'. He was, however, very disappointed not to be able to return to London. 'There go 5,000 francs fallen into the Channel,' he wrote to Caplet, on 3 June 1913 (1957*a*, p. 65). And to Toulet, on 18 August 1913: 'I am bored with not knowing where to put myself, sick, as well as many other things besides, and these things are as miserable as they are burdensome . . .' (1929, p. 81).

At Moscow he was as unhappy as a lost child. He unburdened his heart to Emma, on 4 December 1913:

We have dinner. There are two bottles of Evian just like we have. It is stupid, but that makes me want to cry . . . I see your dear face on the station platform, your lovely eyes filled with tears and that last kiss your hands sent me (that really hurts badly). . . . This trip *which should help us out* . . . it must perhaps be considered like a sort of treatment prescribed by life for our love, from which it will emerge, not more beautiful, for that would be to misjudge it, but adorned with that 'patina' that testifies to one's having suffered for the thing that one loves best in the world. (1957*b*, pp. 102–5)

---

[1] In a letter dated 25 Nov. 1913 to a certain M. Bertault, he referred to his financial problems in these terms:

I was coming back from the A. du P. [Avenir du Prolétariat], and I saw B. It was not a good thing. His greeting was evasive and he hid himself behind the 'committee'. Moreover, he placed my letter on the desk of 'the man whom you know' . . . that seems unpropitious to me and what is to become of us in such hands? . . . (formerly in the collection of P. Vallery-Radot).

['Recueillement', *Cinq Poèmes de Charles Baudelaire*, No. 4.]

He was frantically uneasy when he had no news of her for two days. Of the trip to The Hague and Amsterdam, between 28 February and 2 March 1914, Gustave Doret reports:

While he played the three *Préludes* on the piano, I received the sad impression of the physical discomfort that he sought to control . . . We scoured the stores to find the prettiest Dutch dolls for his dear daughter Chouchou. I was very struck by his depressed manner, by his indecision, and by his almost childlike distress when the time came to take leave of one another on the station platform . . .[2]

In 1914 more works were added to Debussy's catalogue: some transcriptions for violin and piano, studied with the violinist Arthur Hartmann: 'La Fille aux cheveux de lin', 'Minstrels', and 'Il pleure dans mon cœur'; the orchestral sketch of *La Boîte à joujoux*; the completion of the *Six Épigraphes antiques* for piano four-hands (four of them derived from a score written in 1900, *Incidental music for Les Chansons de Bilitis*); and, in November, the *Berceuse heroïque* for piano. At the beginning of February the publisher Dorbon had fruitlessly sought permission to print *Monsieur Croche antidilettante*. Debussy was in no mood to see the 'formless proof-sheets' of the texts of his musical criticism again. He asked Laloy to spare him an hour, nevertheless, so that they could determine how Monsieur Croche would die. Gradually, as the months passed, his pain wore him down.

The wind rose to a tempest the day that Mme Caillaux killed the director of *Le Figaro*. On 15 June a terrifying storm burst over the Ile-de-France; and on 28 June the assassinations at Sarajevo occurred. These threats hanging over Parisian heads weighed upon Debussy, as he wrote to Godet on 14 July 1914: 'For four and a half months I have been able to accomplish nothing! Naturally these things lead to miserable family squabbles, to hours when one thinks of little else but suicide as the way out. For a long time now, I must admit, I have been lost, I have felt myself frightfully impaired' (1942, p. 141).

Debussy considered, however, a project with d'Annunzio. The subject of this third drama is unknown, but it went down the drain because the poet demanded a subsidy twice that which the composer had suggested for them both.*

Debussy's last professional trip was one to London, undertaken on 16 July 1914, where he gave a concert at Sir Edgar Speyer's home on the 17th. Upon his return, having congratulated Widor (on 23 July) upon his nomination as permanent secretary of the Académie des Beaux-Arts, he

---

[2] Paraphrased from G. Doret, *Temps et contretemps* (Fribourg, 1942), 192.

* [For speculation about this project see Orledge, *Debussy and the Theatre*, p. 277.]

received from the candidate an urgent request to join him. Widor wrote: 'I would be very flattered to serve as your sponsor to the Académie and have you as my successor—with an exemption for making a speech in my praise—you will be received there with open arms. Come to see me, tomorrow if possible . . .'[3]

'Open arms' poses a question. Widor and Fauré, doubtless, would have received Debussy so, Charpentier and Paladilhe perhaps, but certainly not Saint-Saëns and Théodore Dubois. 'The next day I received his visit and his acceptance,' Widor reported, and he went on to suggest tactfully that the war delayed Debussy's joining the Académie,* but Saint-Saëns was unshakeable in his opposition.[4]

From then on, as the summer heat rose, so did the political temperature. 'Paris is becoming more and more hateful to me, and I would like to be able to get away a little. Literally, I cannot endure any more,' Debussy wrote to Durand on 29 July 1914 (1927, p. 122). Then death showed itself in all its hideousness. Juarès was assassinated on 31 July. The war was imminent on 1 August, determined on the 2nd, and it broke out on the 3rd. The Germans invaded France. It was all a terrible shock to Debussy. 'I am nothing more than a poor man whirled like an atom by this frightful cataclysm. What I am doing seems so wretchedly petty to me,' he wrote to Durand on 8 August 1914 (1927, p. 124). Upon the advice of Arthur Fontaine, he took refuge at Angers to escape the threat of an attack by German planes. It was a short but taxing exile. On 21 September 1914 he described his feelings to Durand, speaking of 'two months during which I have not written one note nor touched a piano. It is unimportant I know very well, considering the events, but I cannot stop myself from thinking about it sadly . . . at my age, time lost is time lost forever' (1927, p. 126).

Yet he told his publisher: 'If you have some work to have done, I beg you to think of me.' And in January 1915 Durand entrusted him with the editing of Chopin's piano works. Chopin invigorated Debussy, causing him to move the war back from the foreground of his concerns, and to summon up the slightly melancholy but consoling countenance of Music.

The last flowering of Debussy's creativity occurred in 1915. A whole range of moods bloom in the works of that year: *En blanc et noir*, the Sonata for cello and piano, the Sonata for flute, viola, and harp, the

---

[3] Widor, *Fondations: Portraits de Massenet à Paladilhe*, p. 6. Widor's election as secretary left his chair in the music section empty.

[4] Two bits of evidence show this. The painting section proposed Debussy's election on 24 Nov. 1917. Mme Debussy reminded Widor in early Mar. 1918 that he had proposed her husband four years earlier.

Douze Études, and the *Noël des enfants qui n'ont plus de maisons*.* He also made his last additions to the manuscript of *La Chute de la Maison Usher* and sketched the *Ode à la France*, to a text by Laloy. The year had begun with the sorrow of his mother's death on 23 March, and Emma's mother also died that year. On 30 June 1915 he wrote to Durand: 'Without saying anything about it, I have suffered much from the long drought forced upon my brain by the war. In short, I would like to get away as soon as possible. The house has weighed heavily on my shoulders for a long time' (1927, p. 134).

At last he was able to escape from Paris on 12 July and went to Pourville, near Dieppe, and there he stayed for three months in the villa 'Mon Coin', where he felt himself at home, peaceful, with the pleasure of a garden which 'does not have the proud formality of a garden designed by Le Nôtre...'† and from which he could gaze at 'the expanse of the sea'.[5]

He had not been there two weeks before he finished two of the three 'caprices' that make up *En blanc et noir*. Surely he was acquainted with Goya's *Caprices* and *The Disasters of War*. In August he also completed the Sonata for cello and piano, which is so full of masculine imagination. He endured 'the painful uneasiness of this war', and found some solace in the garden of 'Mon Coin', facing the sea. He wrote to Durand on 12 August 1915: 'The trees are good friends ... These last days I have cursed the sullen sea to the point of weeping! Today, it is so beautiful as to surpass any comparison' (1927, p. 144).

A little less than two months before the end of his holiday, he was thinking already of the heart-break of leaving. He was aghast at the rapid passage of time. His letter of 19 August 1915 to Durand gives a touching impression of Debussy, by then condemned, overcome by a disease of which he was unaware: 'The days pass with a wrenching quickness, and I no longer have time to busy myself with the garden...' (1927, p. 146).

He congratulated himself that he felt 'his creative power moving headlong. May it endure, Lord!' He continued the composition of the *Études* and of the Sonata for flute, viola, and harp. On 4 September 1916 he asked Godet if this sonata did not remind him 'of a very antique Claude Debussy, he of the *Nocturnes*, or so it seems to me' (1942, p. 158). He was afraid of coming back to Paris and 'of finding there again that factory of nothingness' which his study had become for him. He told Durand in his letter of 1 September 1915: 'If I had lots of money, I would

---

[5] The villa 'Mon Coin' belonged to the librettist Paul Milliet-Monchecourt.

* [There were also two short works for piano: *Page d'album* and *Élégie*.]
† [Le Nôtre designed the gardens at Versailles.]

buy 'Mon Coin' straight off in gratitude for having found again there the ability to think and to work' (1927, p. 149).

Emma was happy to see that his inspiration had returned, and she helped her husband with her care and belief in him. In turn, he gave her a copy of the *Études*, inscribed for the collection of 'p[etite[m[ienne]' and thanked her 'for the best of collaborations: her little ears that were conscientious and alert, her enduring kindness—her husband—Claude Debussy'. Then, on 22 August, upon a hasty sketch of the étude 'Pour les sixtes', he wrote: 'For you, Petite Mienne, this "étude", in expectation of the others and for good wishes on my birthday ... Are you not my only earthly blessing and the beauty of my spiritual life?'[6]

Beside the sea which moves without let-up, he felt the necessity of work, jealous of the freedom that his dreadful sickness seemed to take away. He wrote to Inghelbrecht on 20 September 1915, sounding as though he had already placed his foot upon the final path. 'Farewell to the countless sounds of the sea, which advise so imperiously not to lose one's time' (1980, p. 260). He finished the *Études* on 27 September 1915, and into them he had put 'much love and faith.'[7] But the days were passing, and the first fires of October lit up the countryside. He wrote to Durand on 27 September 1915: 'I feel ripe with life under the open sky among the secret trees.' He wrote to him again in early October: 'I am taking advantage of my last days of freedom, thinking of Paris as a kind of open prison ... I am writing all the music that comes to mind, like a fury, but a bit sadly, too ... Farewell to the sea, farewell to calm ... (1927, pp. 155, 157).

Farewell to life, he might have added as well, if he had known that the last work he wrote at 'Mon Coin', the Sonata for flute, viola, and harp, would be his final homage to that place. It is a beguiling composition, original, and of incomparable charm, lightened with restrained joy, but somewhat unreal as well, a bit uneasy, all of it veiled by a sincere melancholy that the choice of instruments had suggested and which yields the unmistakable declaration of Debussy, here proclaimed by a harp figure and earnestly uttered by the viola, in the deeply felt phrase at the end of the Interlude, where the musician exalts the beauty of the world and accepts the uncompromising absolute.[8]

[6] Documents published by A. Mantelli in *L'Approdo musicale* (Turin, 1959), nos. 7–8.
[7] Walter Rummel played the first performance of the *Études*, 14 Dec. 1916. In his letter dated 26 Nov. 1916 to the pianist, Debussy specified: 'You can certainly announce "first performance" for the *Études* of C. D., as long as they have not been played on Sirius or Aldebaran.'
[8] It is astonishing that Émile Vuillermoz (1957, pp. 131–2), who often gives unexpected opinions, could actually go so far as to claim that this admirable Sonata, as well as the sonatas for violin and for cello, and even the *Noël* are musically of no importance.

The letter he wrote to Durand at the beginning of October 1915 was terribly sad; in it one feels the shadow of approaching death. 'Here there are no longer curtains on the windows, and like a cat I am saddened by the sight of a trunk. The little garden of the avenue du Bois is going to seem a still smaller "little garden"!' (1927, p. 157).

He steeped himself then in *La Chute de la Maison Usher*, but 'the fateful hour of leaving draws near'. Debussy stopped working. He saturated himself with the air and the characteristic features of 'Mon Coin'; he was filled with an indescribable pleasure in living, which he associated with the Creator, whom he did not want to name. On 14 October he returned to Paris; happily the weather was fine. He confessed to Godet: '[At 'Mon Coin'] I found again the ability to think in musical terms, something that had not happened to me for a year ... Then, I wrote like a fury or like one who is doomed to die the next morning' (1942, p. 144). In fact, his illness then entered an acute phase. In November he was examined by Drs Crespel and Desjardins, who diagnosed a cancer. On 28 November 1915 he confessed to Gabriel Fauré: 'The day of the 26 has really knocked me out, and ever since I have suffered like a dog ...'

An operation was scheduled for 7 December 1915. On the 2nd he played *En blanc et noir* with Louis Aubert, from the proof-sheets at Maison Durand. And at beginning of the same month, he wrote the words and music to the touching *Noël des enfants qui n'ont plus de maisons*, which would have its first performance on 9 April 1916,* sung by a children's choir conducted by Jane Montjovet from the piano, at a concert organized by the Amitiés Franco-étrangères in the Grand Amphithéâtre at the Sorbonne.

* [Roger Nichols (*Debussy's Letters* (London, 1987, p. 312 n.) states that the first performance of the *Noël* (for solo voice and piano) was given by Mme Rollan-Mauger 'on 9 Mar. 1916 at the Casino Saint Pierre in Geneva'.]

'...cette vieille servante...'

FROM then on Debussy's life was a long Calvary, that increased his intense reserve. He wrote to his old friend Godet, on 4 January 1916: 'There are wretched reasons for my silence ... I have been sick for a long time. Not enough exercise, with the usual results, but I lived with that without wanting to stop what I was doing. Abruptly, everything worsened and then, an operation, miserable moments, painful consequences, etc....' (1942, p. 147).

On 18 January 1916 Mme Debussy informed Pasteur Vallery-Radot, then serving at the front, of her husband's illness in this way: 'He is getting along much better, but I am impatient to see him less listless and out of this bed of pain.' She sent him further word of the invalid on 25 February: 'Terrible itching, provoked by the disobedient Maître, causes real torture...' And again on 6 March: 'The itching and the burning afflict my dear patient. Only since yesterday do I find him improved. There have been dreadful days, for him particularly ... He is getting along better today, but he has become so thin and pale...'

As Debussy wrote to Gabriel Fauré on 9 January 1916: 'I am still, to my great regret, in the hands of some surgeons, physicians, and other assassins. Although they measure out the truth to me in very small doses, I am much afraid of being laid up for one more month by these deplorable events.' He told Godet, on 4 February 1916: 'I began a new treatment a little while ago. It is all surrounded by mystery, and I am recommended to have patience ... Good Lord! where will I find patience after sixty days of miscellaneous tortures?' (1942, p. 149). He wrote to Godet again on 3 March 1916: 'All in all, I am not appreciably better. This operation has released other discomforts, and the refrain of all that is always the same: "Have patience...", without knowing exactly where this patience will lead me' (1942, p. 151).

On 8 June 1916 he informed Durand: 'One asks oneself whether this

['...cette vieille servant...' comes from *Pelléas*, near the beginning of Act IV, sc. 2. The quotation, one of Arkël's lines, refers to 'death's old serving-maid'. Debussy used this phrase in his letter of 4 Sept. 1916 to Godet: 'My illness—death's old serving-maid—has chosen me as a testing ground' (1980, p. 274).]

disease is not incurable. It would be better to let me know it right away. "Then, oh, then!" (as poor Golaud says)' (1927, p. 165). A week later, there was a slight improvement: 'I am getting along better, but not enough to sing of a victory ... Will I ever recover my drive, this desire always to go further, which for me took the place of bread and wine?' (1942, p. 155).

He was able to go to Francis Planté's recital, where he saw Widor, who was 'profoundly moved by his thinness and weakness'. Debussy was well aware that his condition was grave, as his letter to Durand, dated 3 July 1916, reveals: 'If I must soon die, I hope at least that I have tried to do my duty' (1927, p. 166).

His legal problems with his first wife continued unabated. In an unpublished letter of 21 July 1916 he mentioned that he had lost his appeal and complains of being abandoned, acknowledging that an artist was certainly less appealing than a model. In August his health showed an undeniable improvement. He was able to work, to play, even to sing, but he slept little and was readily unnerved, as he told Durand in a letter of 4 September. 'What awful weather! ... The sound of the rain on the ground and on the roofs is insupportable' (1927, p. 168).

The doctors prescribed a change of scene. On 6 October 1916 he went to Le Moulleau, near Arcachon, with Emma and Chouchou. Ten days later, however, he was ready to return home. The previous year at Pourville, before his operation, he had dreaded going back to Paris. Now he wrote to Durand, on 16 October: 'I am in a hurry to get back to my old house, with all its shortcomings, its dullness, its bugles.* It knows me better than this reckless holiday, which has disappointed me and done poorly by me' (1927, p. 170).

He began his Sonata for violin and piano, but was pleased with only half of it. While he was at Cap Féret he found the germinal idea for the finale. He wrote to Godet, on 6 October 1916: 'I miss Pourville and "Mon Coin" very much ... I am an old sick man ... Now, what I am writing always seems to stem from yesterday, never from tomorrow' (1942, pp. 159–60). His face was terribly gloomy in the photograph which shows him seated beside Chouchou in the pine woods of Le Moulleau. When he returned to Paris on 24 October 1916, Emma thought he was better. 'He is working, goes out and has taken up his life again,' if it was possible to call that continually painful condition from which he could not free himself a life. He felt as though he had a weight upon his head, as he wrote to Godet on 3 December 1916: 'There is something broken in this

* [The bugles were used on the little railway line that encircled Paris and which ran quite close to Debussy's house.]

strange mechanism which was my brain' (1942, p. 162). On 10 December 1916 he heard his Sonata for flute, viola, and harp at Durand's, and wrote about it to Godet the following day. 'It [the Sonata] . . . is by a Debussy whom I no longer recognize . . . It is fearfully gloomy,'[1] The 'other' Debussy was just as unrecognizable. This letter to Godet continues on the 11th: 'What a life! What days! Worn out with vain pursuits, not tired enough to sleep. Then I wait for tomorrow somehow or other, and it begins all over again' (1942, pp. 164, 166).

His pain was terrible, overwhelming, D.-E. Inghelbrecht and his wife Colette* have given testimony of it, when they had dinner with Debussy: 'Then, sometimes, he begged us to leave him alone. He foresaw the fearful crisis. "I feel that I am going to become nasty . . "' Other times, we saw him drowsing in his armchair. Then we gradually stopped talking and quietly left the room in order to allow him to prolong his respite from pain.'[2]

On 21 December 1916 he participated at the matinée concert given as a benefit for the Vêtement du Prisonnier de Guerre, playing *En blanc et noir* with Roger-Ducasse, and he accompanied Rose Féart in *Le Promenoir des deux amants*, the *Noël des enfants qui n'ont plus de maisons*, and the *Chansons de Bilitis*.[3]

The doctors had not improved his condition appreciably. A year after he had been operated upon, they, without telling him, gave him one more year to live. Little by little, the news got about that he was very sick, but only a few were aware that the illness was fatal. Eugène Berteaux saw him arrive at one of the meetings of the Conseil supérieur des Beaux-Arts one morning in 1917:

He was very emaciated, his complexion sallow and ashen, his smile bitter, his breathing short. 'I am not at all well,' he told me . . . 'Positively, I believe that there is only time to work . . . Yes, I would like to hatch something fantastic, something devilish but vivacious, with much sweetness and light around it.' . . . 'And *Pelléas*?' I asked him, disturbed to see him suffering. 'Oh, *Pelléas* . . . so far away . . . so far . . .' . . . He climbed the three flights of stairs laboriously. And that was the last time I saw him. A few days later, I visited my friend, Dr Crespel, his doctor, who, very moved and with his finger on his lips, answered me: 'You

---

[1] Manuel de Falla would speak of it later to Jean-Aubry in a voice full of emotion. 'It is music for Paradise.'

[2] G. and D.-E. Inghelbrecht, *Claude Debussy* (Paris, 1953), 247.

[3] Perhaps it was on this occasion that, according to Jane Bathori, Gide showed himself very embarrassed on hearing the *Chansons de Bilitis*, not knowing whether he should approve of this music.

---

* [Colette Steinlen was the first Mme Inghelbrecht.]

guessed it. Nothing to be done . . . His case is hopeless.' . . . 'Is he suffering?' I wanted to know. 'Has he long?' 'He will suffer in a few months,' Crespel confided, 'but I know his heroism and modest pride so well that I would predict to you that, right up to the end, he will pretend to ignore his illness.'[4]

At the end of January 1917 extreme cold numbed Paris. There was a drastic shortage of coal. The war wore on. In spite of an admirable vigorous harshness and some moment of heart-breaking pain, the Sonata for violin was proving unbalanced. A passionate farewell to life zigzags energetically across the three movements, as though to escape the halo that threatens to surround them. The Finale extricates itself from it only by means of a crazy gallop, followed by a sudden dive that cuts short the final farewell.[5] Debussy finished the work at the end of March, and heard it at Durand's, on a grey, snowy day. He played it himself with the violinist Gaston Poulet on 5 May 1917 at its first public performance. He wrote to Godet, on 7 June, that he had composed this Sonata only 'to rid myself of it' (1942, p. 174). But a week later, receiving it in published form, he confessed his feelings to Durand: 'In spite of my sad frame of mind, it was all the same a real joy' (1927, p. 180).

On 9 March 1917 he attended a concert for the 'Aide affectueuse aux Musiciens', in the course of which the charming Sonata for flute, viola, and harp had its first public performance. A week later there was another benefit concert, the programme including *Le Promenoir des deux amants*, the *Six Épigraphes antiques*, and the Quartet—this last General Mangin* would never tire of hearing, according to Jacques Durand. There were still other concerts, including two great galas, d'Indy–Debussy festivals from which people had to be turned away. Gabriel Fauré invited Debussy himself, who refused, on 29 April, saying:

My hesitation to answer your kind letter, dear Maître and friend, comes from the very humble reason that I no longer know how to play the piano well enough to chance performing my *Études*. . . . In public, I am seized by a particular phobia: There are too many keys; I no longer have enough fingers; and suddenly I no longer know where the pedals are. It is sad and absolutely painful . . . (1980, p. 277).

On 20 May 1917 Debussy wrote to Toulet, thanking him for his news, which awakened precious memories: 'your delicate scrawl moved me

---

[4] E. Berteaux, *En ce temps-là* (Paris, 1946), 208–9.

[5] Debussy worked hard over his Finale, revised the version made at Cap Féret, and came back to it and modified it. Dukas wrote to him about 6 Apr. 1917. 'I am sure that, among your six versions of the Finale of this sonata, there are five good ones, and the sixth is excellent.'

---

* [A First World War hero, famous for his role in the Battle of Verdun.]

deeply ... I saw again the stifling Bar de la Paix, the crowded Weber; all those places marked with your presence in letters of fire (yes, monsieur). And yet nothing is left of the good old days ...' (1929, pp. 101–2).

Truly they were far from the happy time of *Pelléas*. After a recital by Walter Rummel in June 1917, where works of Johann Sebastian Bach and Claude Debussy were both on the programme, on 28 June, the latter sent warm thanks to his interpreter:

You go from the greatest to the littlest without perceptible strain. Thus you understand the soul of the great Sebastian Bach and that of the little Claude Debussy, in such a way that for a moment they seem to find themselves on the same plane in the public's mind ... For that as for all things, be infinitely thanked, my dear friend ... (1980, p. 282).

That same month he started thinking again about Rosalind of *As You Like It*, a project first discussed thirty years before. There was an interview with Firmin Gémier,* and there were new conferences with Toulet. Debussy informed him in a letter of 9 July 1917: 'I have too great a desire to write this music not to consent to some sacrifices' (1929, p. 111); however, Toulet would not discuss the project. He knew the truth about the health of his unfortunate friend, and his own was no better. On 6 August 1917 Debussy half gave up the project. 'It would be more useful to wait until we are both more certain of ourselves' (1929, p. 114). They saw each other again, during the summer of 1917. On 2 July the Debussy family had left for Saint-Jean-de Luz, where they stayed for three months at the Chalet Habas. That it was a gloomy visit we learn from a letter he wrote to Durand on 22 July: 'I feel only a dreadful tiredness and this distaste for activity that my last illness has left me ... I feel that I bore everybody. If anyone believes that I am enjoying myself, Good Lord!' (1927, p. 183).

He wrote to him again in September of that year: 'Here I wake up tired, irritated, before even knowing what kind of a day it will be ... Where are the beautiful months of 1915? ... I thought I was back in the saddle again and had overcome the bad luck ... What has happened since? I scarcely dare think about it!' (1927, pp. 186–87).

He already had the look of death. Maurice Boucher, who saw him at Saint-Jean-de-Luz, has drawn this ominous picture of him:

The last time that I met him was at Saint-Jean-de-Luz, a year before his death. He walked with difficulty, leaning upon a stick. He paused a few moments facing the sea. His gaze was lost in the distance, and he lowered it only to look at the

* [Gémier had been the director of the Théâtre de la Renaissance and since 1906 of the Théâtre Antoine.]

children playing on the beach. He avoided people. Was it the anguish of approaching death and of tasks left incomplete? There was something tragic on his face and in his appearance: the amber face with its powerful angles, the forehead modelled as though by Rodin's thumbs, the eyes sunken beneath jealous lids.... Even his clothing gave him a look of bitter sadness and restlessness. This man dressed in black who went down to a shore flecked with sunlight, wearing city clothes, and a crushed felt hat on his head, who spoke to no one and soon left as his carriage moved off at a trot to a house chosen for its isolation among the greenery, all this made one think of some character from a fantastic tale.[6]

During this painful holiday he found the strength to play his Sonata for violin again with Gaston Poulet, and Francis Planté performed the 'Toccata', 'Mouvement', and 'Reflets dans l'eau'. Debussy had feared wryly that the pianist Marguerite Long would be a fellow-tenant at the Chalet Habas. As she was, she came to see him, and, for the sake of peace, he finally gave in and coached her in some of his works, notably *L'Isle joyeuse* and the *Études*.[7] There scarcely remained time for him from then on to busy himself seriously with the little *Concerts* that he planned and which he perhaps only announced to Jacques Durand in order to soothe his 'editorial hunger'.

As in 1915, on the eve of his departure for Paris he was again seized with the feeling, the anguish, associated with leave-takings, of the passage of time that would never return. He wrote to Durand on 7 October 1917: 'Soon there will be a replay of the scene with the trunks, which is so disheartening! More disheartening than ever, this year, when I shall bring back no harvest' (1927, p. 189).

Coming back to his old Paris, and this time as if returning to the fold, crossing the threshold of his home he was struck to see how dreary the annual neglect of his little garden seemed. As he wrote in his last letter to Godet, dated 31 October 1917: 'Lost beneath dead leaves, our garden seemed abandoned' (1942, p. 178).

Just as lightning at night suddenly exposes the livid reality of objects, so Debussy, in the space of a second, felt the great sense of loss; death had settled down quietly in the little garden of the avenue du Bois. But the man marked by death, by the dreadful bearer of the scythe, never saw her beside him. Debussy did not suspect that he had entered his home for the last time.

[6] M. Boucher, *Claude Debussy* (Paris, 1930), 33.
[7] In her memoirs (*Au piano avec Claude Debussy* (Paris, 1960), 67), Marguerite Long takes pleasure in 'embroidering' her conversations with Debussy.

22

'Pour un tombeau sans nom'

———◆◆►———

As You Like It and *La Boîte à joujoux* were among the works Debussy mentioned in his last letter, of 1 November 1917, to Jacques Durand; it is possible that he had also looked again at *La Chute de la Maison Usher*: 'for so many fine projects I have now only my wretched health, which is irritated by the slightest shock, by the least change in the weather...' (1927, p. 190).

He received Marguerite Long again, who played, on 16 November 1917, three of the *Études* at the Societé Nationale. From that time on he kept to his bed, his strength failing. His disease forced him to keep a debilitating prone position, which sleepless nights made worse.

The tragic Sonata for violin is his last composition. It is the story of Debussy's struggle against death, and in it can be heard despairing cries.[1] Isolated at Etcheberria under the torrential November rains, Toulet asked for 'a photo of you three'. His wife received it from Mme Debussy with a letter filled with alarm and grief:

His strength is very slow in coming back, and then it is so long since it began to leave him, that one will have to have patience and wait ... You who know so much about worries—of all sorts—know that I have them all—without exception ... Here, often without coal, the house is unbearable—except for Claude's room. Chouchou is well and sleeps peacefully. She is rather badly brought up, but where to find the time to try to prevent that? Her parents are not exactly full of humour every day ... (1929, p. 119)

[1] The Violin Sonata was given its first American performance by Eddy Brown and Louis Gruenberg, 11 Nov. 1917, at Carnegie Hall, New York. The work provoked astonishment in the pages of *Musical America* (10 Nov. 1917, p. 38):

Claude Debussy has meant for us a free, untrammeled impressionist, a leader in modern musical thought, a composer at times of great spiritual beauty and power. And so when we find him writing today a sonata in three movements ... we instinctively feel he is tying himself down to a form that hampers him and acts in opposition to firing his imagination.

The article is signed with the initials A.W.K.

['Pour un tombeau sans nom', *Six Épigraphes antiques*, No. 2.]

A little powdery snow fell on Paris in the middle of December. When 1918 began, the war had lasted 1,248 days. Mme Debussy wrote to Mme Toulet on 3 January 1918:

This new year is full of mystery and, for me, I would add anguish.

My husband is better—perhaps. I no longer know what to believe, always having such sad surprises. But be assured that I feel sorry for him with my whole soul. ... I am growing desperate at not finding anything that might cure him. (1929, p. 121)

A week later she wrote to Pasteur Vallery-Radot: 'The Maître seems better to me—he is eating, reading, singing!—but he is often in pain from his illness and still cannot sit up in his bed. Moreover, nothing has been found to relieve this exhausting enteritis.'

Toulet sent his most recent book, *Comme une fantaisie*, and spoke again of *As You Like It*, hiding his grief beneath a forced humour. German planes swooped over Paris, and people died in the raids. The winter weighed heavily. Pasteur Vallery-Radot could no longer keep his secret or his feelings to himself, and on 8 February, he wrote to Toulet:

I have seen Claude Debussy. Alas, what you have been told is only too true. It is frightfully sad. Eighteen months ago, you know, he had an operation upon his rectum. I knew at the time, in confidence, from someone who could not misinform me, what it really was. Did Mme Debussy then know the truth or not? or did she have the courage to pretend not to know? I do not know which. I have seen her several times. I acted as though I knew nothing, and she did likewise. In Paris, the rumours started to circulate that he had the frightful illness. Each time anyone asked me, I answered that it was not true. It seemed better to leave people in ignorance until the end. When you wrote to me, I did not tell you all that I knew, for I had been told in confidence. Today, the sad truth is too well known by everyone. Mme Debussy herself, without uttering the word, has spoken to me about it. What anxiety I had and what anxiety you must feel. But all that is between ourselves. When you are in contact with him and Mme Debussy, act as though you are unaware of the true facts of his condition. He does not know, I believe. As for her, she wants still to feign ignorance.

He had radium treatments eighteen months ago and he was better as a result.—I saw him in his bed several days ago, very thin, but not too discouraged. What a sad situation! I have felt such grief from it that I cannot express it to you. And all the things that will disappear with him, all the projects that he had formulated two years ago! As if this war did not kill enough people, this illness had to strike a man like him. What injustice, what blindness of fate!

There were announcements of a festival of French music, with appearances by Rose Féart, Claude Debussy, and Gaston Poulet, on 10 March 1918 and also on the 17th (for the 19th). It was a noble deception, designed to delude an invalid who retained complete consciousness. There was a Franck–Debussy Festival on 13 March, and Pierné paid his deeply felt respects by conducting 'Ibéria' on the 17th. These were the first testimonies to the master who was soon to disappear. Laloy writes:

The Opéra, however, was preparing a revival of [Rameau's] *Castor et Pollux*, and its dress rehearsal was held Thursday, 21 March 1918, in the afternoon because of the fear of evening alerts for air raids. It was one of Debussy's last disappointments that he could not be present. Trying to smile, he said to me faintly, seeing me ready to depart: 'Bien le bonjour à Monsieur Castor.'*

When Viñes went to see him, Debussy asked him to play the *Études* for him one last time, and the upright piano was brought into his bedroom. That occasion must have produced deep emotions for both of them. And for the composer particularly, because hearing 'Pour les arpèges composés' must have recalled those deeply happy days at Pourville and the villa 'Mon Coin'.[2]

There were last visits from Inghelbrecht and from Durand, on 23 March, the latter reporting: 'He told me that it was all over, that he knew it was a question of hours, a very short time now. Alas, it was true. When I denied it, he made me a sign that he wanted to embrace me. Then he asked me to hand him a cigarette his last consolation . . .'[3]

Therefore, he knew that he was going to die. He accepted it as he had accepted everything else, because for him death was not the nothingness of the old ruined House of Usher, nor the conventional prospect of Paradise; rather it was the eternity promised to the immortal servants of music.

Widor and Marcel Baschet had managed on 11 March 1918 to have him agree to submit his candidacy to the Académie. It seems that it was on the day before his death that Debussy signed the letter to the Académie that Mme Debussy had written for him, and his signature gives no hint of his condition. On that same Sunday a German canon, firing from a distance to some seventy-two miles, killed ten people in Paris. It seemed like a *coup de grâce* for Debussy.

The following day, 25 March 1918, Pasteur Vallery-Radot was at Debussy's bedside.† The patient dozed, without seeming in pain; he was going away without a sound, like Mélisande. His hands were trembling,

---

[2] 'Mon Coin' was burned during the Second World War. Its garden remains as it was, looking down to the sea, like the stage picture at the end of Act I of *Pelléas*.

[3] J. Durand, *Souvenirs d'un éditeur de musique* (2nd ser.; Paris, 1925), 91.

---

* [Dietschy gave a misleading account of this anecdote. In its place we have substituted the first-hand report of Laloy, *La Musique retrouvée*, p. 228.]

† [According to P. Vallery-Radot (1957*b*, p. 66), Mme Debussy and Roger-Ducasse were there also. Caplet came in later.]

his breathing was shallow; it stopped at ten in the evening. Later on, André Caplet and Roger-Ducasse came. Chouchou was sad, without completely understanding what had happened. (Chouchou Debussy was to die sixteen months later, on 16 July 1919, in the arms of her stepsister, Dolly de Tinan, of a severe case of diphtheria.)

At Debussy's funeral, Alfred Debussy came straight from the trenches, arriving just as the procession was starting out. Most of the friends were there as well: Henri de Régnier, Louis Laloy, Gabriel Pierné, Pasteur Vallery-Radot, André Caplet, Gustave Samazeuilh, even the faithful Chevillard, who had such problems understanding the Maître. Paul Dukas almost fainted with grief. The erstwhile comrade Satie did not attend.

Fifty people left the house for Père-Lachaise cemetery, where it was noted that the government representative, the Minister of Public Instruction, had dropped out, as well as thirty other fashionable people. In 1867, at Baudelaire's funeral, the proportions were just about the same. It seems quite appropriate. The day Debussy died, 25 March 1918, eternal springtime was already trembling deep within the earth, and the night that followed was full of stars.

Catalogue of Works

CATALOGUE OF COMPOSITIONS:
PUBLISHED, UNPUBLISHED, INCOMPLETE

Notes

COLUMN 1: Entry numbers are followed in parenthesis by the corresponding number of Lesure's *Catalogue de l'œuvre de Claude Debussy* (Geneva, 1977).

COLUMN 2: Current published titles are used; former titles are cross-referenced to current ones.

COLUMN 5: Dates in italics indicate publication in a periodical or dissertation.

COLUMN 6: Performance dates are of the first public ones.

COLUMN 7: Numbers refer to entries in column 1, indicating, in sequence, the titles included in a set or larger work.

COLUMN 8: Names in parentheses indicate the source of a subject rather than the author of a specific text.

COLUMN 9: Names of dedicatees are given in Debussy's wording. (Names in parentheses indicate dedicatees on manuscripts presented by Debussy.)

COLUMN 11: MS and MSS refer to Debussy's autographs; MSS indicates that both the piano and orchestral scores are in the same location.

Dates of composition and of first performance as well as location of manuscripts have all been brought up to date.

Abbreviations

acc.	accompaniment	orig.	originally
bar.	baritone	perf.	performance
bn.	bassoon	pf.	pianoforte
compl.	completed	publ.	published
d.b.	double bass	rev.	revised, revision
frag.	fragment	sax.	saxophone
hn.	horn	sep.	separate
hpd.	harpsichord	tpt.	trumpet
inc.	incomplete	trans.	translation
instr.	instrument(s)	va.	viola
movt.	movement(s)	var.	various
ob.	oboe	vc.	violoncello
orch.	orchestra, orchestral,	vn.	violin
	orchestrated	2-h	2-hands
		4-h	4-hands

Library sigla

AN	Archives Nationales, Paris
BB	Bibliotheca Bodmeriana, Cologny-Geneva
BFL	Bibliothèque Musicale François Lang, Royaumont
BL	British Library, London
BN	Bibliothèque Nationale, Paris
BO	Bibliothèque de l'Opéra, Paris
ESM	Eastman School of Music, Rochester
HL	Houghton Library, Harvard University, Cambridge
LC	Library of Congress, Washington
MT	Musée Tchaikovsky, Klin, USSR
NEC	New England Conservatory of Music, Boston
NL	Newberry, Library, Chicago
NYP	New York Public Library, New York
PC	Private Collection
PLU	Present Location Unknown
PML	Pierpont Morgan Library, New York
SMF	Stiftelsen Musikkulturens främjande, Stockholm
SUC	Stanford University, California
SW	Stadtbibliothek Winterthur, Switzerland
UMA	University of Michigan, Ann Arbor
UTA	University of Texas, Austin

1. No.	2. Title	3. Genre	4. Composed	5. Publ.	6. 1st perf.
1 (L 16)	*Aimons-nous et dormons*	voice & piano	1880	1933	
2 (L 79)	*Âme évaporée, L'*	voice & piano			
3 (L 38)	'Andante'	orch. suite for piano 4-hands	1881	*1987*	
4 (L 36*bis*)	*Andante cantabile*	piano 4-hands	*c.*1882	*1987*	
5 (L 76)	*Angélus, Les*	voice & piano	1891	1891	
6 (L 53)	*Apparition*	voice & piano	1884	*1926*, 1969	17 May 1926
7 (L 66)	*Arabesques, Deux*	piano	1888–91	1891	23 May 1894 (2nd only)
8 (L 46)	*Archet, L'*	voice & piano	1881		
9	*Ariettes*	voice & piano	1885–7	1888	2 Feb. 1889 (2 of them)
10 (L 60)	*Ariettes oubliées*	voice & piano	rev. 1903	1903	
11 (L 118)	'Auprès de cette grotte sombre'	voice & piano	1904	1910	14 Jan. 1911
12 (L 63)	*Axël*	opera	*c.*1888		
13 (L 50)	'Bacchanale'	orchestra	*c.*1883		
14 (L 55*bis*)	*Baisers, Les*	voice & piano	1881		
15 (L 64)	'Balcon, Le'	voice & piano	1888	1890	
16 (L 70)	*Ballade*	piano	1890	1891; 1903	
17 (L 1)	*Ballade à la lune*	voice & piano	*c.*1879		
18 (L 119)	'Ballade des femmes de Paris'	voice & piano	1910	1910	18 Nov. 1910
19 (L 119)	'Ballade de Villon à s'amye'	voice & piano	1910	1910	16 Jan. 1911
20 (L 119)	'Ballade que Villon feit a la requeste de sa mère'	voice & piano	1910	1910	16 Jan. 1911

7. No. in set	8. Text by	9. Dedication	10. Orch. by	11. Remarks
	T. de Banville	Paul Vidal		MS in PC
				see 'Romance' (265)
No. 2, *Triomphe de Bacchus*	(T. de Banville)			MS in PML
				MS in PML
	G. Le Roy			MS in PML
No. 4, *Chansons de jeunesse*	S. Mallarmé	Mme Vasnier		MS in LC
			G. J. Roberts	MS in BN
	C. Cros			MS in BN
38, 143, 196, 50, 133, 299	P. Verlaine			MSS—see sep. entries (rev. as *Ariettes oubliées*)
38, 143, 196, 50, 133, 299	P. Verlaine	Mary Garden 1903	see sep. entries	rev. versions of *Ariettes*
No. 1, *Promenoir des deux amants*	T. Lhermite	Emma Claude Debussy . . . p.m.	L. Beydts	MS in BN (also No. 2, *Chansons de France*)
	V. de L'Isle-Adam			MS—PLU (one scene only?)
No. 4, *Première Suite d'orchestre*				MS—PLU
	T. de Banville	Mme Vasnier		MS in PC
No. 1, *Poèmes de Baudelaire*	C. Baudelaire	Étienne Dupin	L. Aubert	MS in BN; PML
		Mme Ph. Hottinguer		MS—PLU (orig. *Ballade slave*)
	A. de Musset			MS—PLU
No. 3, *Ballades de Villon*	F. Villon		Debussy	MSS in BN
No. 1, *Ballades de Villon*	F. Villon		Debussy	MSS in BN
No. 2, *Ballades de Villon*	F. Villon		Debussy	MSS in BN

1. No.	2. Title	3. Genre	4. Composed	5. Publ.	6. 1st perf.
21 (L 119)	*Ballades de François Villon, Trois*	voice & piano	1910	1910	16 Jan. 1911
22 (L 50)	'Ballet'	orchestra	*c.*1883		
23 (L 65)	'Ballet'	piano 4-hands	1888–9	1889	23 May 1894
24 (L 58)	*Barcarolle*	voice & piano	*c.*1885		
25 (L 6)	*Beau soir*	voice & piano	1886	1891	
26 (L 74)	*Belle au bois dormant, La*	voice & piano	1890	1902	
27 (L 93)	*Berceuse* pour *La Tragédie de la mort*	solo voice	1899		17 Dec. 1992
28 (L 132)	*Berceuse héroïque*	piano	1914	*1914*, 1915	26 Oct. 1915
29 (L 96)	'Bilitis'	incidental music	1900–1	1971 (compl. by Hoérée)	7 Feb. 1901; 10 Apr. 1954 (compl. by Boulez)
30 (L 128)	*Boîte à joujoux, La*	ballet	1913	1913	10 Dec. 1919
31 (L 123)	'Brouillards'	piano	1911–12	1913	5 Mar. 1913
32 (L 123)	'Bruyères'	piano	1911–12	1913	8 Apr. 1913
33 (L 28)	*Calmes dans le demi-jour* ('En sourdine')	voice & piano	1882	*1942*, 1944	14 Mar. 1939
34 (L 123)	'Canope'	piano	1911–12	1913	12 June 1913
35 (L 5)	*Caprice*	voice & piano	1880	*1966*	12 Dec. 1974
36 (L 117)	'Cathédrale engloutie, La'	piano	1909–10	1910	25 May 1910
37 (L 117)	'Ce qu'a vu le vent d'ouest'	piano	1909–10	1910	26 July 1910
38 (L 60)	'C'est l'extase langoureuse'	voice & piano	1887; rev. 1903	1888; 1903	
39 (L 96)	'Chanson'	incidental music	1900–1	1971 (compl. by Hoérée)	7 Feb. 1901; 10 Apr. 1954 (compl. by Boulez)

7. No. in set	8. Text by	9. Dedication	10. Orch. by	11. Remarks
19, 20, 19	F. Villon		Debussy	MSS in BN
No. 2, *Première Suite d'orchestre*				MS—PLU
No. 4, *Petite Suite*			H. Busser	MS in BN
	E. Guinand			MS—PLU
	P. Bourget			MS—PLU
	E.-V. Hyspa			MS in PC
	R. Peter	René (Peter)		MS in LC
		Albert Ier de Belgique et ses soldats	Debussy	MS in BN (pf.); BO (orch.)
No. 6, *Les Chansons de Bilitis*	P. Louÿs		Debussy–Boulez; Debussy–Hoérée	MSS in BN (compl. by Boulez; Hoérée)
	A. Hellé		Debussy–A. Caplet	MSS in BN
No. 1, *Préludes*, II				MS in BN; PC (sketch)
No. 5, *Préludes*, II				MS in BN
	P. Verlaine			MS in PC (publ. title of early version of 'En sourdine')
No. 10, *Préludes*, II				MS in BN
	T. de Banville	Mme Vasnier		MS in BN
No. 10, *Préludes*, I			H. Busser	MS in PC
No. 7, *Préludes*, I	(H. C. Anderson)			MS in PC
No. 1, *Ariettes oubliées*	P. Verlaine	Mary Garden 1903	A. Caplet	MS in BN; BFL
No. 4, *Les Chansons de Bilitis*	P. Louÿs		Debussy–Boulez; Debussy–Hoérée	MSS in BN (compl. by Boulez; Hoérée) (adapted as No. 3, *Épigraphes antiques*)

1. No.	2. Title	3. Genre	4. Composed	5. Publ.	6. 1st perf.
40 (L 42)	'Chanson espagnole'	2 equal voices & piano	1883	1980, 1983	unknown, but BBC Radio 3, 16 Dec. 1984
41 (L 47)	*Chanson triste*	voice & piano	1881		
42	*Chansons*	voice & piano	1883–4	1980,[1] 1983	see sep. entries
43 (L 90)	*Chansons de Bilitis*	voice & piano	1897–8	1899	17 Mar. 1900
44 (L 96)	*Chansons de Bilitis, Les, Incidental music for*	incidental music	1900–1	1971 (compl. by Hoérée)	7 Feb. 1901; 10 Apr. 1954 (compl. by Boulez)
45 (L 92)	*Chansons de Charles d'Orléans, Trois*	4 voices a cappella	1898 (1, 3) 1908 (2)	1908	9 Apr. 1909
46 (L 102)	*Chansons de France, Trois*	voice & piano	1904	1904	6 Feb. 1906
47	*Chansons de jeunesse, Quatre*	voice & piano	1881–4	*1926*, 1969	see sep. entries
48 (L 96)	'Chant pastorale'	incidental music	1900–1	1971 (compl. by Hoérée)	7 Feb. 1901; 10 Apr. 1954 (compl. by Boulez)
49	*Chevaux de bois*, 1st version	voice & piano	1885		
50 (L 60)	'Chevaux de bois', 2nd version	voice & piano	1887; rev. 1903	1888; 1903	
51 (L 90)	'Chevelure, La'	voice & piano	1897	*1897*, 1899	17 Mar. 1900
52 (L 113)	*Children's Corner*	piano	1906–8	1908	18 Dec. 1908
53 (L 35)	*Chœur des brises*	choral	1882		
54 (L 112)	*Chute de la Maison Usher, La*	opera	1908–17	1979	27 Nov. 1959; 1 Dec. 1977[3]
55 (L 32)	'Clair de lune', 1st version	voice & piano	1882	*1926*, 1969	unknown, but BBC Radio 3, 16 Dec. 1984

[1] This edition, in which the first versions of Nos. 205 and 318 were included, was withdrawn. These two songs were omitted in the 1983 edition. The references in column 7 are to the late edition.

[3] The case of *La Chute* is complicated. The performance of 27 Nov. 1959, cited by Dietschy (p. 264), almost certainly refers to one with piano accompaniment. On 25 Feb. 1977 the Abbate edition, orchestrated by Abbate and Robert Kyr, was sung and staged.

7. No. in set	8. Text by	9. Dedication	10. Orch. by	11. Remarks
No. 2, *Chansons*	A. de Musset	Mme Vasnier		MS in BN (No. 7, *Vasnier Songbook*)
	M. Bouchor			MS in BN (sketch)
54, 40, 264, 183, 267, 258 (205, 318 in 1980 edn. only)	see sep. entries	Mme Vasnier		MS in BN (Nos. 6–13, *Vasnier Songbook*)
28, 51, 309	P. Louÿs		M. Delage	see sep. entries
8, 62, 63, 39, 203, 29, 310, 66, 93, 76, 297, 214	P. Louÿs		Debussy–Boulez; Debussy–Hoérée	MSS in BN (compl. by Boulez; Hoérée)[2]
8, 253, 320	C. d'Orléans	see sep. entries		MS in BN
05, 134, 220	see sep. entries	Mme S. Bardac		MS in BN
02, 55, 212, 6	see sep. entries	Mme Vasnier		see sep. entries
No. 1, *Les Chansons de Bilitis*	P. Louÿs		Debussy–Boulez; Debussy–Hoérée	MSS in BN (compl. by Boulez; Hoérée) (adapted as No. 1, *Épigraphes antiques*)
	P. Verlaine	Bachelet		MS in BN; PML
No. 4, *Ariettes oubliées*	P. Verlaine	Mary Garden 1903	M. Rosenthal	MS in BFL
No. 2, *Chansons de Bilitis*	P. Louÿs	Mme A. Peter (*1897*)	M. Delage	MS in BN
1, 158, 283, 287, 164, 132		Chouchou	A. Caplet	MSS in BN (except No. 3)
	L. Bouilhet			MS in SUC (sketch)
	Poe–Debussy		J. Allende-Blin	MS in BN (inc.); UTA (text)
No. 2, *Chansons de jeunesse*	P. Verlaine	Mme Vasnier		MS in BN; NL (N. 4, *Vasnier Songbook*)

On 23 Apr. 1977 this edition, orchestrated by Abbate and Robert Bailey, was performed in concert as an orchestral suite.

[2] Both Boulez and Hoérée have constructed versions of the missing celesta part.

1. No.	2. Title	3. Genre	4. Composed	5. Publ.	6. 1st perf.
56 (L 80)	'Clair de lune', 2nd version	voice & piano	1891	1903	
57 (L 75)	'Clair de lune'	piano	1890–1905	1905	
58 (L 79)	'Cloches, Les'	voice & piano	1886	1891	
59 (L 111)	'Cloches à travers les feuilles'	piano	1907	1908	21 Feb. 1908
60 (L 117)	'Collines d'Anacapri, Les'	piano	1909	1910	14 Jan. 1911
61 (L 104)	'Colloque sentimental'	voice & piano	1904	1904	23 June 1904
62 (L 96)	'Comparaisons, Les'	incidental music	1900–1	1971 (compl. by Hoérée)	7 Feb. 1901; 10 Apr. 1954 (compl. by Boulez)
63 (L 96)	'Contes, Les'	incidental music	1900–1	1971 (compl. by Hoérée)	7 Feb. 1901; 10 Apr. 1954 (compl. by Boulez)
64 (L 39)	'Coquetterie posthume'	voice & piano	1883	1980, 1983	?14 Mar. 1939
65 (L 65)	'Cortège'	piano 4-hands	1888–9	1889	23 May 1894
66 (L 96)	'Courtisanes égyptiennes, Les'	incidental music	1900–1	1971 (compl. by Hoérée)	7 Feb. 1901; 10 Apr. 1954 (compl. by Boulez)
67 (L 118)	'Crois mon conseil, chère Climène'	voice & piano	1910	1910	14 Jan. 1911
68 (L 62)	Damoiselle élue, La	cantata	1887–8; rev. 1902	1893; 1903	8 Apr. 1893
69 (L 20)	Daniel	cantata	1882		
70 (L 69)	Danse	piano	1890	1891	10 Mar. 1900
71 (L 9)	Danse bohémienne	piano	1880	1932	
72 (L 117)	'Danse de Puck, La'	piano	1910	1910	25 May 1910
73 (L 103)	'Danse profane', II	harp & orch.	1904	1904	6 Nov. 1904

7. No. in set	8. Text by	9. Dedication	10. Orch. by	11. Remarks
No. 3, *Fêtes galantes*, I	P. Verlaine	Mme Arthur Fontaine		MS in PC
No. 3, *Suite bergamasque*			A. Caplet	MS—PLU
No. 2, *Deux Romances*	P. Bourget			MS in BN
No. 1, *Images*, II	(L. Laloy)	Alexandre Charpentier		MS in BN
No. 5, *Préludes*, I				MS in PC
No. 3, *Fêtes galantes*, II	P. Verlaine	A.l.p.M. (Mme Bardac)	L. Beydts	MS in BN; PML (early version)
No. 2, *Les Chansons de Bilitis*	P. Louÿs		Debussy–Boulez; Debussy–Hoérée	MSS in BN (compl. by Boulez; Hoérée)
No. 3, *Les Chansons de Bilitis*	P. Louÿs		Debussy–Boulez; Debussy–Hoérée	MSS in BN (compl. by Boulez; Hoérée)
No. 1, *Chansons*	T. Gautier	Mme Vasnier		MS in BN (No. 6, *Vasnier Songbook*)
No. 2, *Petite Suite*			H. Busser	MS in BN
No. 8, *Les Chansons de Bilitis*	P. Louÿs		Debussy–Boulez; Debussy–Hoérée	MSS in BN (compl. by Boulez; Hoérée) (adapted as No. 2, *Épigraphes antiques*)
No. 2, *Promenoir des deux amants*	T. Lhermite	Emma Claude Debussy . . . p.m.	L. Beydts	MS in BN
	D. G. Rossetti	Paul Dukas	Debussy	MS in BN; PML (short score)
	E. Cicile			MS in PC (inc. short score)
		Mme Ph. Hottinguer	M. Ravel	MS—PLU (orig. *Tarentelle styrienne*)
				MS—PLU
No. 11, *Préludes*, I	(Shakespeare)			MS in PC
No. 2, *Deux Danses*		Gustave Lyon		MS in BN

1. No.	2. Title	3. Genre	4. Composed	5. Publ.	6. 1st perf.
74 (L 103)	'Danse sacrée', I	harp & orch.	1904	1904	6 Nov. 1904
75 (L 103)	*Danses, Deux*, for harp & string orchestra	harp & orch.	1904	1904	6 Nov. 1904
76 (L 96)	'Danseuse aux crotales, La'	incidental music	1900–1	1971 (compl. by Hoérée)	7 Feb. 1901; 10 Apr. 1954 (compl. by Boulez)
77 (L 117)	'Danseuses de Delphes'	piano	1909	1910	25 May 1910
78 (L 78)	*Dans le jardin*	voice & piano	1903	1905	
79 (L 109)	'De l'aube à midi sur la mer'	orchestra	1903–5	1905	15 Oct. 1905
80 (L 84)	'De fleurs'	voice & piano	1893	1895	17 Feb. 1894
81 (L 84)	'De grève'	voice & piano	1892	1895	?16 Jan. 1904
82 (L 84)	'De rêve'	voice & piano	1892	1895	
83 (L 84)	'De soir'	voice & piano	1893	1895	17 Feb. 1894
84 (L 117)	'Des pas sur la neige'	piano	1909	1910	29 Mar. 1911
85 (L 101)	*Diable dans le beffroi, Le*	opera	1902–11		
86 (L 109)	'Dialogue du vent et de la mer'	orchestra	1903–5	1905	15 Oct. 1905
87 (L 51)	*Diane au bois*	cantata	1883–6		BBC Radio 3, 9 Nov. 1968
88 (L 92)	'Dieu! qu'il la fait bon regarder'	4 voices a cappella	1898	1908	9 Apr. 1909
89 (L 36)	*Divertissement*	piano 4-hands	1884		
90 (L 38)	'Divertissement'	orch. suite for piano 4-hands	1882	1928 (pf., orch.) *1987* (pf.)	2 Apr. 1928 (orch.)
91 (L 113)	'Doctor Gradus ad Parnassum'	piano	1908	1908	18 Dec. 1908
92 (L 99)	*D'un cahier d'esquisses*	piano	1903	*1904*, 1904	20 Apr. 1910

7. No. in set	8. Text by	9. Dedication	10. Orch. by	11. Remarks
No. 1, *Deux Danses*		Gustave Lyon		MS in BN
74, 73		Gustave Lyon		MS in BN
No. 10, *Les Chansons de Bilitis*	P. Louÿs		Debussy–Boulez; Debussy–Hoérée	MSS in BN (compl. by Boulez; Hoérée) (adapted as No. 4, *Épigraphes antiques*)
No. 1, *Préludes*, I			H. Forterre	MS in PC
	P. Gravollet			MS—PLU
No. 1, *La Mer*		Jacques Durand		MS in BN; ESM (short score)
No. 3, *Proses lyriques*	Debussy	Mme E. Chausson (Mme M. A. Fontaine)	Roger-Ducasse	MS in PC; BN
No. 2, *Proses lyriques*	Debussy	Raymond Bonheur	Roger-Ducasse	MS—PLU (text publ. in *1892*)
No. 1, *Proses lyriques*	Debussy	V. Hoquet	Roger-Ducasse	MS in PC (text publ. in *1892*)
No. 4, *Proses lyriques*	Debussy	Henry Lerolle (Mme M. A. Fontaine)	Roger-Ducasse	MS in BN
No. 6, *Préludes*, I				MS in PC
	Poe–Debussy			MS in BN (sketch & inc. text)
No. 3, *La Mer*		Jacques Durand		MS in BN; ESM (short score)
	T. de Banville			MS in PML (frag.); BN (frag.)
No. 1, *Chansons de C. d'Orléans*	C. d'Orléans	(Lucien Fontaine)		MS in BN; PC
				MS in BN (inc.)
No. 1, *Triomphe de Bacchus*	(T. de Banville)		M. F. Gaillard	MS in PML (tempo: 'Allegro')
No. 1, *Children's Corner*		Chouchou	A. Caplet	MS in BN
				MS—PLU

1. No.	2. Title	3. Genre	4. Composed	5. Publ.	6. 1st perf.
93 (L 96)	'Eau pure du bassin, L''	incidental music	1900–1	1971 (compl. by Hoérée)	7 Feb. 1901; 10 Apr. 1954 (compl. by Boulez)
94 (L 81)	'Échelonnement des haies, L''	voice & piano	1891	1901	6 Dec. 1905
95 (L 49)	*Églogue*	2 voices	1881		
96 (L 138)	*Élégie*	piano	1915	*1916*; 1978	
96 *bis*	Elfes, Les	voice & piano	1881		
97 (L 65)	'En bateau'	piano 4-hands	1888–9	1889	23 May 1894
98 (L 134)	*En blanc et noir*	2 pianos	1915	1915	22 Jan. 1916
99 (L 57)	*Enfant prodigue, L'*	cantata	1884; rev. 1906–8	1884; 1908	27 June 1884
100 (L 28)	*En sourdine*, 1st version	voice & piano	1882		unknown, but BBC Radio 3, 14 Dec. 1984
101 (L 80)	'En sourdine', 2nd version	voice & piano	1891–2	1903	
102 (L 131)	*Épigraphes antiques, Six*	piano 2- and 4-hands	1914	1915	17 Mar. 1917
103 (L 100)	*Estampes*	piano	1903	1903	9 Jan. 1904
104 (L 111)	'Et la lune descend sur le temple qui fut'	piano	1907	1908	21 Feb. 1908
105 (L 136*bis*)	*Étude retrouvée*	piano	1915	1980	30 May 1980
106 (L 136)	*Études (Douze), Book I*	piano	1915	1916	14 Dec. 1916
107 (L 136)	*Études (Douze), Book II*	piano	1915	1916	14 Dec. 1916
108 (L 127)	'Éventail'	voice & piano	1913	1913	21 Mar. 1914
109 (L 107)	'Fanfare' (d'ouverture)	incidental music	1904–6	1926	22 Oct. 1926

7. No. in set	8. Text by	9. Dedication	10. Orch. by	11. Remarks
No. 9, *Les Chansons de Bilitis*	P. Louÿs		Debussy–Boulez; Debussy–Hoérée	MSS in BN (compl. by Boulez; Hoérée)
No. 3, *Mélodies (de Verlaine)*	P. Verlaine	Robert Godet (Lucien Fontaine)		MS in BN; PC
	L. de Lisle			MS in BN
				MS—PLU
	L. de Lisle			MS in BN (inc.)
No. 1, *Petite Suite*			H. Busser	MS in BN
3 untitled movements		A. Kussewitsky (1); Jacques Charlot (2); I. Stravinsky (3)		MS in BN; PLU
	E. Guinand	Ernest Guiraud		MS in BN (1st Prix de Rome)
	P. Verlaine	Mme Vasnier		MS in BN (No. 2, *Vasnier Songbook*); PC; PML; HL (inc.)
No. 1, *Fêtes galantes*, I	P. Verlaine	Mme Robert Godet (Mlle C. Stevens)		MS in UTA; PML (× 2)
221, 239, 237, 222, 223, 238	(P. Louÿs)		E. Ansermet	MS in BN
200, 288, 153		J.-É. Blanche		MS in BN
No. 2, *Images*, II		Louis Laloy		MS in BN
No. 11, *Études*, II, early version				MS in PML
228, 236, 233, 234, 232, 230		Frédéric Chopin		MS in BN; also see sep. entries
229, 226, 231, 235, 227, 225		Frédéric Chopin		MS in BN; also see sep. entries
No. 3, *Poèmes de Mallarmé*	S. Mallarmé	Stéphane Mallarmé et Mme E. Bonniot (née G. Mallarmé)		MS in BN
No. 1, *Musique pour 'Le Roi Lear'*	(Shakespeare)		Roger-Ducasse	MS—PLU

1. No.	2. Title	3. Genre	4. Composed	5. Publ.	6. 1st perf.
110 (L 73)	*Fantaisie* for piano & orchestra	orchestra	1889–90	1920; rev. 1968	20 Nov. 1919
111 (L 21)	*Fantoches*, 1st version	voice & piano	1882		unknown, but BBC Radio 3, 16 Dec. 1984
112 (L 80)	'Fantoches', 2nd version	voice & piano	1891	1903	
113 (L 104)	'Faune, Le'	voice & piano	1904	1904	23 June 1904
114 (L 123)	'Fées sont d'exquises danseuses, Les'	piano	1911–12	1913	5 Apr. 1913
115 (L 50)	'Fête'	orchestra	*c.*1883		
116 (L 23)	'Fête galante'	voice & piano	1882	1984	12 May 1882
117 (L 91)	'Fêtes'	orchestra	1897–9	1900; rev. 1930; new rev. 1964	9 Dec. 1900
118 (L Ann. IV)	*Fêtes galantes*	opera-ballet	?1912–15		
119 (L 80)	*Fêtes galantes*, series I	voice & piano	1891–2	1903	
120 (L 104)	*Fêtes galantes*, series II	voice & piano	1904	1904	23 June 1904
121 (L 123)	'Feuilles mortes'	piano	1911–12	1913	5 Mar. 1913
122 (L 123)	'Feux d'artifice'	piano	1913?	1913	5 Apr. 1913
123 (L 33)	*Fille aux cheveux de lin, La*	voice & piano	1881		
124 (L 117)	'Fille aux cheveux de lin, La'	piano	1910	*1910*, 1910	26 July 1910
125 (L 7)	*Fleur des blés*	voice & piano	1881	1891	
126 (L 48)	*Fleur des eaux*	voice & piano	1881		
127 (L 25)	*Flots, palmes, sables*	voice & piano	1882		?16 Nov. 1947
128 (L 90)	'Flûte de Pan, La'	voice & piano	1897	1899	17 Mar. 1900
129 (L 123)	'"General Lavine" —eccentric'	piano	1911–12	1913	8 Apr. 1913

7. No. in set	8. Text by	9. Dedication	10. Orch. by	11. Remarks
		René Chansarel		MS in PC (orch.); BL (2 pianos)
	P. Verlaine	Mme Vasnier		MS in BN (No. 5, *Vasnier Songbook*); PML
No. 2, *Fêtes galantes*, I	P. Verlaine	Mme Lucien Fontaine	M. Rosenthal	MS in PML
No. 2, *Fêtes galantes*, II	P. Verlaine	A.l.p.M. (Mme Bardac)	R. Manuel	MS in BN
No. 4, *Préludes*, II	(A. Rackham)			MS in BN
No. 1, *Première Suite d'orchestre*				MS—PLU
No. 7, *Poèmes de Banville*	T. de Banville	Mme Vasnier		MS in PC; BFL (adapted as No. 3, *Petite Suite*)
No. 2, *Nocturnes*		Georges Hartmann; (Lilly-Lilo)		MS in PC; LC (short score)
	L. Laloy (after P. Verlaine)			MS in BN (inc.)
101, 112, 56	P. Verlaine	see sep. entries	see sep. entries	MS in PC
148, 113, 61	P. Verlaine	A.l.p.M. (Mme Bardac)	see sep. entries	MS in BN
No. 2, *Préludes*, II				MS in BN; PC (sketch)
No. 12, *Préludes*, II				MS in BN
	L. de Lisle	Mme Vasnier		MS in PML
No. 8, *Préludes*, I	(L. de Lisle)			MS in PC
	A. Girod	Mme É. Deguingand		MS—PLU
	M. Bouchor			MS in BN (sketch)
	A. Renaud	Mme Vasnier		MS in PC (see also *Mélodie persane*)
No. 1, *Chansons de Bilitis*	P. Louÿs		M. Delage	MS in BN (× 2) (*Flûte de Pan*, orig. title of *Syrinx*)
No. 6, *Préludes*, II	(Ed Lavine)			MS in BN

1. No.	2. Title	3. Genre	4. Composed	5. Publ.	6. 1st perf.
130 (L 122)	'Gigues'	orchestra	1909–12	1913	26 Jan. 1913
131 (L 41)	*Gladiateur, Le*	cantata	1883		23 June 1883
132 (L 113)	'Golliwogg's Cake-walk'	piano	1908	1908	18 Dec. 1908
133 (L 60)	'Green'	voice & piano	1886; rev. 1903	1888; 1903	
134 (L 102)	'Grotte, La'	voice & piano	1904	1904	27 May 1904
135 (L 64))	'Harmonie du soir'	voice & piano	1889	1890	
136 (L 20*bis*)	*Hélène*	choral	1881		
137 (L 115)	*Hommage à Haydn*	piano	1909	*1910*, 1910	11 Mar. 1911
138 (L 110)	'Hommage à Rameau'	piano	1904–5	1905	14 Dec. 1905
139 (L 123)	'Hommage à S. Pickwick Esq. P.P.M.P.C.'	piano	1911–12	1913	12 June 1913
140 (L 37)	*Hymnis*	incidental music	1882		
141 (L 122)	'Ibéria'	orchestra	1905–8	1910	20 Feb. 1910
142 (L 37)	'Il dort encore'	voice & piano	1882	1984	28 Apr. 1985
143 (L 60)	'Il pleure dans mon cœur'	voice & piano	1887; rev. 1903	1888; 1903	
144 (L 110)	*Images*, I (1st series)	piano	1904–5	1905	14 Dec. 1905 (No. 2); 6 Feb. 1906 (Nos. 1 & 3)
145 (L 111)	*Images*, II (2nd series)	piano	1907	1908	21 Feb. 1908
146 (L 87)	*Images (oubliées)*	piano	1894	1977	1978
147 (L 122)	*Images pour orchestre*	orchestra	1905–12	1913	26 Jan. 1913
148 (L 104)	'Ingénus, Les'	voice & piano	1904	1904	23 June 1904

7. No. in set	8. Text by	9. Dedication	10. Orch. by	11. Remarks
No. 1, *Images pour orchestre*				MS in BN; PML (short score) (orig. 'Gigues tristes')
	E. Moreau			MS in BN
No. 6, *Children's Corner*		Chouchou	A. Caplet	MS in BN
No. 5, *Ariettes oubliées*	P. Verlaine	Mary Garden 1903	A. Caplet	MS in BFL; PLU
No. 2, *Chansons de France*	T. Lhermite	Mme S. Bardac	L. Beydts	MS in BN (also No. 1, *Promenoir des deux amants*)
No. 2, *Poèmes de Baudelaire*	C. Baudelaire	Étienne Dupin		MS in BN
	L. de Lisle			MS—PLU (frag.)
		Hommage à Joseph Haydn		MS in PC
No. 2, *Images*, I				MS in BN
No. 9, *Préludes*, II	(C. Dickens)			MS in BN
see 142, 195	T. de Banville	Mme Vasnier		MS—PLU (scenes I, II, VII +)
No. 2, *Images pour orchestre*				MS in BN; PML (short score, movts. 2, 3)
No. 5, *Poèmes de Banville*	T. de Banville	Mme Vasnier		MS in BB (from *Hymnis*, scene I)
No. 2, *Ariettes oubliées*	P. Verlaine	Mary Garden 1903		MS in BN
257, 138, 182				MS in BN
59, 104, 219		see sep. entries		MS in BN
160, 298, 254		Mlle Yvonne Lerolle		MS in PML (orig. *Images*)
130, 141, 273		Emma Claude Debussy (No. 3)		MS in BN
No. 1, *Fêtes galantes*, II	P. Verlaine	A.l.p.M. (Mme Bardac)		MS in BN

1. No.	2. Title	3. Genre	4. Composed	5. Publ.	6. 1st perf.
149 (L 27)	*Intermezzo*	cello & orch.	1882	1944 (vc. & pf.)	
150 (L 40)	*Invocation*	men's chorus & orch.	1883	1928 (pf. acc.); 1957 (orch.)	2 Apr. 1928
151 (L 106)	*Isle joyeuse, L'*	piano	1903–4	1904	10 Feb. 1905
152 (L 19)	*Jane*	voice & piano	1881	*1966*, 1982	29 June 1938
153 (L 100)	'Jardins sous la pluie'	piano	1903	1903	9 Jan. 1904
154 (L 64)	'Jet d'eau, Le'	voice & piano	1889	1890	15 May 1905
155 (L 118)	'Je tremble en voyant ton visage'	voice & piano	1910	1910	14 Jan. 1911
156 (L 126)	*Jeux*	ballet	1912–13	1912	15 May 1913
157 (L 109)	'Jeux de vagues'	orchestra	1903–5	1905	15 Oct. 1905
158 (L 113)	'Jimbo's Lullaby'	piano	1908	1908	18 Dec. 1908
159 (L 125)	*Khamma*	ballet	1911–12	1916 (pf.)	15 Nov. 1924 26 Mar. 1947 (ballet)
160 (L 87)	'Lent (mélancolique et doux)'	piano	1894	1977	
161 (L 22)	'Lilas, Le'	voice & piano	1882	1984	29 June 1938
162 (L 97)	*Lindaraja*	2 pianos	1901	1926	28 Oct. 1926
163 (L 114)	*Little Nigar, The*	piano	1909	1909, 1934	
164 (L 113)	'Little Shepherd, The'	piano	1908	1908	18 Dec. 1908
165 (L 2)	*Madrid, Princesse des Espagnes*	voice & piano	1879		
166 (L 29)	*Mandoline*	voice & piano	1882	*1890*, 1890	16 Jan. 1904
167 (L 77)	*Marche des anciens comtes de Ross*				

7. No. in set	8. Text by	9. Dedication	10. Orch. by	11. Remarks
	(H. Heine)			MS—PLU (orch.); PML (pf. 4-h); PC (vc. & pf.)
	A. de Lamartine			MS in BN (orch.); PML (pf. 4-h)
			B. Molinari	MS in BN
	L. de Lisle	Mme Vasnier		MS in PC
No. 3, *Estampes*		J.-É. Blanche		MS in BN (from No. 3, *Images (oubliées)*)
No. 3, *Poèmes de Baudelaire*	C. Baudelaire	Étienne Dupin	Debussy– A. Caplet	MSS in BN
No. 3, *Promenoir des deux amants*	T. Lhermite	Emma Claude Debussy ... p.m.	L. Beydts	MS in BN
	(Nijinsky + ?Diaghilev)	Mme Jacques Durand		MS in BN; PML; SW (short score)
No. 2, *La Mer*		Jacques Durand		MS in BN; ESM (short score)
No. 2, *Children's Corner*		Chouchou	A. Caplet	MS in BN
	(W. L. Courtney & Maude Allan)		Debussy– C. Koechlin	MS in UTA; BN (scenario)
No. 1, *Images (oubliées)*		Mlle Yvonne Lerolle		MS in PC
No. 3, *Poèmes de Banville*	T. de Banville			MS in PC
				MS—PLU
				MS—PLU (wrongly *Le Petit Nègre*)
No. 5, *Children's Corner*		Chouchou	A. Caplet	MS in BN
	A. de Musset	P. Vidal et Passerieu		MS in PML (frag. of music only)
	P. Verlaine	Mme Vasnier	L. Beydts	MS in BN; HL (No. 3, *Vasnier Songbook*)
				see *Marche écossaise*

1. No.	2. Title	3. Genre	4. Composed	5. Publ.	6. 1st perf.
168 (L 77)	*Marche écossaise sur un thème populaire*	piano 4-hands	1891; 1903; 1908 (orch.)	1891 (pf.); 1911 (orch.)	16 Jan. 1909 (pf.); 19 Apr. 1913 (orch.)
169 (L 38)	'Marche et Bacchanale'	orch. suite for piano 4-hands	*c.*1882		
170 (L 124)	*Martyre de Saint Sébastien, Le*	incidental music	1911	1911	22 May 1911
171 (L 105)	*Masques*	piano	1903–4	1904	10 Feb. 1905
172 (L 67)	*Mazurka*	piano	?1890	1904	
173 (L 25)	*Mélodie persane*	harp	1882		
174 (L 81)	*Mélodies (de Verlaine), Trois*	voice & piano	1891	1901	see sep. entries
175 (L 65)	'Menuet'	piano 4-hands	1888–9	1889	23 May 1894
176 (L 75)	'Menuet'	piano	1890–1905	1905	
177 (L 109)	*Mer, La*	orchestra	1903–5	1905	15 Oct. 1905
178 (L 81)	'Mer est plus belle, La'	voice & piano	1891	1901	16 Jan. 1904
179 (L 117)	'Minstrels'	piano	1910	1910	29 Mar. 1911
180 (L 108)	*Morceau de concours*	piano	1904	*1905*, 1980	30 May 1980
181 (L 64)	'Mort des amants, La'	voice & piano	1887	1890	
182 (L 110)	'Mouvement'	piano	1904–5	1905	6 Feb. 1906
183 (L 44)	'Musique'	voice & piano	1883	1980, 1983	14 Mar. 1939
184 (L 107)	*Musique pour 'Le Roi Lear'*	incidental music	1904–8	1926	22 Oct. 1926
185 (L 82)	*Nocturne*	piano	1892	*1892*, 1892	
186 (L 26)	*Nocturne et Scherzo*	cello & piano	1882		12 May 1882 (vn. & pf.)
187 (L 91)	*Nocturnes (Trois)* for violin & orch.	orchestra	1894–5		

7. No. in set	8. Text by	9. Dedication	10. Orch. by	11. Remarks
		General Meredith Read	Debussy	MSS—PLU (orig. *Marche des anciens comtes de Ross*)
No. 4, *Triomphe de Bacchus*	T. de Banville			MS—PLU
	G. d'Annunzio		Debussy– A. Caplet	MS in BO
				MS in BN
				MS—PLU
	(A. Renaud)			MS in PC (accomp. for *Flots, palmes, sables*)
178, 293, 94	P. Verlaine	see sep. entries		MSS in BN; PC (No. 3)
No. 3, *Petite Suite*			H. Busser	MS in BN (based on 'Fête galante' (116)
No. 2, *Suite bergamasque*			G. Cloëz	MS—PLU
79, 157, 86		Jacques Durand		MSS in BN; ESM (short score)
No. 1, *Mélodies (de Verlaine)*	P. Verlaine	Ernest Chausson		MS in BN
No. 12, *Préludes*, I				MS in PC; ESM (vn. & pf.)
				MS—PLU (orig. *Pièce pour piano*)
No. 5, *Poèmes de Baudelaire*	C. Baudelaire	Étienne Dupin		MS in BN
No. 3, *Images*, I				MS in BN
No. 4, *Chansons*	P. Bourget	Mme Vasnier		MS in BN (No. 9, *Vasnier Songbook*)
109, 289	(Shakespeare)		Roger-Ducasse	MS—PLU[4]
				MS—PLU
				MS in BN (vc. & pf.)
				MS—PLU (became *Nocturnes?*)

[4] Four bars of a *Prélude*, dated 'July 1908', are reproduced in Boucher, *Claude Debussy* (1930), plate XLIII.

1. No.	2. Title	3. Genre	4. Composed	5. Publ.	6. 1st perf.
188 (L 91)	*Nocturnes*	orch. & women's chorus	1897–9	1900; rev. 1930; new rev. 1964	27 Oct. 1901
189 (L 139)	*Noël des enfants qui n'ont plus de maisons*	voice & piano	1915	1916	9 Mar. 1916
190 (L 130)	*No-ja-li*	ballet	1914		
191 (L 91)	'Nuages'	orchestra	1897–9	1900; rev. 1930; new rev. 1964	9 Dec. 1900
192 (L 4)	*Nuit d'étoiles*	voice & piano	1880	1882	
193 (L 94)	*Nuits blanches* (1 & 2)	voice & piano	1899–1902	1911	18 Oct. 1991
194 (L 141)	*Ode à la France*	choral	1916–17	1928	2 Apr. 1928
195 (L 37)	'Ode bachique'	2 voices & piano	*c.*1882		
196 (L 60)	'Ombre des arbres, L'	voice & piano	1885; rev. 1903	1888; 1903	
197 (L 123)	'Ondine'	piano	1911–12	1913	12 June 1913
198 (L 12*bis*)	*Ouverture de Diane*	2 pianos	1881		
199 (L 133)	*Page d'album*	piano	1915	1933, 1980	24 Mar. 1917
200 (L 100)	'Pagodes'	piano	1903	1903	9 Jan. 1904
201 (L 130)	*Palais du silence, Le*				
202 (L 31)	'Pantomime'	voice & piano	1883	*1926*, 1969	unknown, but BBC Radio 3, 16 Dec. 1984
202 *bis*	*Papillons, Les*	voice & piano	1881		18 Feb. 1962
203 (L 96)	'Partie d'osselets, La'	incidental music	1900–1	1971 (compl. by Hoérée)	7 Feb. 1901; 10 Apr. 1954 (compl. by Boulez)
204 (L 75)	'Passepied'	piano	1890–1905	1905	
205 (L 45)	'Paysage sentimentale'	voice & piano	1883; rev. 1891, 1902	*1891*; 1902; 1980 (1883 version)	unknown, but BBC Radio 3, 16 Dec. 1984 (1883 version)
206 (L 88)	*Pelléas et Mélisande*	opera	1893–1902	1902 (pf.); 1904 (orch.)	30 Apr. 1902

7. No. in set	8. Text by	9. Dedication	10. Orch. by	11. Remarks
191, 117, 286		Georges Hartmann; (Lilly-Lilo)		MS in PC; LC (short score)
	Debussy		D.-E. Inghelbrecht	MSS in BN
	G. de Feure			MS in BN (sketch) (orig. *Le Palais du Silence*)
No. 1, *Nocturnes*		Georges Hartmann; (Lilly-Lilo)		MS in PC; LC (short score)
	T. de Banville	Mme Moreau-Sainti		MS in PC (1st publ. composition)
	Debussy			MS in PC; BO (frag.)
	L. Laloy		M. F. Gaillard	MS in BN (orch. sketches, inc.)
from *Hymnis*, scene VII	T. de Banville	Mme Vasnier		MS in PML
No. 3, *Ariettes oubliées*	P. Verlaine	Mary Garden 1903		MS in PML
No. 8, *Préludes*, II				MS in BN
	(T. de Banville)			MS in BN
		Emma Debussy		MS in BN (orig. *Pièce pour piano*)
No. 1, *Estampes*		J.-É. Blanche	A. Caplet	MS in BN
				see *No-ja-li*
No. 1, *Chansons de jeunesse*	P. Verlaine	Mme Vasnier		MS in BN (No. 1, *Vasnier Songbook*)
	T. Gautier	Mme Vasnier		MS in NYP
No. 5, *Les Chansons de Bilitis*	P. Louÿs		Debussy–Boulez; Debussy–Hoérée	MSS in BN (compl. by Boulez; Hoérée)
No. 4, *Suite*			G. Cloëz	MS–PLU
No. 5, *Chansons* (1883 version in 1980 edn. only)	P. Bourget	Mme Vasnier (1883); Mlle Jeanne Andrée (1891)		MS in BN (1883 version) (No. 10, *Vasnier Songbook*)
	M. Maeterlinck	Georges Hartmann et André Messager		MS in BN; PC; PML; UTA

1. No.	2. Title	3. Genre	4. Composed	5. Publ.	6. 1st perf.
207 (L 120)	*Petite Pièce* for clarinet & piano	chamber music	1910	1910	10 July 1910
208 (L 65)	*Petite Suite*	piano 4-hands	1888–89	1889	23 May 1894
209 (L 114)	*Petit Nègre, Le*				
210 (L 108)	*Pièce pour piano*				
211 (L 133)	*Pièce pour piano (pour l'œuvre du 'Vêtement du blessé')*				
212 (L 15)	'Pierrot'	voice & piano	1882	*1926*; 1969	
213 (L 127)	'Placet futile'	voice & piano	1913	1913	21 Mar. 1914
214 (L 96)	'Pluie au matin, La'	incidental music	1900–1	1971 (compl. by Hoérée)	7 Feb. 1901; 10 Apr. 1954 (compl. by Boulez)
215 (L 121)	*Plus que lente, La*	piano	1910	1910	
216	*Poèmes de Banville, Sept*	voice & piano	*c.*1880–2	1984	see sep. entries
217 (L 64)	*Poèmes de Charles Baudelaire, Cinq*	voice & piano	1887–89	1890	
218 (L 127)	*Poèmes de Stéphane Mallarmé, Trois*	voice & piano	1913	1913	21 Mar. 1914
219 (L 111)	'Poissons d'or'	piano	1907	1908	21 Feb. 1908
220 (L 102)	'Pour ce que Plaisance est morte'	voice & piano	1904	1904	6 Feb. 1906
221 (L 131)	'Pour invoquer Pan, Dieu du vent d'été'	piano 2- or 4-hands	1914	1915	17 Mar. 1917
222 (L 131)	'Pour la danseuse aux crotales'	piano 2- or 4-hands	1914	1915	17 Mar. 1917
223 (L 131)	'Pour l'égyptienne'	piano 2- or 4-hands	1914	1915	17 Mar. 1917

7. No. in set	8. Text by	9. Dedication	10. Orch. by	11. Remarks
				MS in AN (Concours at the Conservatoire)
97, 65, 175, 23			H. Busser	MS in BN
				see *The Little Nigar*
				see *Morceau de concours*
				see *Page d'album*
No. 3, *Chansons de jeunesse*	T. de Banville	Mme Vasnier		MS in LC
No. 2, *Poèmes de Mallarmé*	S. Mallarmé	Stéphane Mallarmé et Mme E. Bonniot (née G. Mallarmé)		MS in BN
No. 12, *Les Chansons de Bilitis*	P. Louÿs		Debussy–Boulez; Debussy–Hoérée	MSS in BN (compl. by Boulez; Hoérée); (adapted as No. 6, *Épigraphes antiques*)
			Debussy	MSS in BN
260, 295, 161, 282, 142, 274, 116	T. de Banville	see sep. entries		see sep. entries
15, 135, 154, 256, 181	C. Baudelaire	Étienne Dupin	Debussy–A. Caplet (No. 3)	MSS in BN
296, 213, 108	S. Mallarmé	Stéphane Mallarmé et Mme E. Bonniot (née G. Mallarmé)		MS in BN
No. 3, *Images*, II		Ricardo Viñes		MS in BN
Rondel II, *Chansons de France*, No. 3)	C. d'Orléans	Mme S. Bardac		MS in BN
No. 1, *Épigraphes antiques*	(P. Louÿs)		E. Ansermet	MS in BN (derived from No. 1, *Les Chansons de Bilitis*)
No. 4, *Épigraphes antiques*	(P. Louÿs)		E. Ansermet	MS in BN (derived from No. 10, *Les Chansons de Bilitis*)
No. 5, *Épigraphes antiques*	(P. Louÿs)		E. Ansermet	MS in BN

1. No.	2. Title	3. Genre	4. Composed	5. Publ.	6. 1st perf.
224 (L 95)	*Pour le piano*	piano	1894–1901	1901	11 Jan. 1902
225 (L 136)	'Pour les accords'	piano	1915	1916	14 Dec. 1916
226 (L 136)	'Pour les agréments'	piano	1915	1916	14 Dec. 1916
227 (L 136)	'Pour les arpèges composés'	piano	1915	1916	14 Dec. 1916
228 (L 136)	'Pour les cinq doigts'	piano	1915	1916	14 Dec. 1916
229 (L 136)	'Pour les degrés chromatiques'	piano	1915	1916	14 Dec. 1916
230 (L 136)	'Pour les huit doigts'	piano	1915	1916	14 Dec. 1916
231 (L 136)	'Pour les notes répétées'	piano	1915	1916	14 Dec. 1916
232 (L 136)	'Pour les octaves'	piano	1915	1916	14 Dec. 1916
233 (L 136)	'Pour les quartes'	piano	1915	1916	14 Dec. 1916
234 (L 136)	'Pour les sixtes'	piano	1915	1916	14 Dec. 1916
235 (L 136)	'Pour les sonorités opposées'	piano	1915	1916	14 Dec. 1916
236 (L 136)	'Pour les tierces'	piano	1915	1916	14 Dec. 1916
237 (L 131)	'Pour que la nuit soit propice'	piano 2- and 4-hands	1914	1915	17 Mar. 1917
238 (L 131)	'Pour remercier la pluie au matin'	piano 2- and 4-hands	1914	1915	17 Mar. 1917
239 (L 131)	'Pour un tombeau sans nom'	piano 2- and 4-hands	1914	1915	17 Mar. 1917
240 (L 75)	'Prélude'	piano	1890–1905	1905	
241 (L 95)	'Prélude'	piano	1901	1901	11 Jan. 1902
242 (L 86)	*Prélude à 'L'Après-midi d'un faune'*	orchestra	1892–4	1895	22 Dec. 1894
243 (L 117)	*Préludes*, Book I	piano	1909–10	1910	see sep. entries
244 (L 123)	*Préludes*, Book II	piano	1911–13	1913	see sep. entries

7. No. in set	8. Text by	9. Dedication	10. Orch. by	11. Remarks
241, 276, 308		see sep. entries	M. Ravel (No. 2)	MS in PC
No. 12, *Études*, II		Frédéric Chopin		MS in BN; BFL
No. 8, *Études*, II		Frédéric Chopin		MS in BN; BFL
No. 11, *Études*, II		Frédéric Chopin		MS in BN; BFL
No. 1, *Études*, I		Frédéric Chopin		MS in BN
No. 7, *Études*, II		Frédéric Chopin		MS in BN; BFL
No. 6, *Études*, I		Frédéric Chopin		MS in BN; BFL
No. 9, *Études*, II		Frédéric Chopin		MS in BN; BFL
No. 5, *Études*, I		Frédéric Chopin		MS in BN; BFL
No. 3, *Études*, I		Frédéric Chopin		MS in BN; BFL
No. 4, *Études*, I		Frédéric Chopin		MS in BN
No. 10, *Études*, II		Frédéric Chopin		MS in BN; BFL
No. 2, *Études*, I		Frédéric Chopin		MS in BN, BFL
No. 3, *Épigraphes antiques*	(P. Louÿs)		E. Ansermet	MS in BN (derived from No. 4, *Les Chansons de Bilitis*)
No. 6, *Épigraphes antiques*	(P. Louÿs)		E. Ansermet	MS in BN (derived from No. 12, *Les Chansons de Bilitis*)
No. 2, *Épigraphes antiques*	(P. Louÿs)		E. Ansermet	MS in BN (derived from Nos. 7 & 8, *Les Chansons de Bilitis*)
No. 1, *Suite bergamasque*			G. Cloez	MS—PLU
No. 1, *Pour le piano*		Mlle M. W. de Romilly		MS in PML
	(S. Mallarmé)	Raymond Bonheur (Gaby (Dupont) (1899))		MS in BN; PC (2 pianos); PML (short score)
7, 319, 317, 294, 60, 84, 37, 124, 284, 36, 72, 179			H. Busser (No. 10)	MS in PML
1, 121, 252, 114, 32, 129, 306, 197, 139, 34, 307, 122			H. Busser (No. 3)	MS in BN

1. No.	2. Title	3. Genre	4. Composed	5. Publ.	6. 1st perf.
245 (L 116)	*Première Rapsodie* for clarinet with piano (or orch.)	chamber music; orchestra	1909–10	1910	16 Jan. 1911
246 (L 50)	*Première Suite d'orchestre*	orchestra	c.1883		
247 (L 24)	*Printemps, Le*	women's chorus & orch.	1882		
248 (L 56)	*Printemps, Le* (L'aimable printemps)	chorus & orch.	1884		17 May 1884
249 (L 61)	*Printemps*	symphonic suite with chorus	1887; rev. 1912	1904 (pf.); 1913 (orch.)	18 Apr. 1913 (orch.)
250 (L 118)	*Promenoir des deux amants, Le*	voice & piano	1904, 1910	1910	14 Jan. 1911
251 (L 84)	*Proses lyriques*	voice & piano	1892–3	1895	see sep. entries
252 (L 123)	'Puerta del Viño, La'	piano	1911–12	1913	5 Mar. 1913
253 (L 92)	'Quant j'ai ouy le tabourin'	4 voices a cappella	1908	1908	9 Apr. 1909
254 (L 87)	'Quelques aspects de "Nous n'irons plus au bois"'	piano	1894	1977	
255 (L 98)	*Rapsodie* for orchestra & saxophone	orchestra	1903–11	1919	17 May 1904
256 (L 64)	'Recueillement'	voice & piano	1889	1890	
257 (L 110)	'Reflets dans l'eau'	piano	1904–5	1905	6 Feb. 1906
258 (L 55)	'Regret'	voice & piano	1884	1980, 1983	14 Mar. 1939
259 (L 50)	'Rêve'	orchestra	c.1883		
260 (L 8)	'Rêverie'	voice & piano	1880	1984	28 Apr. 1985
261 (L 68)	*Rêverie*	piano	1890	1895	27 Feb. 1899
262 (L 72)	*Rodrigue et Chimène*	opera	1890–2		14 May 1993
263 (L 107)	*Roi Lear, Le*				
264 (L 43)	'Romance' (Silence ineffable)	voice & piano	1883	1980, 1983	14 Mar. 1939

7. No. in set	8. Text by	9. Dedication	10. Orch. by	11. Remarks
		P. Mimart	Debussy	MSS in BN (Concours at the Conservatoire, 14 July 1910)
15, 22, 259, 13				MSS—PLU (orch. & 2 pianos)
				see *Salut printemps*
	J. Barbier			MS in BN; PML (chorus & pf., inc.); PC (frag.)
	(Botticelli-M. Baschet)	Auguste Durand	H. Busser–Debussy	MS in UTA (pf. 4-h & chorus)
11, 67, 155	T. Lhermite	Emma Claude Debussy ... p.m.	L. Beydts	MS in BN
82, 81, 80, 83	Debussy	see sep. entries	Roger-Ducasse	MSS—see sep. entries
No. 3, *Préludes*, II			H. Busser	MS in BN
No. 2, *Chansons de C. d'Orléans*	C. d'Orléans			MS in BN
No. 3, *Images (oubliées)*		Mlle Yvonne Lerolle		MS in PC
	(commissioned by Mrs Elise Hall)	Mme Elise Hall		MS in NEC (inc.); BN
No. 4, *Poèmes de Baudelaire*	C. Baudelaire	Étienne Dupin		MS in BN
No. 1, *Images*, I				MS in BN
No. 6, *Chansons*	P. Bourget	Mme Vasnier		MS in BN (No. 13, *Vasnier Songbook*)
No. 3, *Première Suite d'orchestre*				MS—PLU
No. 1, *Poèmes de Banville*	T. de Banville			MS in PC
				MS—PLU
	C. Mendès	Mlle Gabrielle Dupont (1890)		MS in PML (inc. short score)
				see *Musique pour 'Le Roi Lear'*
No. 3, *Chansons*	P. Bourget	Mme Vasnier		MS in BN (No. 8, *Vasnier Songbook*)

1. No.	2. Title	3. Genre	4. Composed	5. Publ.	6. 1st perf.
265 (L 79)	'Romance' (L'Âme évaporée)	voice & piano	1884	1891	
266 (L 52)	'Romance—Musique pour éventail'				
267 (L 54)	'Romance d'Ariel, La'	voice & piano	1884	1980, 1983	unknown, but BBC Radio 3, 16 Dec. 1984
268 (L 79)	*Romances, Deux*	voice & piano	1886	1891	
269 (L 30)	*Rondeau*	voice & piano	1881	1932	
270 (L 102)	'Rondel I'				
271 (L 102)	'Rondel II'				
272 (L 17)	*Rondel chinois*	voice & piano	1881		
273 (L 122)	'Rondes de printemps'	orchestra	1905–9	1910	2 Mar. 1910
274 (L 13)	'Roses, Les'	voice & piano	1882	1984	12 May 1882
275 (L 24)	*Salut printemps*	women's chorus & orch.	1882	1928 (pf.) 1956 (orch.)	2 Apr. 1928
276 (L 95)	'Sarabande'	piano	1894–1901	*1896*; 1901	11 Jan. 1902
277 (L 89)	*Saulaie, La*	solo voice (bar) & orch.	1896–1900		
278 (L 83)	*Scènes au crépuscule, Trois*	orchestra	1892–3		
279 (L 38)	'Scherzo'	orch. suite for piano 4-hands	*c.*1882		
280 (L 26)	Scherzo	cello & piano	1882		
281 (L 14)	*Séguidille*	voice & piano	1882		
282 (L 34)	'Sérénade'	voice & piano	1882	1984	29 June 1938

7. No. in set	8. Text by	9. Dedication	10. Orch. by	11. Remarks
No. 1, *Romances, Deux*	P. Bourget			MS in BN
No. 6, *Chansons* (1980 edn.)				title in *Vasnier Songbook*; see 'Voici que le printemps'
No. 5, *Chansons*	P. Bourget	Mme Vasnier		MS in BN (No. 12, *Vasnier Songbook*)
58, 265	P. Bourget			MS in BN
	A. de Musset	Alexandre de Meck		MS—PLU
No. 1, *Chansons de France*				see 'Le temps a laissié son manteau'
No. 3, *Chansons de France*				see 'Pour ce que Plaisance est morte'
	unknown	Mme Vasnier		MS in LC
No. 3, *Images pour orchestre*		Emma Claude Debussy		MS in BN
No. 6, *Poèmes de Banville*	T. de Banville	Mme Vasnier		MS in SMF
	Comte de Ségur			MS in BN (orch.); PML (pf.); (orig: *Le Printemps*)
No. 2, *Pour le piano*		Mme E. Rouart (née Y. Lerolle)	M. Ravel	MS in PC (rev. of No. 2, *Images (oubliées)*)
	D. G. Rossetti (trans. P. Louÿs)			MS in SUC (frag.); St-G (frag);[1] BN (text)
	(H. de Régnier)			MS in BN (sketch); (?became *Nocturnes*)
No. 3, *Triomphe de Bacchus*	(T. de Banville)			MS—PLU
				see *Nocturne et Scherzo*
	T. Gautier	Mme Vasnier		MS in PC
No. 4, *Poèmes de Banville*	T. de Banville	Mme Vasnier		MS in PC (inc.)

[1] Maison Claude Debussy, Saint-Germain-en-Laye.

1. No.	2. Title	3. Genre	4. Composed	5. Publ.	6. 1st perf.
283 (L 113)	'Serenade for the Doll'	piano	1906	1906, 1908	18 Dec. 1908
284 (L 117)	'Sérénade interrompue, La'	piano	1909–10	1910	14 Jan. 1911
285 (L 43)	'Silence ineffable'				14 Mar. 1939
286 (L 91)	'Sirènes'	women's chorus & orch.	1897–9	1900; rev. 1930; new rev. 1964	27 Oct. 1901
287 (L 113)	'Snow is Dancing, The'	piano	1908	1908	18 Dec. 1908
288 (L 100)	'Soirée dans Grenade, La'	piano	1903	1903	9 Jan. 1904
289 (L 107)	'Sommeil de Lear, Le'	incidental music	1904–6	1926	22 Oct. 1926
290 (L 135)	Sonata for cello & piano	chamber music	1915	1915	24 Mar. 1917
291 (L 137)	Sonata for flute, viola, & harp	chamber music	1915	1916	9 Mar. 1917
292 (L 140)	Sonata for violin & piano	chamber music	1916–17	1917	5 May 1917
293 (L 81)	'Son du cor s'afflige, Le'	voice & piano	1891	1901	16 Jan. 1904
294 (L 117)	'Sons et les parfums tournent dans l'air du soir, Les'	piano	1910	1910	29 Mar. 1911
295 (L 11)	'Souhait'	voice & piano	1881	1984	29 June 1938
296 (L 127)	'Soupir'	voice & piano	1913	1913	21 Mar. 1914
297 (L 96)	'Souvenir de Mnasidica, Le'	incidental music	1900–1	1971 (compl. by Hoérée)	7 Feb. 1901; (compl. by Boulez)
298 (L 87)	'Souvenir du Louvre'	piano	1894	*1896*; 1977	
299 (L 60)	'Spleen'	voice & piano	1888; rev. 1903	1888; 1903	
300 (L 85)	String Quartet, Op. 10	chamber music	1892–3	1894	29 Dec. 1893

7. No. in set	8. Text by	9. Dedication	10. Orch. by	11. Remarks
No. 3, *Children's Corner*		Chouchou	A. Caplet	MS—PLU
No. 9, *Préludes*, I				MS in PC
				see 'Romance' (264)
No. 3, *Nocturnes*		Georges Hartmann; (Lilly Lilo)		MS in PC; LC (short score)
No. 4, *Children's Corner*		Chouchou	A. Caplet	MS in BN
No. 2, *Estampes*		J.-É. Blanche (Pierre Louÿs)	H. Busser	MS in BN
No. 2, *Musique pour 'Le Roi Lear'*	(Shakespeare)		Roger-Ducasse	MS—PLU
		Emma Claude Debussy (p.m.)		MS in BN; PLU; SW (sketch)
		Emma Claude Debussy (p.m.)		MS in BN; PLU
		Emma Claude Debussy (p.m.)		MS in BN; PLU
No. 2, *Mélodies (de Verlaine)*	P. Verlaine	Robert Godet		MS in BN
No. 4, *Préludes*, I	(C. Baudelaire)			MS in PC
No. 2, *Poèmes de Banville*	T. de Banville			MS in PC
No. 1, *Poèmes de Mallarmé*	S. Mallarmé	Stéphane Mallarmé et Mme E. Bonniot (née G. Mallarmé)		MS in BN
No. 11, *Les Chansons de Bilitis*	P. Louÿs		Debussy–Boulez; Debussy–Hoérée	MSS in BN (compl. by Boulez; Hoérée)
No. 2, *Images (oubliées)*		Mlle Yvonne Lerolle		MS in PC (publ. as *Sarabande*, early version of No. 2, *Pour le piano*)
No. 6, *Ariettes oubliées*	P. Verlaine	Mary Garden 1903		MS in BFL
		Quatuor Ysaÿe		MS in BN

1. No.	2. Title	3. Genre	4. Composed	5. Publ.	6. 1st perf.
301 (L 75)	*Suite bergamasque*	piano	1890–1905	1905	
302 (L 10)	Symphony in B minor	piano 4-hands	1880–81	1933; 1965	27 Jan. 1937
303 (L 129)	*Syrinx*	flute	1913	1927	1 Dec. 1913
304 (L 69)	*Tarentelle styrienne*				
305 (L 102)	'Temps a laissié son manteau, Le'	voice & piano	1904	1904	15 May 1905
306 (L 123)	'Terrasse des audiences du clair de lune, La'	piano	1911–12	1913	5 Apr. 1913
307 (L 123)	'Tierces alternées, Les'	piano	1913?	1913	12 June 1913
308 (L 95)	'Toccata'	piano	1901	1901	11 Jan. 1902
309 (L 90)	'Tombeau des naïades, Le'	voice & piano	1898	1899	17 Mar. 1900
310 (L 96)	'Tombeau sans nom, Le'	incidental music	1900–1	1971 (compl. by Hoérée)	7 Feb. 1901; 10 Apr. 1954 (compl. by Boulez)
311 (L 18)	*Tragédie*	voice & piano	1881		
312 (L 3)	Trio in G for piano, violin, & cello	chamber music	1880	1986	20 Oct. 1985
313 (L 12)	*Triolet, à Philis*				
314 (L 38)	*Triomphe de Bacchus*	orch. suite for piano 4-hands	1882	1928 (pf., orch.); *1987* (pf.)	2 Apr. 1928
315 (L 71)	*Valse romantique*	piano	1890	1890	
316	*Vasnier Songbook*	voice & piano	1882–4	1980 & 1983 (partial)	unknown, but BBC Radio 3, 16 Dec. 1984
317 (L 117)	'Vent dans la plaine, Le'	piano	1909	1910	29 Mar. 1911
318 (L 52)	'Voici que le printemps'	voice & piano	1884; rev. 1902	1902; 1980 (1884 version)	unknown, but BBC Radio 3, 16 Dec. 1984 (1884 version)
319 (L 117)	'Voiles'	piano	1909	1910	25 May 1910

7. No. in set	8. Text by	9. Dedication	10. Orch. by	11. Remarks
240, 176, 57, 204			see sep. entries	MS—PLU
		Mme de Meck		MS in MT
	(G. Mourey) (for *Psyché*)	Louis Fleury		MS—PLU (orig. *Flûte de Pan*)
				see *Danse*
'Rondel I', *Chansons de France*, No. 1	C. d'Orléans	Mme S. Bardac		MS in BN
No. 7, *Préludes*, II	(R. Puaux)			MS in BN
No. 11, *Préludes*, II				MS in BN
No. 3, *Pour le piano*		N. G. Coronio		MS in PC
No. 3, *Chansons de Bilitis*	P. Louÿs	(Mme Lucien Fontaine)	M. Delage	MS—PLU
No. 7, *Les Chansons de Bilitis*	P. Louÿs		Debussy–Boulez; Debussy–Hoérée	MSS in BN (compl. by Boulez; Hoérée) (adapted as No. 2, *Épigraphes antiques*)
	L. Valade (after H. Heine)	Mme Vasnier		MS in PC
		Émile Durand		MS in PML (movt. 1); UMA (movts. 2–4)
				see *Zéphyr*
90, 3, 279, 169	T. de Banville		M. F. Gaillard	MS in PML (movts. 1, 2) (see (90), (30))
		Mlle Rose Depecker		MS—PLU
202, 100, 166, 55, 111, 64, 40, 264, 183, 205, 318, 267, 258	see sep. entries	Mme Vasnier		MS in BN (orig. *Chansons*)
No. 3, *Préludes*, I	(Favart)			MS in PC
No. 6, *Chansons* (1884 version in 1980 edn. only)	P. Bourget	Mme Vasnier		MS in BN (1884 version) (No. 11, *Vasnier Songbook*)
No. 2, *Préludes*, I				MS in PC

1. No.	2. Title	3. Genre	4. Composed	5. Publ.	6. 1st perf.
320 (L 92)	'Yver, vous n'estes qu'un villain'	4 voice a cappella	1898	1908	9 Apr. 1909
321 (L 12)	*Zéphyr*	voice & piano	1881	1932	
322 (L 59)	*Zuleima*	choral	1885–6		?Dec. 1886

7. No. in set	8. Text by	9. Dedication	10. Orch. by	11. Remarks
No. 3, *Chansons de C. d'Orléans*	C. d'Orléans	Lucien Fontaine		MS in BN; PC
	T. de Banville			MS in PC (orig. *Triolet, à Philis*)
	G. Boyer (after H. Heine)			MS—PLU

CATALOGUE OF PROJECTS:
ABANDONED, NEVER STARTED, REJECTED

Note

COLUMN 1: Entry numbers followed by (L Ann. IV) refer to the list in Lesure's *Catalogue de l'œuvre de Claude Debussy*, p. 153, entitled *Projets non réalisés*.

1. No.	2. Title	3. Genre	4. Considered	5. Text by	6. Remarks
1 (L Ann. IV)	'Amour masqué, L''				See *Masques et bergamasques*
2 (L Ann. IV)	*Amphion*	opera	*c.*1900	P. Valéry	never started
3 (L Ann. IV)	*Aphrodite*	ballet	1896–7	P. Louÿs	never started
4 (L Ann. IV)	*As You Like It*	incidental music	1886	M. Vaucaire (after Shakespeare)	never started
5	*As You Like It*	incidental music	1917	Shakespeare (trans. P.-J. Toulet)	never started
6	*Ballet persan*	ballet	1912	P.-J. Toulet	abandoned
7	'Ballet rosso-vénitien'				see *Masques et bergamasques*
8	*Briséis*	opera	1903	C. Mendès and Mikhaël (after Goethe)	(completion of opera by Chabrier)
9 (L Ann. IV)	*Cendrelune*	opera	1895–8	P. Louÿs	never started
10	*Chat botté, Le*	?opera	1909	G. Mourey	rejected
11 (L Ann. IV)	*Chevalier d'or, Le*	pantomime	1897	Mme J.-L. Forain	never started
12 (L Ann. IV)	*Comme il vous plaira*	opera	1902	Shakespeare (trans. P.-J. Toulet)	never started

1. No.		2. Title	3. Genre	4. Considered	5. Text by	6. Remarks
13		*Concerts*	piano & orch.	1917		never started
14	(L Ann. IV)	*Crimen amoris*	opera	1912–14	C. Morice (after P. Verlaine)	abandoned; became *Fêtes galantes* (118)[1]
15		*Dame à la faulx, La*	incidental music	1911	Saint-Pol-Roux	never started
16		*Danseuse, La*	ballet	1894	P. Louÿs	abandoned
17	(L Ann. IV)	*Daphnis et Chloé*	ballet	1895–8	P. Louÿs (after Longus)	never started
18	(L Ann. IV)	*Dionysos*	incidental music	1904	J. Gasquet	never started
19		*Don Juan*	opera	?1903	?Byron or Molière	never started
20		*Drame cosmogonique*	theatre	?1908	J.-É. Blanche	abandoned
21		*Drame fantastique*	theatre	?1917	Debussy	abandoned
22		*Drame indien*	theatre	?1914	G. d'Annunzio	never started
23	(L Ann. IV)	*Embarquement pour ailleurs, L'*	incidental music	1891	G. Mourey	never started
24	(L Ann. IV)	'Éternelle aventure, L''				see *Masques et bergamasques*
25		*Fille de Pasiphaé, La*	incidental music	1898	V. de Balbiani	rejected
26	(L Ann. IV)	*Florise*	?incidental music	c.1882	T. de Banville	abandoned
27	(L Ann. IV)	*Grande Bretèche, La*	opera	1895	H. de Balzac	never started
28	(L Ann. IV)	*Histoire de Tristan, L'*	opera	1907–9	G. Mourey (after J. Bédier)	abandoned, forbidden by the author
29		*Huon de Bordeaux*	?opera	1909	G. Mourey	rejected
30		*Joyzelle*	opera	?1903	M. Maeterlinck	never started

[1] See Catalogue of Compositions: Published, Unpublished, Incomplete.

1. No.		2. Title	3. Genre	4. Considered	5. Text by	6. Remarks
31		*Marchand de rêves, Le*	?opera	1909	G. Mourey	rejected
32	(L Ann. IV)	*Masques et bergamasques*	ballet	1909–10	Debussy	abandoned; scenario publ. 1910; MS in UTA[2]
33		*Mille et une nuits de n'importe où et d'ailleurs*	incidental music	?1897, ?1901	R. Peter	rejected
34	(L Ann. IV)	*Noces de Sathan, Les*	incidental music	1892	J. Bois	rejected
35		*Orestie, L'*	opera	1909	L. Laloy (after Aeschylus)	never started
36		*Oedipe à Colonne*	incidental music	1894	Sophocles (trans. P. Louÿs & A.-F. Herold)	abandoned
37	(L Ann. IV)	*Orphée*	ballet	c.1895	P. Valéry	never started
38	(L Ann. IV)	*Orphée-Roi*	opera	1907–9	V. Segalen	never started
39		*Pèlerin d'amour, Le*	incidental music	1902–3	V.-E. Michele	abandoned
40		*Poème*	violin & orch.	c.1912–14		abandoned
41	(L Ann. IV)	*Princesse Maleine, La*	opera	1891	M. Maeterlinck	abandoned, forbidden by the author
42		*Pygmalion*	ballet	1911	(after Rameau)	never started
43	(L Ann. IV)	'Reine des Aulnes, La'				see *Cendrelune*
44	(L Ann. IV)	'Roi des Aulnes, Le'				see *Cendrelune*
45	(L Ann. IV)	*Salammbô*	opera	1886	G. Flaubert	abandoned
46	(L Ann. IV)	*Siddhartha*	opera	1907–10	V. Segalen	abandoned
47	(L Ann. IV)	Sonata for vn. & pf.	chamber music	1894		never started

[2] University of Texas at Austin.

1. No.		2. Title	3. Genre	4. Considered	5. Text by	6. Remarks
48	(L Ann. IV)	Sonata No. 4 for ob., hn, & hpd.	chamber music	1915–18		never started
49	(L Ann. IV)	Sonata No. 5 for tpt., cl., bn., & pf.	chamber music	1915–18		never started
50	(L Ann. IV)	Sonata No. 6 for several instr. & d.b.	chamber music	1915–18		never started
51		String Quartet, No. 2	chamber music	1894		never started
52		Symphony[3]	orchestra	1890	(E. A. Poe)	abandoned
53		*Tania*	opera	1914–16	?Russian author	rejected
54		*Tentation de St-Antoine, La*	incidental music	1895	G. de Voisins	rejected
55	(L Ann. IV)	*Uns et les autres, Les*	opera	1896	P. Verlaine	never started
56		*Valse*	piano	1894		abandoned
57		*Valse*	2 pianos	1905		abandoned
58	(L Ann. IV)	*Voyage de Pausole, Le*	symphonic suite	1901	P. Louÿs	abandoned

[3] This may well be the first manifestation of what developed into *La Chute de la Maison Usher* and *Le Diable dans le beffroi*.

LIST OF
DEBUSSY'S WRITINGS

1. Unpublished Plays
(Written with René Peter)

*Les Mille et une nuits de n'importe où et d'ailleurs (c.*1897).
Les 'Frères en art' (F.E.A.), (1897–8; rev. Debussy *c.*1903).
*Le Roman de Rosette (c.*1898–1901).
*L'Utile aventure (c.*1898).
*L'Herbe tendre (c.*1899).
*Esther et la maison de fous (c.*1899).

2. Librettos

La Chute de la Maison Usher (incomplete).
Le Diable dans le beffroi (scenario).
(These have been published in Lockspeiser, *Debussy et Edgar Poe* (Monaco, 1962).)

3. Criticism

Monsieur Croche antidilettante (Paris, 1921; 2nd edn., 1926; 1950); trans. N. Douglas
    as *Monsieur Croche the Dilettante-hater* (London, 1927).
Monsieur Croche et autres écrits, Introduction and notes by F. Lesure (Paris, 1971;
    2nd edn., rev. & enl. 1987); trans. and ed. R. L. Smith as *Debussy on Music*
    (London and New York, 1977).

4. Texts for songs

Proses lyriques (1892–3).
*Nuits blanches (c.*1900).
Noël des enfants qui n'ont plus de maisons (1915).

5. Ballet scenario

Masques et bergamasques (Paris, 1910).

6. Editor's Preface

Preface to Durand edition of Chopin's piano works (Paris, 1915).

Select Bibliography

INTRODUCTORY NOTE

The sources of the quotations from the various collections of Debussy's letters are indicated in the text by their year of publication.

1927   *Lettres de Claude Debussy à son éditeur*, ed. J. Durand (Paris, 1927).

1929   *Correspondance de Claude Debussy et P.-J. Toulet*, ed. H. Martineau (Paris, 1929).

1938   *L'Enfance de Pelléas: Lettres de Claude Debussy à André Messager*, ed. J. André-Messager (Paris, 1938).

1942   *Claude Debussy: Lettres à deux amis: Soixante-dix-huit lettres inédites à Robert Godet et G. Jean-Aubry*, ed. G. Jean-Aubry (Paris, 1942).

1945   *Correspondance de Claude Debussy et Pierre Louÿs*, ed. H. Borgeaud (Paris, 1945).

1948   *Debussy et d'Annunzio: Correspondance inédite*, ed. G. Tosi (Paris, 1948).

1957a   *Claude Debussy: Lettres inédites à André Caplet*, ed. E. Lockspeiser (Monaco, 1957).

1957b   *Lettres de Claude Debussy à sa femme Emma*, ed. P. Vallery-Radot (Paris, 1957).

1962   'Correspondance de Claude Debussy et de Louis Laloy (1902–1914)', *RdM: Claude Debussy 1862–1962: Textes et documents inédits*, ed. F. Lesure, 48 (1962), 3.

1980   *Claude Debussy: Lettres 1884–1918*, ed. F. Lesure (Paris, 1980).

1987   *Debussy Letters*, ed. F. Lesure and R. Nichols (London, 1987).

A SELECTIVE BIBLIOGRAPHY

Abbate, C., '*Tristan* in the Composition of *Pelléas*', *19th Century Music*, 5 (1981–2), 117–41.

Ackere, J. van, *Claude Debussy* (Antwerp, 1949).

—— *Pelléas et Mélisande* (Brussels, 1952).

Almendra, J. d', *Les Modes grégoriens dans l'œuvre de Claude Debussy* (2nd edn., rev. & enl., Paris, 1950).

Alshvang, A., *Klod Debussyi, Zizn, deyatelnost mirovozzrenie in tvortschestvo* (Moscow, 1935).

Arconada, M., *En torno a Debussy* (Madrid, 1926–7).

Ashbrook, W., 'A Study in Estrangement', *Opera News*, 24/11 (16 Jan. 1960), 8–9.

Astruc, G., *Le Pavillon des fantômes* (Paris, 1929).

Austin, W. (ed.), *Debussy: Prelude to 'The Afternoon of a Faun'* (New York, 1970).

Avant-scène, L', Opéra, 'Pelléas et Mélisande', 9 (Paris, 1977).

Barraqué, J., *Debussy* (Paris, 1962; trans. R. Toop, London, 1972).

Bathori, J., *Sur l'interprétation des mélodies de Claude Debussy* (Paris, 1953).

Bernac, P., *The Interpretation of French Song* (London, 1970).

Bertaux, E., *En ce temps-là* (Paris, 1946).

Blanche, J.-É., *La Pêche aux souvenirs* (priv. pub., n.d.; rev., Paris, 1949).

Bois, J., *Les Noces de Sathan* (Paris, 1892).

Bonheur, R., 'Souvenirs et impressions d'un compagnon de jeunesse', *ReM: La Jeunesse de Claude Debussy* (1 May 1926), 3–9.

Bonmariage, S., *Catherine et ses amis* (Gap, 1949).

Boucher, M., *Claude Debussy* (Paris, 1930).

Brussel, R., 'Claude Debussy et Paul Dukas', *ReM: La Jeunesse de Claude Debussy* (1 May 1926), 99–109.

Burnand, R., *La Vie quotidienne en France de 1870 à 1900* (Paris, 1947).

Busser, H., 'Souvenirs de jeunesse sur Claude Debussy' in A. Martin (ed.) *Catalogue de l'Exposition Debussy 1942* (Paris, 1942), vi–viii.

—— *De Pelléas aux Indes galantes* (Paris, 1955).

Cahiers Debussy, Nos., 1–3, 1974–6; Nouvelle série Nos. 1–9, 1977–85.

Caillard, C. F., and **Bérys, J. de,** *Le Cas Debussy* (Paris, 1910).

Chantavoine, J., 'Pelléas et Mélisande', in *Petit Guide de l'amateur de musique*, 2 (Paris, 1948, 1953).

Chennevière, D., *Claude Debussy et son œuvre* (Paris, 1913).

Clive, H. P., *Pierre Louÿs (1870–1925), A Biography* (Oxford, 1978).

Cobb, M. G., *The Poetic Debussy: A Collection of His Song Texts and Selected Letters* (Boston, 1982).

—— 'Claude Debussy to Claudius and Gustave Popelin: Nine Unpublished Letters', *19th Century Music*, 18 (Summer 1989), 39–48.

Colette, *Journal à rebours* (Paris, 1941; 2nd edn., 1974).

Constant, P., *Le Conservatoire National de Musique* (Paris).

Cooper, M., *French Music from the Death of Berlioz to the Death of Fauré* (London, 1951).

Cortot, A., 'La Musique pour piano de Claude Debussy', *ReM: Numéro spécial consacré à Debussy* (1 Dec. 1920), 127–50; trans. V. Edgell as *The Piano Music of Debussy* (London, 1922).

—— *La Musique française de piano* (Paris, 1930; 5th edn., 1948).

—— 'Un drame lyrique de Claude Debussy (*Rodrigue et Chimène*)', *Inédits sur Claude Debussy*, Collection Comœdia-Charpentier (Paris, 1942), 13–16.

Cox, D., *Debussy Orchestral Music* (BBC Music Guides; London, 1974; Seattle, 1975).

Daly, W.-H., *Debussy: A Study in Modern Music* (Edinburgh, 1908).

Danckert, W., *Claude Debussy* (Berlin, 1950).

Dawes, F., *Debussy Piano Music* (London, 1969; 2nd edn., 1975).

Debussy, C., *Monsieur Croche antidilettante* (Paris, 1921; 2nd edn., 1926; 1950); trans. N. Douglas as *Monsieur Croche the Dilettante-hater* (London, 1927).

—— *Monsieur Croche et autres écrits*, introduction and notes by F. Lesure (Paris, 1971; 2nd edn., rev. & enlarged, 1987); trans. and ed. R. L. Smith as *Debussy on Music* (London and New York, 1977).

Decsey, E., *Claude Debussy*, 2 vols. (Graz, 1933; 2nd edn., 1936, 1949).

Denis, M., *Henri Lerolle et ses amis* (Paris, 1932).

Dietschy, M., 'The Family and Childhood of Debussy', trans. E. Lockspeiser, *Musical Quarterly*, 46 (July 1960), 301–14.

Donnay, M., *Autour du Chat Noir* (Paris, 1926).

Doret, G., *Temps et contretemps* (Fribourg, 1942).

Douliez, P., *Claude Debussy* (Haarlem, 1954).

Dumesnil, M., *How to Play and Teach Debussy* (New York, 1932).

—— *Claude Debussy, Master of Dreams* (New York, 1940).

Durand, J., *Quelques souvenirs d'un éditeur de musique*, i (Paris, 1924).

—— *Souvenirs d'un éditeur de musique* (2nd ser., Paris, 1925).

Eaton, Q., *The Boston Opera Company* (New York, 1965).

Emmanuel, M., *Pelléas et Mélisande* (Paris, 1926; 2nd edn., 1950).

—— 'Entretiens inédits d'Ernest Guiraud et de Claude Debussy (1889–1890)', *Inédits sur Claude Debussy*, Collection Comœdia-Charpentier (Paris, 1942), 25–6.

Estrade-Guerra, O. d', 'Les Manuscrits de *Pelléas et Mélisande*', *ReM* (Carnet Critique), 235 (1957), 5.

Fabian, L. *Claude Debussy und sein Werk* (Munich, 1923).

Faure, M., *Musique et société du Second Empire aux années vingt* (Paris, 1985).

Ferchault, G., *Claude Debussy: 'Musicien français'* (Paris, 1948).

Gaïanus, *see* Paglia, C.

Garden, M., and Biancolli, L., *Mary Garden's Story* (New York, 1951).

Gatti-Casazza, G., *Memories of Opera* (New York, 1941; London, 1977).

Gauthier, A., *Debussy: Documents iconographiques* (Geneva, 1952).

Gianturco, E., *Claude Debussy* (Naples, 1923).

Gilman, L., *Debussy's Pelléas et Mélisande: A Guide to the Opera* (New York, 1907).

Godet, R., 'Le Lyrisme intime de Debussy', *ReM: Numéro spéciale consacré à Debussy* (1 Dec. 1920), 167–90.

Goléa, A., *Pelléas et Mélisande* (Paris, 1952).

—— *Claude Debussy* (Paris, 1966).

—— *Claude Debussy: Pelléas et Mélisande* (Geneva, 1983).

Goubault, C., *Claude Debussy* (Paris, 1986).

Gourdet, G., *Debussy* (Paris, 1970).

Grayson, D. A., *The Genesis of Debussy's 'Pelléas et Mélisande'* (Ann Arbor, 1986).

Gysi, F., 'Claude Debussy', *Neujahrsblätter der Allgemeinen Musikgesellschaft* (Zurich, 1926).

Hardeck, E., *Untersuchungen zu Klavierliedern C. Debussys* (Regensburg, 1967).

Harvey, H. B., *Claude de France: The Story of Debussy* (New York, 1948).

Hertrich, C., *Claude Debussy: Génie du symbolisme musical* (Saint-Etienne, 1944).

Hirsbrunner, T., *Debussy und seine Zeit* (Berne, 1981).

Holloway, R., *Debussy and Wagner* (London, 1979).

Honegger, A., *Incantation aux fossiles* (Lausanne, 1948).

Howat, R., *Debussy in Proportion: A Musical Analysis* (Cambridge and Boston, 1983).

Inédits sur Claude Debussy, Collection Comœdia-Charpentier (Paris, 1942) (articles by Cortot, Emmanuel, Martin, Peter).

Inghelbrecht, G., and **Inghelbrecht, D.-E.,** *Claude Debussy* (Paris, 1953).

Jankélévitch, V., *Debussy et le mystère* (Neuchâtel, 1949; 2nd. edn., 1962).

—— *La Vie et la mort dans la musique de Debussy* (Neuchâtel, 1968).

—— *Debussy et le mystère de l'instant* (Paris, 1976).

Jardillier, R., *Claude Debussy* (Dijon, 1922).

—— *Pelléas* (Paris, 1927).

Jarocinski, S., *Debussy, a impressionizm i symbolizm* (Cracow, 1966); trans. T. Douchy as *Debussy, impressionisme et symbolisme* (Paris, 1971); trans. from French, R. Myers as *Debussy, Impressionism and Symbolism* (London, 1975).

—— *Debussy, kronika, zycia, dziela, epoki* (Cracow, 1972).

Jean-Aubry, G., *La Musique et les nations* (Paris, 1922).

Joly-Segalen, A., and **Schaeffner, A.,** *Segalen et Debussy* (Monaco, 1961).

Keil, W., *Untersuchungen zur Entwicklung des frühen Klavierstils von Debussy und Ravel* (Wiesbaden, 1982).

Ketting, P., *Claude-Achille Debussy* (Amsterdam, 1941); trans. W. A. G. Doyle-Davidson as *Claude-Achille Debussy* (New York and Stockholm, 1947).

Koechlin, C., *Debussy* (Paris, 1927, 1941, 1956).

Kolsch, H. F., *Der Impressionismus bei Debussy* (Düsseldorf, 1937).

Kounitskaia, R. I., *O romantitcheskoi i poetike v tvortchestve Debussy* (Moscow, 1982).

Kremlev, Y., *Klod Debussy* (Moscow, 1963).

Laloy, L., *Claude Debussy* (Paris, 1909).

—— *Debussy* (Paris, 1944).

—— *La Musique retrouvée, 1902–1927* (Paris, 1928; 2nd edn. rev. & enl., 1974).

Leblanc, G., *Souvenirs* (Paris, 1931).

Lépine, J., *La Vie de Claude Debussy* (Paris, 1930).

Lesure, F., 'Bibliographie Debussyste', *ReM: Claude Debussy 1862–1962. Textes et documents inédits*, 48 (1962), 129–43.

—— *Claude Debussy, Catalogue de l'exposition de la Bibliothèque Nationale* (Paris, 1962).

—— *Catalogue de l'œuvre de Claude Debussy* (Geneva, 1977).

—— *Iconographie musicale: Debussy* (Geneva, 1975; Paris, 1980).

—— *Claude Debussy avant 'Pelléas' ou les années symbolistes* (Paris, 1992).

—— *Claude Debussy, Correspondence (1884–1918)* (Paris, 1993).

—— and **Cogeval, G.,** *Debussy e il simbolismo* (Rome, 1984).

Liebich, L., *Claude-Achille Debussy* (London, 1908; 2nd edn., 1925).

Liess, A., *Claude Debussy, Das Werk im Zeitbild* (Strasbourg, 1936).

—— *Claude Debussy und das deutsche Musikschaffen* (Würzburg, 1939).

Lifar, S., *Histoire du Ballet Russe* (Paris, 1950).

Lockspeiser, E., *Debussy* (London, 1936, 2nd edn. 1944; 3rd edn. rev., 1951, 1962; 4th edn. rev., 1962, 1966; 5th edn. rev. by R. L. Smith, 1980).

—— *Debussy et Edgar Poe* (Monaco, 1962).

—— *Debussy: His Life and Mind* (2 vols.; London 1962–5; vol. 1, 1962, 2nd edn. 1966; vol. 2, 1965; both repr. with corrections, 1978).

—— *Claude Debussy: sa vie et sa pensée*, trans. L. Dilé, with analysis of works by H. Halbreich (Paris, 1980).

Long, M., *Au piano avec Claude Debussy* (Paris, 1960); trans. O. Senior-Ellis as *At the piano with Debussy* (London, 1972).

Lugné-Poe, A., *Sous les étoiles* (Paris, 1933).

Malipiero, R., *Claude Debussy* (Brescia, 1948, 1959).

Martin, A., 'Commentaire sur un visage', *Inédits sur Claude Debussy*, Collection Comœdia-Charpentier (Paris, 1942), 17–24.

—— (ed.), *Claude Debussy: Catalogue de l'Exposition organisée du 2 au 17 mai 1942 au Foyer de l'Opéra-Comique* (Paris, 1942) with comments by Busser, Cocteau, and Poulenc.

Mauclair, C., 'Claude Debussy et les poètes', in *Festival Claude Debussy: Programme et Livre d'or des souscripteurs* (Paris, 17 June 1932).

Millan, G., *Pierre Louÿs ou le culte de l'amitié* (Aix-en-Provence, 1979).

Muhlfeld, L., *Le Monde où l'on imprime* (Paris, 1897).

Musik-Konzepte, 1–2 (Special Debussy issue) (Munich, 1977).

Myers, R., *Debussy* (London, 1948; New York, 1949).

—— *Claude Debussy: The Story of his Life and Work* (London, 1972).

Nectoux, J.-M., 'Debussy et Fauré', *Cahiers Debussy*, Nouvelle série, No. 3 (1979), 13–30.

Nichols, R., *Debussy* (London, 1973).

—— 'Claude Debussy', *The New Grove Twentieth-century French Masters*, work-list, R. Nichols and R. Orledge (London and New York, 1986).

—— and **Smith, R. L.,** *Claude Debussy: 'Pelléas et Mélisande'* (Cambridge, 1989).

Oleggini, L., *Au cœur de Claude Debussy* (Paris, 1947).

Omaggio a Claude Debussy, prix de Rome 1884, articles by G. Cogeval, E. Giachery, G. Lanza Tomasi, F. Lesure, F. C. Ricci, J. Risset, J. Roy, and A. Teste (Rome, 1984).

Orledge, R., *Debussy and the Theatre* (Cambridge, 1982).

Oulmont, C., *Musique de l'amour*, i. (Paris, 1935).

Paglia, C. (Gaïanus, pseud.) *Strauss, Debussy e compagnia bella* (Bologna 1913; 2nd edn., 1919).

Paoli, R., *Debussy* (Florence, 1940, 1947; 2nd edn., 1951).

Pasler, J., 'Pelléas and Power: Forces behind the Reception of Debussy's Opera', *19th Century Music*, 10/3 (Spring, 1987), 243–64.

Perrachio, L., *L'opera pianistica di Claude Debussy* (Milan, 1924).

Peter, R., *Claude Debussy* (Paris, 1931; rev. edn., 1944, 1952).

—— 'Ce que fut la "Générale" de *Pelléas et Mélisande'*, *Inédits sur Claude Debussy*, Collection Comœdia-Charpentier (Paris, 1942), 3–10.

Pierné, G., 'Souvenirs d'Achille Debussy', *ReM: La Jeunesse de Claude Debussy* (1 May 1926), 10–11.

Pommer, M., *Claude Debussy für Sie portraitiert* (Leipzig, 1983).

Poniatowski, A., *D'un siècle à l'autre* (Paris, 1948).

Prunières, H., 'À la Villa Medicis', *ReM: La Jeunesse de Claude Debussy* (1 May 1926), 23–42 (includes 12 letters to M. Vasnier).

Réalités Hachette, *Debussy* (Collections Génies et Réalités) (Paris, 1972) (includes articles by Bouchourechliev, Collins, Février, Goléa, Halbreich, Jullien, Le Roux, Lesure, Samuel, and Schneider).

Revue belge de musicologie, 'Souvenir et présence de Debussy' (Brussels, 1962), 43 (includes articles by Deliège, Keczkmeti, van den Linden, Ruwett, and Souris).

Revue de musicologie, 'Claude Debussy 1862–1962. Textes et documents inédits', ed. F. Lesure (1962) (includes 81 letters to Louis Laloy).

Revue internationale de musique française, 1/2, 'Le Journal inédit de Ricardo Viñes (Ravel, Debussy, Duparc)' (June, 1980).

Revue musicale, 'Numéro spécial consacré à Debussy' (1 Dec. 1920) (includes articles by Cortot, Godet, Inghelbrecht, Jean-Aubry, Laloy, Peter, Suarès, and Vuillermoz).

Revue musicale, Numéro spécial, 'La Jeunesse de Claude Debussy' (1 May 1926) (includes articles by Bonheur, Brussel, Emmanuel, Godet, Koechlin, Messager, Pierné, Prunières, Régnier, Vasnier, and Vidal).

Revue musicale, 'Claude Debussy 1862–1962. Livre d'or', No. 258 (1964) (includes articles by Gervais, Jankélévitch, Sauguet, and Vallery-Radot).

Ricci, F. C., *Claude Debussy* (Bari, 1975).

Ricou, G., 'La Générale de "Pelléas et Mélisande"', in R. Ricou (ed.), *Histoire du théâtre lyrique en France depuis les origines jusqu'à nos jours*, (Paris, 1935–8), iii. 69.

Rivière, J., *Études* (Paris, 1925, 1944).

Robert, G., *La Musique à Paris (1895–1896)* (Paris, 1896).

Rolland, R., *Journal des années de guerre (1914–1918)* (Paris, 1952).

Romilly, Mme G. de, 'Debussy professeur, par une de ses élèves', *Cahiers Debussy*, Nouvelle série, No. 2 (1978), 3–10.

Rootzen, K. W., *Claude Debussy* (Stockholm, 1948).

Rutz, H., *Claude Debussy, Dokumente seines Lebens und Schaffens* (Munich, 1954).

Sabaneyev, L., *Klod Debussy* (Moscow, 1922); Eng. trans. S. W. Prinz in *Music and Letters*, 10 (1929), 1.

Sachs, M., *Au temps du Bœuf sur le Toit* (Paris, 1939).

Saint-Marceaux, Mme de, 'Debussy à travers le journal de Mme de Saint-Marceaux (1894–1911)', *Cahiers Debussy*, 3 (1976), 5–10.

Samazeuilh, G., *Musiciens de mon temps* (Paris, 1947).

Santen, R. van, *Claude Debussy* (The Hague, 1926; 2nd edn. rev. by B. van den Sigtenhorst-Meyer, 1947).

Schaeffner, A., 'Debussy et ses rapports avec la musique russe', in P. Souvt-chinsky (ed.), *Musique russe*, i. (Paris, 1953).

—— *Essais de musicologie et autres fantaisies* (Paris, 1980).

Schaeffner, G., *Claude Debussy und das Poetische* (Bern, 1943).

Schallenberg, E. W., *Een muzikaal evangelie: 'Pelléas et Mélisande'* (Leiden, 1950).

Schmitz, E. R., *The Piano Works of Claude Debussy* (New York, 1950; corrected edn., 1966).

Séré, O., *Musiciens français d'aujourd'hui* (Paris, 1921).

Settaccioli, G., *Debussy è un innovatore?* (Rome, 1910).

Smith, R. L., 'La genèse de *La Damoiselle élue*', *Cahiers Debussy*, Nouvelle série No. 4–5 (1980–1), 3–18.

—— 'Debussy and the Pre-Raphaelites', *19th Century Music*, 5 (1981–2), 95–109.

Sousa Rodriguès, L. de, *Debussy compositor frances* (Oporto, 1945).

Strobel, H., *Claude Debussy* (Zurich, 1940, 1942, 1943; rev., 1948).

—— *Claude Debussy*, trans. A. Cœuroy (Paris, 1943; new rev. edn., 1952).

Suarès, A., *Debussy* (Paris, 1922; rev. 1936, 1949).

—— *Cette âme ardente* (Paris, 1954).

Tatry, R., *Claude Debussy* (Paris, 1957).

Terrasson, R., *Pelléas et Mélisande ou l'initiation* (Paris, 1982).

Thompson, O., *Debussy: Man and Artist* (New York, 1937; new edn., 1967).

Tiénot, Y., and **d'Estrade-Guerra, O.,** *Debussy: L'Homme, son œuvre, son milieu* (Paris, 1962).

Tinan, Mme G. de, 'Memories of Debussy and His Circle', *Recorded Sound*, no. 50–1 (1973), 158–63.

Ujfallussy, J., *Claude-Achille Debussy* (Buda-Pesth, 1959).

Vallas, L., *Debussy, 1862–1918* (Paris, 1927).

—— *Les Idées de Claude Debussy* (Paris, 1927); trans. M. O'Brien as *The Theories of Claude Debussy, Musicien français* (London, 1929; New York, 1967).

—— *Claude Debussy et son temps* (Paris, 1932; rev. edn., 1958); trans. M. and G. O'Brien as *Claude Debussy, His Life and Works* (London, 1933; New York, 1973).

—— *Achille-Claude Debussy* (Paris, 1944, 1949).

Vallery-Radot, P., *Tel était Claude Debussy* (Paris, 1958).

Vasnier, M., 'Debussy à dix-huit ans', *ReM: La Jeunesse de Claude Debussy* (1 May 1926), 17–22.

Verhaar, A., *Het leven van Claude Debussy* (The Hague, 1951).

Verlaine, Ex-Mme P., *Mémoires de ma vie*, ed. F. Porché (Paris, 1935).

Vidal, P., 'Souvenirs d'Achille Debussy', *ReM: La Jeunesse de Claude Debussy* (1 May 1926), 11–16.

Vuillermoz, É., *Claude Debussy*, Conférence prononcée le 15 avril 1920 aux Concerts Historiques Pasdeloup (Paris, 1920).

—— *Claude Debussy* (Geneva, 1957; rev. Paris, 1962).

Weber, E. (ed.), *Debussy et l'évolution de la musique au XXe Siècle*, Colloques Internationaux de la CNRS (Paris, 1965).

Wenk, A. B., *Debussy and the Poets* (Berkeley, 1976).

—— *Claude Debussy and Twentieth-Century Music* (Boston, 1983).

Wessem, C. van, *Claude Debussy* (Baarn, 1920).

Widor, C.-M., *Fondations: Portraits de Massenet à Paladilhe* (Paris, 1927).

Wolff, S., *Un demi-siècle d'Opéra-Comique: 1900–1950* (Paris, 1953).

Ysaÿe, A., *Eugène Ysaÿe, sa vie, son œuvre, son influence* (Brussels, 1947).

Zagwijn, H., *Debussy* (The Hague, 1940).

Zelling, A., *Claude Debussy* (The Hague, 1918).

INDEX

Musical and literary works are listed under the composer or author